From the Library of:

Van Stelle

THE SPIRIT OF THE DISCIPLINES

Exercise thyself unto godliness. For bodily exercise profiteth little: but godliness is profitable unto all things, having promise of the life that now is, and of that which is to come.

ST. PAUL, (I TIMOTHY 4:7–8)

Know well that the enemy laboureth in all wise to stay thy desire in good and to make thee void of all good exercise.

THOMAS À KEMPIS
(IMITATION OF CHRIST III, 7)

THE SPIRIT
OF THE DISCIPLINES

Understanding
How God Changes Lives

Dallas Willard

1817

Harper & Row, Publishers, San Francisco

New York, Grand Rapids, Philadelphia, St. Louis
London, Singapore, Sydney, Tokyo, Toronto

For John and Rebecca
in hope that they may live abundant life in
the easy yoke and
the light burden of Christ

Grateful acknowledgment is given for the use of an excerpt from "Little Gidding" in *Four Quartets,* copyright 1943 by T. S. Eliot; renewed 1971 by Esme Valerie Eliot. Reprinted by permission of Harcourt Brace Jovanovich, Inc.

Library of Congress Cataloging-in-Publication Data
Willard, Dallas, 1935-
    The spirit of the disciplines.

    Bibliography: p.
    1. Spiritual life—Baptist authors.   I. Title.
BV4501.2.W533   1988   248.4   86-45033
ISBN 0-06-069441-6

        90   91   92   HC   10   9   8   7   6

Table of Contents

Acknowledgments

My special thanks to several people who read parts or all of the chapters to follow and gave me advice—always useful, though not always followed: Larry Burtoft, John D. Carter, Trevor Hudson, James M. Houston, Klaus Issler, Tudor Lance, J. P. Moreland, Ann Moru, Bruce Narramore, Raymond Neal, Dirk Nelson, Gary Rapkin, Bill Roth, Lynda Stephenson, Art and Barbara Sward, Jane Lakes Willard, J. I. Willard, Rebecca Willard, Gary Wyner, and numerous participants in the fellowships of Woodlake Avenue Friends, Woodland Hills Presbyterian, Rolling Hills Covenant, Faith Evangelical, and Valley Vista Christian Community.

Unless otherwise indicated, all scripture quotations are from the King James Version (occasionally adapted by the author).

The dove descending breaks the air
With flame of incandescent terror
Of which the tongues declare
The one discharge from sin and error.
The only hope, or else despair
   Lies in the choice of pyre or pyre—
   To be redeemed from fire by fire.

   Who then devised the torment? Love.
Love is the unfamiliar Name
Behind the hands that wove
The intolerable shirt of flame
Which human power cannot remove.
   We only live, only suspire
   Consumed by either fire or fire.

T. S. ELIOT, *LITTLE GIDDING*, IV

Preface

The modern age is an age of revolution—revolution motivated by insight into the appalling vastness of human suffering and need. Pleas for holiness and attacks on sin and Satan were used for centuries as the guide and the cure for the human situation. Today such pleas have been replaced with a new agenda. On the communal level, political and social critiques yield recipes for revolutions meant to liberate humankind from its many bondages. And on the individual level various self-fulfillment techniques promise personal revolutions bringing "freedom in an unfree world" and passage into the good life. Such are modern answers to humanity's woes.

Against this background a few voices have continued to emphasize that the cause of the distressed human condition, individual and social—and its only possible cure—is a *spiritual* one. But what these voices are saying is not clear. They point out that social and political revolutions have shown no tendency to transform the heart of darkness that lies deep in the breast of every human being. That is evidently true. And amid a flood of techniques for self-fulfillment there is an epidemic of depression, suicide, personal emptiness, and escapism through drugs and alcohol, cultic obsession, consumerism, and sex and violence—all combined with an inability to sustain deep and enduring personal relationships.

So obviously the problem *is* a spiritual one. And so must be the cure.

But if the cure is spiritual, how does modern Christianity fit into the answer? Very poorly, it seems, for Christians are among those caught up in the sorrowful epidemic just referred to. And that fact is so prominent that modern thinking has come to view the Christian faith as powerless, even somehow archaic, at the very least irrelevant.

Yet even though the church's track record for solving social and individual ills may not appear historically outstanding, we believe that it holds the *only* answer—still. What then is keeping Christianity from being that guide to life which it alone can be? Christianity can only succeed as a guide for current humanity if it does two things.

First, it must take the need for human transformation as seriously as do modern revolutionary movements. The modern negative critique of Christianity arose in the first place because the church was not faithful to its own message—it failed to take human transformation seriously as a real, practical issue to be dealt with in realistic terms. Fortunately, there are today many signs that the church in all its divisions is preparing to correct this failure.

Second, it needs to clarify and exemplify realistic methods of human transformation. It must show how the ordinary individuals who make up the human race today can become, through the grace of Christ, a love-filled, effective, and powerful community.

This book offers help with this second task. Here I want to deal with methods for the spiritual life, for the life present in the Christian gospel. We *can* become like Christ in character and in power and thus realize our highest ideals of well-being and well-doing. That is the heart of the New Testament message.

Do you believe this is possible?

My central claim is that we *can* become like Christ by doing one thing—by following him in the overall style of life he chose for himself. If we have faith in Christ, we must believe that he knew how to live. We can, through faith and grace, become like Christ by practicing the types of activities he engaged in, by arranging our whole lives around the activities he himself practiced in order to remain constantly at home in the fellowship of his Father.

What activities did Jesus practice? Such things as solitude and silence, prayer, simple and sacrificial living, intense study and meditation upon God's Word and God's ways, and service to others. Some of these will certainly be even more necessary to us than they were to him, because of our greater or different need. But in a balanced life of such activities, we will be constantly enlivened by "The Kingdom Not of This World"—the Kingdom of Truth as seen in John 18:36–37.

But history keeps a heavy hand upon our present thoughts and feelings. Such a faith as just described is strongly opposed today by powerful tendencies around us. Faith today is treated as something that only *should* make us different, not that actually *does* or *can* make us different. In reality we *vainly* struggle against the evils of this world, waiting to die and go to heaven. Somehow we've gotten the idea that the essence of faith is entirely a mental and inward thing.

I don't think anyone wanted or planned this state of affairs. We have simply let our thinking fall into the grip of a false opposition of grace to "works" that was caused by a mistaken association of works with "merit." And history has only made things worse. It has built a wall between faith and grace, and what we actually *do*. Of course we know there *must* be some connection between grace and life, but we can't seem to make it intelligible to ourselves. So, worst of all, we're unable to use that connection as the basis for specific guidance as to how to enter into Christ's character and power.

Today, we think of Christ's power entering our lives in various ways—through the sense of forgiveness and love for God or through the awareness of truth, through special experiences or the infusion of the Spirit, through the presence of Christ in the inner life or through the power of ritual and liturgy or the preaching of the Word, through the communion of the saints or through a heightened consciousness of the depths and mystery of life. All of these are doubtlessly real and of some good effect. However, neither individually nor collectively do any of these ways reliably produce large numbers of people who really are like Christ and his closest followers throughout history. That is statistically verifiable *fact*.

I believe our present difficulty is one of misunderstanding how our experiences and actions enable us to receive the grace of God. There is a deep longing among Christians and non-Christians alike for the personal purity and power to live as our hearts tell us we should. What we need is a deeper insight into our practical relationship with God in redemption. We need an understanding that can guide us into constant interaction with the Kingdom of God as a real part of our daily lives, an *ongoing spiritual presence* that is at the same time a *psychological reality.* In other words, we must develop a psychologically sound theology of the spiritual life and of its disciplines to guide us.

In the pages that follow, I have tried to deal with the most basic points about our relationship to God. I have first tried to clarify the nature of spiritual life itself, to show how it is the fulfillment of the human body and how our body is a primary *resource* for the spiritual life. Then I offer a perspective on the idea of "spiritual discipline," and why the disciplines became for all practical purposes lost to us in Western Christianity. Next, I explain the major groups of disciplines relevant to us today, and then conclude by emphasizing how a widespread transformation of character through wisely disciplined discipleship to Christ can transform our world—how it can disarm the structural evils that have always dominated humankind and now threaten to destroy the earth.

So while I write to teach, to add to our knowledge, my ultimate aim is to change our *practice* radically. This book is a plea for the Christian community to place the disciplines for the spiritual life at the heart of the gospel. When we call men and women to life in Christ Jesus, we are offering them the greatest opportunity of their lives—the opportunity of a vivid companionship with him, in which they will learn to be like him and live as he lived. This is that "transforming friendship" explained by Leslie Weatherhead. We *meet* and *dwell* with Jesus and his Father in the disciplines for the spiritual life.

As our meeting place, the disciplines are part of the good news of new life. We should practice them and then invite others to join us there.

I want us to take the disciplines that seriously. I want to inspire Christianity today to remove the disciplines from the category of historical curiosities and place them at the center of the new life in Christ. Only when we do, can Christ's community take its stand at the present point of history. Our local assemblies must become academies of life as it was meant to be. From such places there can go forth a people equipped in character and power to judge or guide the earth.

Multitudes are now turning to Christ in all parts of the world. How unbearably tragic it would be, though, if the millions of Asia, South America and Africa were led to believe that the best we can hope for from The Way of Christ is the level of Christianity visible in Europe and America today, a level that has left us tottering on the edge of world destruction. The world can no longer be left to mere diplomats, politicians, and business leaders. They have done the best they could, no doubt. But this is an age for spiritual heroes—a time for men and women to be heroic in faith and in spiritual character and power. The greatest danger to the Christian church today is that of pitching its message *too low.*

Holiness and devotion must now come forth from the closet and the chapel to possess the street and the factory, the schoolroom and boardroom, the scientific laboratory and the governmental office. Instead of a select few making religion their life, with the power and inspiration realized through the spiritual disciplines, all of us can make our daily lives and vocations be "the house of God and the gate of heaven." It can—and must—happen. And it will happen. The living Christ will make it happen through us as we dwell with him in life appropriately disciplined in the spiritual Kingdom of God.

The Spirit of the Disciplines is nothing but the love of Jesus, with its resolute will to be like him whom we love. In the fellowship of the burning heart, "exercise unto godliness" is our way of receiving ever more fully the grace in which we stand, rejoicing in the hope of the glory of God (Rom. 5:2). The chapters that follow are written to aid you in understanding the absolute necessity of the spiritual disciplines for our faith, and the revolutionary results of practicing these disciplines intelligently and enthusiastically through a full, grace-filled, Christlike life.

1. The Secret of the Easy Yoke

Take my yoke upon you, and learn of me; for I am meek and lowly in heart: and you shall find rest unto your souls. For my yoke is easy, and my burden is light.

MATTHEW 11:29–30

His commands are not burdensome.

1 JOHN 5:3, NIV

A more reasonable estimate of human costs and values will lead us to think that no labour is better expended than that which explores the way to the treasure-houses of the spirit, and shows mankind where to find those goods which are increased by being shared, and which none can take from us.

WILLIAM RALPH INGE

"Christianity has not so much been tried and found wanting, as it has been found difficult and left untried." So said that insightful and clever Christian, G. K. Chesterton. Whether or not he was totally serious, there is almost universal belief in the immense difficulty of being a *real* Christian. The vast, grim "cost of discipleship" is something we hear constantly emphasized. Chesterton's observation can at least be taken as reflecting the attitude of many serious people toward The Way of Christ.

But it must not be left to stand as the whole truth. We would do far better to lay a clear, constant emphasis upon the cost of *non-*discipleship as well. As Søren Kierkegaard reminds us, "It costs a man just as much or even more to go to hell than to come to heaven. Narrow, exceedingly narrow is the way to perdition!"[1]

Proverbs 13:15 tells us that it is the way of the transgressor that is hard. We can also learn this by candid observation of life. Actually, a large part of the Old Testament book of Proverbs merely records the results of such observation. The whole book is a song of praise for the path of the righteous over that of the wicked, leaving no doubt in which life, joy and strength are to be found.

To depart from righteousness is to choose a life of crushing burdens, failures, and disappointments, a life caught in the toils of endless problems that are never resolved. Here is the source of that unending soap opera, that sometimes horror show known as normal human life. The "cost of discipleship," though it may take all we have, is small when compared to the lot of those who don't accept Christ's invitation to be a part of his company in The Way of life.

The words of Jesus quoted above from Matthew 11:29–30 present an alternative to the desolation of life lived apart from God. Yet, in all honesty, most Christians probably find both Jesus' statement and its reiteration by the author of 1 John (5:3) to be more an expression of a hope or even a mere *wish* than a statement about the substance of their lives. To many, Jesus' words are frankly bewildering. We hear them often quoted, because the idea they express is obviously one that attracts and delights, but there seems to be something about the way we approach them, something about what we think it means to walk with Christ and obey him, that prevents most of us from entering into the reality which they express. The ease, lightness, and power of his Way we rarely enjoy, much less see, as the pervasive and enduring quality of our street-level human existence.

So we do not have the strength we should have, and Jesus' commandments become overwhelmingly burdensome to us. In fact, many Christians cannot even believe he actually intended for us to carry them out. So what is the result? His teachings are treated as a mere ideal, one that we may better ourselves by aiming for but know we are bound to fall glaringly short of.

It's a familiar story. "We're only human," we say, and "to err is human." Such pronouncements may be for another age or "dispensation," we may think—or possibly they're for when we are in heaven. But they cannot be for us now. Not really. Jesus could not have imposed anything that *hard* upon us. And beside, we're in a period of grace—we are saved by grace, not by anything we do—so obedience to Christ is actually not necessary. And it is so hard, anyway; it cannot be expected of us, much less enjoyed by us.

And so we reason. All of our reasonings cannot, however, remove the thought that Jesus calls us to follow him—to follow him now, not after death.

No one denies that we would be far better off and our world an immeasurably better place, if we were to conform in deed and spirit to who he is and what he taught. And all of our lack of understanding doesn't cancel his offer of an easy yoke and a light burden, in which our souls can find rest. That offer, like his call to follow him, is clearly made to us here and now, in the midst of this life where we labor and bear impossible burdens and cry out for rest. It's true. It's real. We have only to grasp the secret of entering into that easy yoke.

What then is the secret? There is a simple answer to this all-important question. It is one that can be introduced and even made completely clear, by comparing some facts with which we are all familiar

Think of certain young people who idolize an outstanding baseball player. They want nothing so much as to pitch or run or hit as well as their idol. So what do they do? *When they are playing in a baseball game,* they all try to behave exactly as their favorite baseball star does. The star is well known for sliding head first into bases, so the teenagers do too. The star holds his bat above his head, so the teenagers do too. These young people try anything and everything their idol does, hoping to be like him—they buy the type shoes the star wears, the same glove he uses, the same bat.

Will they succeed in performing like the star, though? We all know the answer quite well. We know that they won't succeed if all they do is try to be like him in the game—no matter how gifted they may be in their own way. And we all understand why. The star performer himself didn't achieve his excellence by trying to behave in a certain way *only during the game*. Instead, he chose an overall life of preparation of mind and body, pouring all his energies into that total preparation, to provide a foundation in the body's automatic responses and strength for his conscious efforts during the game.

Those exquisite responses we see, the amazing timing and strength such an athlete displays, aren't produced and maintained by the short hours of the game itself. They are available to the athlete for those short and all-important hours because of a daily regimen no one sees. For example, the proper diet and rest and the exercises for specific muscles are not a part of the game itself, but without them the athlete certainly would not perform outstandingly. Some of these daily habits may even seem silly to us, but the successful athlete knows that his disciplines must be undertaken, and undertaken rightly, or all his natural talents and best efforts will go down in defeat to others who *have* disciplined themselves in preparation for game time.

What we find here is true of any human endeavor capable of giving significance to our lives. We are touching upon a general principle of human life. It's true for the public speaker or the musician, the teacher or the surgeon. A successful performance at a moment of crisis rests largely and essentially upon the depths of a self wisely and rigorously prepared in the totality of its being— mind and body.

And what is true of specific activities is, of course, also true of life as a whole. As Plato long ago saw, there is an art of living, and the living is excellent only when the self is prepared in all the depths and dimensions of its being.

Further, this is not a truth to be set aside when we come to our relationship with God. We are saved by grace, of course, and by it alone, and not because we deserve it. That is the basis of God's acceptance of us. But grace does *not* mean that sufficient strength and insight will be automatically "infused" into our being in the moment of need. Abundant evidence for this claim is available precisely in the experience of any Christian. We only have to look at the facts. A baseball player who expects to excel in the game without adequate exercise of his body is no more ridiculous than the Christian who hopes to be able to act in the manner of Christ when put to the test without the appropriate exercise in godly living.

As is obvious from the record of his own life, Jesus understood this fact well and lived accordingly. Because of the contemporary bias with which we read the Gospels—a bias we'll be discussing later—we have great difficulty seeing the main emphases in his life. We forget that being the unique Son of God clearly did not relieve him of the necessity of a life of preparation that was mainly spent out of the public eye. In spite of the auspicious events surrounding his birth, he grew up in the seclusion of a simple family in lowly Nazareth. At the age of twelve, as Luke 2:45 tells us, he exhibited astonishing understanding "in the midst of the doctors" in Jerusalem. Yet he returned to his home with his parents and for the next eighteen years was subject to the demands of his family.

Then, after receiving baptism at the hands of his cousin, John the Baptist, Jesus was in solitude and fasted for a month and a half. Afterward, as his ministry proceeded, he was alone much of the time, often spending the entire night in solitude and prayer before serving the needs of his disciples and hearers the following day.

Out of such preparation, Jesus was able to lead a public life of service through teaching and healing. He was able to love his closest companions to the end—even though they often disappointed him greatly and seemed incapable of entering into his faith and works. And then he was able to die a death unsurpassed for its intrinsic beauty and historical effect.

And in this truth lies the secret of the easy yoke: the secret involves living as he lived in the entirety of his life—adopting his overall life-style. Following "in his steps" cannot be equated with behaving as he did when he was "on the spot." To live as Christ lived is to live as he did *all* his life.

Our mistake is to think that following Jesus consists in loving our enemies, going the "second mile," turning the other cheek, suffering patiently and hopefully—while living the rest of our lives just as everyone around us does. This is like the aspiring young baseball players mentioned earlier. It's a strategy bound to fail and to make the way of Christ "difficult and left untried." In truth *it is not the way of Christ* anymore than striving to act in a certain manner in the heat of a game is the way of the champion athlete.

Whatever may have guided us into this false approach, it is simply a mistake. And it will certainly cause us to find Jesus' commands about our actions during specific situations impossibly burdensome—"grievous" as the King James Version of the New Testament puts it. Instead of an easy yoke, all we'll experience is frustration.

But this false approach to following Christ has counterparts throughout human life. It is part of the misguided and whimsical condition of humankind that we so devoutly believe in the power of effort-at-the-moment-of-action alone to accomplish what we want and completely ignore the need for character change in our lives as a whole. The general human failing is to want what is right and important, but at the same time not to commit to the kind of life that will produce the action we know to be right and the condition we want to enjoy. This is the feature of human character that explains why the road to hell is paved with good intentions. We intend what is right, but we avoid the life that would make it reality.

For example, some people would genuinely like to pay their bills and be financially responsible, but they are unwilling to lead the total life that would make that possible. Others would like to have friends and an interesting social life, but they will not adapt themselves so that they become the kind of people for whom such things "come naturally."

The same concept applies on a larger scale. Many people lament the problem of today's tragic sexual behaviors, yet are content to let the role of sex in business, art, journalism, and recreation remain at the depraved level from which such tragedy naturally comes. And others say they would like to get rid of the weapons of warfare, but at the same time they maintain the attitudes and values toward people and nations that make warfare inevitable. We prefer no social unrest or revolution—as long as *our* style of life is preserved.

In his recent book *The Road Less Traveled,* psychiatrist M. Scott Peck observes:

There are many people I know who possess a vision of [personal] evolution yet seem to lack the will for it. They want, and believe it is possible, to skip over the discipline, to find an easy shortcut to sainthood. Often they attempt to attain it by simply imitating the superficialities of saints, retiring to the desert or taking up carpentry. Some even believe that by such imitation they have really become saints and prophets, and are unable to acknowledge that they are still children and face the painful fact that they must start at the beginning and go through the middle.[2]

So, ironically, in our efforts to avoid the necessary pains of discipline we miss the easy yoke and light burden. We then fall into the rending frustration of trying to do and be the Christian we know we ought to be without the necessary insight and strength that only discipline can provide. We become unbalanced and are unable to handle our lives. Dr. Peck reminds us of Carl Jung's penetrating diagnosis: "Neurosis is always a substitute for legitimate suffering."[3]

So, those who say we cannot truly follow Christ turn out to be correct in a sense. We cannot behave "on the spot" as he did and taught if in the rest of our time we live as everybody else does. The "on the spot" episodes are not the place where we can, even by the grace of God, redirect unchristlike but ingrained tendencies of action toward sudden Christlikeness. Our efforts to take control *at that moment* will fail so uniformly and so ingloriously that the whole project of following Christ will appear ridiculous to the watching world. We've all seen this happen.

So, we should be perfectly clear about one thing: Jesus never expected us simply to turn the other cheek, go the second mile, bless those who persecute us, give unto them that ask, and so forth. These responses, generally and rightly understood to be characteristic of Christlikeness, were set forth by him as illustrative of what might be expected of a new kind of person—one who intelligently and steadfastly seeks, above all else, to live within the rule of God and be possessed by the kind of righteousness that God himself has, as Matthew 6:33 portrays.

Instead, Jesus did invite people to follow him into that sort of life from which behavior such as loving one's enemies will seem like the only sensible and happy thing to do. For a person living that life, the hard thing to do would be to hate the enemy, to turn the supplicant away, or to curse the curser, just as it was for Christ. True Christlikeness, true companionship with Christ, comes at the point where it is hard not to respond as he would.

Oswald Chambers observes: "The Sermon on the Mount is not a set of principles to be obeyed apart from identification with Jesus Christ. The Sermon on the Mount is a statement of the life we will live when the Holy Spirit is getting his way with us."[4] In other words, no one ever says, "If you want to be a great athlete, go vault eighteen feet, run the mile under four minutes," or "If you want to be a great musician, play the Beethoven violin concerto." Instead, we advise the young artist or athlete to enter a certain kind of overall life, one involving deep associations with qualified people as well as rigorously scheduled time, diet, and activity for the mind and body.

But what would we tell someone who aspired to live well in general? If we are wise, we would tell them to approach life with this same general strategy. So, if we wish to follow Christ—and to walk in the easy yoke with him—we will have to accept his overall way of life as our way of life *totally.* Then, and only then, we may reasonably expect to know by experience how easy is the yoke and how light the burden.

Some decades ago there appeared a very successful Christian novel called *In His Steps.* The plot tells of a chain of tragic events that brings the minister of a prosperous church to realize how unlike Christ's life his own life had become. The minister then leads his congregation in a vow not to do anything without first asking themselves the question, "What would Jesus do in this case?" As the content of the book makes clear, the author took this vow to be the same thing as intending to follow Jesus—to walk precisely "in his steps." It is, of course, a novel, but even in real life we would count on significant changes in the lives of earnest Christians who took such a vow—just as it happens in that book.

But there is a flaw in this thinking. The book is entirely focused upon trying to do what Jesus supposedly would do in response to *specific choices*. In the book, there's no suggestion that he ever did anything but make right choices from moment to moment. And more interestingly, there is no suggestion that his power to choose rightly was rooted in the kind of overall life he had adopted in order to maintain his inner balance and his connection with his Father. The book does not state that to follow in his steps is to adopt the total manner of life he did. So the idea conveyed is an absolutely fatal one—that to follow him simply means to try to behave as he did when he was "on the spot," under pressure or persecution or in the spotlight. There is no realization that what he did in such cases was, in a large and essential measure, the natural outflow of the life he lived when not on the spot.

Asking ourselves "What would Jesus do?" when suddenly in the face of an important situation simply is not an adequate discipline or preparation to enable one to live as he lived. It no doubt will do some good and is certainly better than nothing at all, but that act alone is not sufficient to see us boldly and confidently through a crisis, and we could easily find ourselves driven to despair over the powerless tension it will put us through.

The secret of the easy yoke, then, is to learn from Christ how to live our total lives, how to invest all our time and our energies of mind and body as he did. We must learn how to follow his preparations, the disciplines for life in God's rule that enabled him to receive his Father's constant and effective support while doing his will. We have to discover how to enter into his disciplines from where we stand today—and no doubt, how to extend and amplify them to suit our needy cases.

This attitude, this action is our necessary preparation for taking the yoke of Christ and is the subject of the rest of this book. We shall be discussing how to actually follow Christ—to live as he lived. This book is intended for those who would be a disciple of Jesus in *deed*.

Do you believe that such a life is possible? I do. Emphatically. I am writing about what it *means* to follow him and about *how* following him fits into the Christian's salvation. I want to explain, with some precision and detailed fullness, how activities such as solitude, silence, fasting, prayer, service, celebration—disciplines for life in the spiritual kingdom of God and activities in which Jesus deeply immersed himself—are essential to the deliverance of human beings from the concrete power of sin and how they can make the experience of the easy yoke a reality in life. By focusing on the whole of Christ's life and the lives of many who have best succeeded in following him, I will outline a *psychologically and theologically sound, testable way* to meet grace and fully conform to him.

The secret of the easy yoke is simple, actually. It is the intelligent, informed, unyielding resolve to live as Jesus lived in all aspects of his life, not just in the moment of specific choice or action. *The secret described in these pages has been placed within your reach.* In the following pages, you will see both why and how that kind of resolve leads to a life with Jesus, as we begin to form a theology of the disciplines for the spiritual life.

NOTES

Epigraph. W. R. Inge, *Personal Religion and the Life of Devotion* (London: Longmans, Green, 1924), 18.
1. Søren Kierkegaard, *For Self-Examination: Recommended for the Times,* trans. Edna and Howard Hong (Minneapolis, MN: Augsburg, 1940), 76–77.
2. M. Scott Peck, *The Road Less Traveled* (New York: Simon & Schuster, 1978), 77.
3. *Ibid.,* 17.
4. Oswald Chambers, *The Psychology of Redemption.* (London: Simpkin Marshall LTD, 1947) 34.

2. Making Theology of the Disciplines Practical

For God has made no promises of mercy to the slothful and negligent. His mercy is only offered to our frail and imperfect, but best endeavours, to practise all manner of righteousness.

WILLIAM LAW

Thus men will lie on their backs, talking about the fall of man, and never make an effort to get up.

HENRY DAVID THOREAU

It was a Bible study at a large Midwestern university in the early sixties. We were mainly graduate students of evangelical background, who met weekly to discuss selected New Testament passages. On this particular occasion we were struggling with 1 John 3:9–10: "No one born of God commits sin; for God's nature abides in him, and he cannot sin because he is born of God. . . . Whoever does not do right is not of God, nor he who does not love his brother" (RSV).

A straightforward reading of the passage seemed to leave this choice: either one is free from sin or one is not a child of God. A very difficult option! But a well-known "saving interpretation" was offered by one of the more sophisticated members of the group. According to it, the form of the Greek verb (*poiei*) translated as "commits" indicates a continuous action. Hence, the *real* meaning had to be that the one who is born of God does not sin all the time or continuously. A short moment of triumph ensued.

But these were bright people, or they would not have been where they were. It was quickly pointed out that even the very ungodly do not sin *all* the time. They have their good moments. How could merely not sinning *continuously* suffice to distinguish the child of God from them? Will the one born of God not sin on

Tuesday, Thursday, and Saturday but sin on Monday, Wednesday, and Friday? Couldn't you kill someone every ten years and still meet the condition of not sinning continuously? Maybe even every five years—or every five weeks?

Further, would it not introduce chaos into the New Testament teachings if we were to add "continuously" in the translation of *every* present indicative active verb? Experimenting with a few test passages showed that it would. But if it is not to be added in every case, why should it be added just in this case—except to relieve the tension between this text and our lives?

Things were beginning to heat up. People began to take sides. Those who thought there must be some important sense in which the child of God might be and should be free from sin were accused of "perfectionism." Someone finally exploded: "Well, are *you* perfect?" But no one assented.

This scene has been played out many times with many variations. It reflects a profound human dilemma that is only intensified by entry into the Christian community. Leo Tolstoy comments in *The Kingdom of God Is Within You* that "all men of the modern world exist in a continual and flagrant antagonism between their consciences and their way of life."[1] There can be little doubt that this continues to be true today and that it is true specifically of modern Christians who live in constant tension between what they know they should be and what they think they can be—as well as what they are.

We believe in our hearts that we should be Christlike, closely following our Lord. However, few of us, if any, can see this as a real possibility for ourselves or others we know well. It does not seem to be something we could realize through definite practical measures we clearly understand and know how to implement.

As a result we find ourselves caught on the horns of a dilemma. If one day I assure my Christian friends that I intend to "quit sinning" and arrive at a stage where I can perfectly follow Jesus Christ, they will most likely be scandalized and threatened—or at least very puzzled. "Who do you think you are?" they would probably say. Or they might think, "What is he really up to?"

But if, on the other hand, I state that I do not intend to stop sinning or that I do not plan ever to follow my Lord in actuality, they will be equally upset. And for good reason. How can Jesus be my Lord if I don't even *plan* to obey him? Would that really differ in substance and outcome from not having him as Lord at all? My Christian fellowship circle will allow me not to follow him and even not to plan to follow him, but they will not permit me to say it.

Yet, I must do one or the other. Either I must intend to stop sinning or *not* intend to stop. There is no third possibility. I must plan to follow Jesus fully or not plan to follow him. But how can I honestly do either? And does not planning to follow him really differ, before God and humanity, from *planning not to follow* him?

The dilemma would be dissolved if we could realistically plan to be like Christ. Perhaps the most difficult of moments in a minister's or teacher's life occurs when, in response to his own sincere preaching or teaching, a listener says: "All right, I really do want to be like Christ. You have convinced me that it is only as I walk with him and become really like him that I can know the fullness of life for which I was created. Now, tell me precisely how to go about it."

The leader can hardly say, "Oh you shouldn't really try to do that!" On the other hand it is the rare leader or teacher today who can calmly say, "Here's how you do it," and state specific tried and true steps actually accessible to the earnest inquirer.

When Christ walked the earth, the Christian method of spiritual growth, through perhaps harsher, seemed much simpler. "I am the light of the world," he says in John 8:12. "Whoever follows me will never walk in darkness, but will have the light of life." To Simon and Andrew fishing, to James and John, to Matthew collecting taxes, he called out: "Follow me!" They obeyed, literally leaving what they were doing to be with him. In this way they learned by observation and direct contact and involvement to do what he did and be as he was. It may have been hard, but a least it was clear-cut and simple.

Today, no less than in Jesus' day, we Christians deeply and inescapably feel the call to follow the Lord who tells us, "You are the light of the world. You are the salt of the earth." But this is very hard to believe or even to take seriously without Christ's physical presence here to reassure and guide us.

How can ordinary human beings such as you and I—who must live in circumstances all too commonplace—follow and become like Jesus Christ? How can we be like Christ always—not just on Sundays when we're on our best behavior, surrounded by others to cheer and sustain us? How can we be like him not as a pose or by a constant and grinding effort, but with the ease and power he had—flowing from the inner depths, acting with quiet force from the innermost mind and soul of the Christ who has become a real part of us? There is no question that we are called to this. It is our vocation as well as our greatest good. And it must be possible. But how?

WHERE IS OUR PRACTICAL THEOLOGY TODAY?

"Theology" is a stuffy word, but it should be an everyday one. That's what practical theology does. It makes theology a practical part of life. A theology is only a way of thinking about and understanding—or misunderstanding—God. Practical theology studies the manner in which our actions interact with God to accomplish his ends in human life.

So everyone has a practical theology, even if it is only the purely negative one of the atheist. And everyone's practical theology vitally affects the course of his or her life. We have some measure of choice in what that theology will be in our own individual case, but we will certainly have a theology. And a thoughtless or uninformed theology grips and guides our life with just as great a force as does a thoughtful and informed one. Our practical theology, then, has the task of answering those questions about how one goes about growing spiritually. And if it is successful, it will resolve for us the dilemma we've discussed.

Practical theology's overall task is, in effect, to develop for practical implementation the methods by which women and men interact with God to fulfill the divine intent for human existence. That intent for the church is twofold: the effective proclamation of the Christian gospel to all humanity, making "disciples" from every nation or ethnic group, and the development of those disciples' character into the character of Christ himself "teaching them to do all things whatsoever I have commanded you" (Matt. 28:20). If these are done well, all else desirable will follow.

The leaders and teachers God gives to his church are, in Paul's words to the Ephesians (4:12), "For the equipping of the saints, for the work of ministry, for building up the body of Christ until we all attain to the unity of the faith and of the knowledge of the Son of God, to mature manhood, to the measure of the stature of the fulness of Christ."

But our practical theology has not always been successful. As the church has moved from period to period in its history, our leaders have not always been sufficiently wise and powerful in their work of equipping the saints. In our immediate past, worldwide evangelism has been strongly emphasized and also quite successful. Perhaps this has been the main task of the church during the last three centuries. We can be happy and thankful for the expansion of the church, both geographically and numerically. But our very zeal and success in this area may deflect us from an adequate emphasis upon the understanding and practice of growth in Christlikeness *after* conversion. Have we done what is necessary to bring the earnest convert into his or her possessions as a child of God, as a brother or sister of Jesus Christ in the new life?

Unfortunately, the answer to this question must be a clear no. It is not an exaggeration to say that this dimension of practical theology is not even taken as a matter of great seriousness by most of our teachers and leaders, probably because it doesn't seem imperative to succeed in doing so immediately. So we can only describe the phrase, "teaching them to do all things whatsoever I have commanded you," as the Great *Omission* from the Great Commission of Matthew 28:19–20.

Too harsh? Simply make an inquiry of your own. Ask your church, "What is our group's plan for teaching our people to do everything Christ commanded?" The fact is that our existing churches and denominations do not have active, well-designed, intently pursued plans to accomplish this in their members. Just as you will not find any national leader today who has a plan for paying off the national debt, so you will not find any widely influential element of our church leadership that has a plan—not a vague wish or dream, but a *plan*—for implementing all phases of the Great Commission.

The American church has overestimated the good that comes from mere scientific progress or doctrinal correctness, or from social progress, missionary work, and evangelism. The church has been shaken to its foundations by ideological, technological, and military movements on a scale never before experienced by humankind, as it has been smothered by mass culture, mindless "prosperity," insipid education, and pseudo-egalitarianism. And as a result, the church at present has lost any realistic and specific sense of what it means for the individual believer to "grow in the grace and knowledge of our Lord and Savior Jesus Christ," as 2 Peter 3:18 expresses it. In fact, it has lost sight of the type of life in which such growth would be a realistic and predictable possibility.

How then could it see the way such growth could be methodically fostered in a routinely effective manner by the ministry and the church's fellowship? Whatever could be learned concerning such matters from the history of the church and from the Bible itself has been generally passed off as somehow irrelevant. Or much worse, this precious information has simply become invisible to the Christian of the modern age.

By the middle of this century, we had lost any recognized, reasonable, theologically and psychologically sound approach to spiritual growth, to really becoming like Christ. Already in the eighteenth century, John Wesley pointed out this trend:

It was a common saying among the Christians of the primitive church, "The soul and the body make a man; the spirit and discipline make a Christian:" implying that none could be real Christians without the help of Christian discipline. But if this be so, is it any wonder that we find so few Christians; for where is Christian discipline?[2]

NEW LIFE BREATHED INTO OLD DISCIPLINES

If Wesley were living today, what would he have to say about the situation in which we find the church? He would at least find much more to be hopeful about in our present situation than in the church of a few years ago. A number of significant changes have occurred in American Protestantism during the last quarter century. None, however, is of greater significance for our own times or of greater potential for future good than the revival of interest in those age-old practices we here refer to as the "disciplines for the spiritual life."

Today, for the first time in our history as a nation, we are being presented with a characteristic range of human behaviors such as fasting, meditation, simple living, and submission to a spiritual overseer, in an attractive light. Though still regarded by too few as essentials of Christian living, such practices are widely studied as possibly one important aid to being an effective Christian. Lectures, seminars, retreats, and books and articles on them enjoy a popularity that was utterly inconceivable fifteen years ago. They are increasingly looked to as a reliable means of growth in spiritual substance toward maturity in Christ.

And this shift of interest and emphasis is most visible with reference to fasting. When Richard Foster published his *Celebration of Discipline* in 1978, he reported that his research could not turn up a single book published on the subject of fasting from 1861 to 1954. But books on this subject now are plentiful. Without any specific effort to collect literature on fasting, I happen to have five recent books concerning it on my desk.[3] And many more discussions on fasting have graced the pages of recent religious periodicals as well as other books.

In the early 1970s, I found myself forced to begin teaching systematically on the disciplines. There seemed no other way to make my hearers understand what life in God's Kingdom as lived and proclaimed by Jesus and his immediate followers was really like.

And there seemed no other way to help them effectively enter into that type of life. Seventeen years of ministerial efforts in a wide range of denominational settings had made it clear to me that what Christians were normally told to do, the standard advice to churchgoers, was not advancing them spiritually.

Of course, most Christians had been told by me as by others to attend the services of the church, give of time and money, pray, read the Bible, do good to others, and witness to their faith. And certainly they should do these things. But just as certainly something more was needed. It was painfully clear to me that, with rare and beautiful exceptions, Christians were not able to do even these few necessary things in a way that was really good for them, as things that would be an avenue to life filled and possessed of God. All pleasing and doctrinally sound schemes of Christian education, church growth, and spiritual renewal came around at last to this disappointing result.

But whose fault was this failure? Try as I might, I was unable to pass this outcome off as a lack of effort on the Christians' part. One of the most discouraging features of ordinary church members' lives is how little confidence in their own abilities for spiritual work, or even church work, they exhibit. Leave the irregular, the half-hearted, and the novices aside for the moment. If the steady, longtime faithful devotees to our ministries are not transformed in the substance of their lives to the full range of Christlikeness, they are being failed by what we are teaching them.

For serious churchgoing Christians, the hindrance to true spiritual growth is not unwillingness. While they are far from perfect, no one who knows such people can fail to appreciate their willingness and goodness of heart. For my part, at least, I could no longer deny the facts. I finally decided their problem was a theological deficiency, a lack in teaching, understanding, and practical direction. And the problem, I also decided, was one that the usual forms of ministry and teaching obviously do not remedy.

As I now see it, and as we will discuss, the gospel preached and the instruction and example given these faithful ones simply do not do justice to the *nature of human personality, as embodied, incarnate.*

And this fact has far reaching implications for the development of human health and excellence.

By contrast, the secret of the standard, historically proven spiritual disciplines is precisely that they *do* respect and count on the bodily nature of human personality. They all deeply and essentially involve bodily conditions and activities. Thus they show us effectively *how* we can "offer our bodies as living sacrifices, holy and acceptable unto God" and how our "spiritual worship" (Rom. 12:1) really is inseparable from the offering up of our bodies in specific physical ways. Paul's teachings, especially when added to his practices, strongly suggest that he understood and practiced something vital about the Christian life that we have lost—and that we must do our best to recover.

And so in the early 1970s, I began to teach the disciplines, at first with a little hesitation and concern about what the response would be. At that time, I was intermittently teaching in several Protestant churches of various denominations. All of them had in common a firmly entrenched tradition of scorn for "ascetic" practices such as solitude, silence, and fasting. My hearers seemed to have two major concerns about them. They wondered how these specific practices could be done except either as a way of meriting forgiveness or as way of extorting favorable actions from God, but to my surprise they offered no out-and-out resistance to the idea of spiritual disciplines. Just the opposite, in fact. My teaching about them almost universally met with a friendly interest and usually with some attempt to learn how to do the things discussed.

WHY THE NEW INTEREST NOW?

A number of factors are at work to explain today's interest in the spiritual disciplines. For one thing, we were in the seventies just emerging from a period in our national history widely perceived as one of the great laxness. The images of hippies, street riots, and Dr. Spock were strongly and negatively fixed in people's minds. There was generally a hunger for order and a somewhat fearful sense that at the foundation of our personal and social life lay forces that, if not carefully channeled, could swallow us up in boredom or in chaos and violence.

But this change in attitude toward the classical spiritual disciplines was also produced by the growth of psychology, and of Christian psychology in particular, as a profession and as a body of knowledge. Here was an event of fundamental importance for the twentieth-century American church. Psychologists, in the very nature of their work, are required to face the *realities* of the Christian soul—all dogmas, professions, and rituals aside—and to propose means of doing something about persons' problems. But this is exactly what the spiritual overseer of past ages tried to do, and though it was not widely studied in the 1960s or 1970s, there is an ocean of literature that relates such work to the earlier recognized disciplines for the spiritual life.

The psychologist's work—indeed, the mere presence of the psychologist in the context of Christian institutions—made it clear to Christians of all denominations and all theological orientations that their "faith and practice" did not necessarily bring peace or health of mind and soul, much less a robust growth toward mature Christlikeness. Many Christians were suddenly prepared to look at traditional methods of spiritual formation. They could not help but see that spiritual growth and vitality stem from what we actually *do* with our lives, from the *habits* we form, and from the *character* that results.

True character transformation begins, we are taught to believe, in the pure grace of God and is continually assisted by it. Very well. But *action* is also indispensable in making the Christian truly a different kind of person—one having a new life in which, as 2 Corinthians 5:17 states, "Old things have passed away and, behold, all things become new." Failure to act in certain definite ways will guarantee that this transformation does not come to pass.

These are two factors in the current change of attitude toward the disciplines, but there is a still more important factor to be considered. There seems to be today nothing less than a widespread shift of religious consciousness and sentiment. What I encountered in the congregations where I ministered in the early seventies was only a part of something much larger that was happening in the flow of American Protestantism and the culture associated with it.

PROTESTANT SECTARIANISM DEFUSED

In our own generation, this specific type of Christianity completed a major phase in its development. In previous times, to be a Protestant and to be a member of a particular Protestant denomination was a very serious matter. On occasion it had been, as history shows, a literal matter of life and death. People were persecuted and even killed over differences of denomination, and those of one denomination rarely held out much hope either for the moral decency or the eternal prospects of those from others. As late as the forties and fifties of this century, intermarriage was strongly discouraged and deep friendships rarely found across denominational lines.

In the sixties and seventies, by contrast, such attitudes effectively disappeared from the American scene. Whatever might be revealed by an in-depth analysis of the causes of this change, it is a fact that during the last two decades we experienced the complete trivialization of sectarian dogmatism along denominational lines. Plenty of battles remained to be fought, of course: liberalism versus fundamentalism, scriptural errancy versus inerrancy, charismatic versus noncharismatic, social activism versus quietism—but they had little or no bearing upon whether one was Lutheran or Methodist, as opposed to Presbyterian, Baptist, or Anglican. Such a radical stretch in thinking was surely a great gain.

However, the general effect was to dull the *specific* character of church life. Just being Baptist or Episcopalian was no longer something to nourish the heart or guide the life. It no longer gave the individual life a form and an identity. Whatever there might be to the Christian Way beyond denominational specifics and being a nice person proved very hard for the ordinary person to grasp, due in part to generations of misguided insistence that all of essential importance lay within *our* denomination. The trivialization of the denominational distinctives left a huge void where little or nothing of specific religious practice was seen to be a matter of life or death. And yet if such practice were not a matter of that—did religion really matter at all, as it truly should?

Even the chief nondenominational religious contrast of the past century—that between the theologically liberal activist and the theologically conservative quietist—had, by the early seventies, also lost most of its substance and urgency for the ordinary churchgoer. Each of the two parties now mainly defined themselves and prided themselves in not being the other.[4] And neither exhibited an inherent richness or strength to mark themselves as transcendent life forces powerful enough to threaten the structures of secular existence.

As Donald E. Miller recently wrote, "The inner reserves of liberal Christianity are largely depleted, drained by too much secular theology and too many radical theologies, and not enough nourishment at the fount of religious experience."[5] But this is not really a new problem for liberal Christianity, which has found it difficult to maintain a rich and rewarding religious experience all along.

Flora Wuellner aptly comments on liberal Protestantism in relation to prayer:

Where is our Christ, who is alive and lives in power? In the preaching of our churches, he has become a beautiful ideal. He has been turned into a myth, embodying a theological concept. The witness to his objective reality has largely been lost. Most liberal Protestant churches have never even heard of the prayer of power in his name. The church has become an organization of well-meaning idealists, working for Christ but far from his presence and power.[6]

As for the conservative side, most conservatives by the early seventies generally accepted that being a Christian had nothing essentially to do with *actually* following or being like Jesus. It was readily admitted that most "Christians" did not really follow him and were not really like him. "Christians aren't perfect, just forgiven" became a popular bumper sticker. (While correct in the letter, this declaration nullifies serious *effort* toward spiritual growth.) The only absolute requirement for being a Christian was that one believe the proper things *about* Jesus.[7] The doctrinal struggles of many centuries—intensified in their impact by the usual intertwinings with political, legal, and even military power, but at the same time drained of religious significance—had transformed saving faith into *mere mental assent* to correct doctrine.

This purely mental view of faith intertwined with another undeniable fact within the conservative and fundamentalist ranks. Regardless of how high a view was professed about the Bible, it was no longer *functionally* authoritative over life on a wide scale. That is to say, it did not in actuality have the effect of bringing the life of the faithful into obvious Christlikeness, whatever the conservatives thought.

How can I claim this? By modest estimate, more than a quarter of the entire population of the United States have professed an evangelical conversion experience. William Iverson wryly observes that "A pound of meat would surely be affected by a quarter pound of salt. If this is real Christianity, the 'salt of the earth,' where is the effect of which Jesus spoke?"[8]

Plus, that mainstay of fundamentalist piety—the revival—was no longer what it used to be. "Revival" in the classical sense of an overwhelming inspiration of God coming upon a large community that moved the whole community toward God has long been replaced. It was replaced by a new form of "revival"—more or less carefully orchestrated evangelistic efforts still called by the old name. As a rule, these new efforts leave not only the communities but also the individuals who make decisions for Christ substantially unchanged from what they were before. Of course, there are always exceptions to this. But painfully little remained of those massive communal responses to the influx of God's Word and Spirit we read about in the New Testament and in more recent periods of church history. Now one can even have an *unsuccessful* "revival," which once you stop to think about it, makes as little sense as the unsuccessful raising of a dead person—that is, no raising at all.

A FAITH THAT TAKES OUR LIVES SERIOUSLY

So what was generally sensed by the early seventies, even where it could not be openly expressed, was the empty and powerless feeling of current Protestantism in the face of life. That's not to say that Protestantism wasn't still very important and the producer of much good. But at that point in our national history there emerged a widespread awareness that this brand of religion, whether of the Right or the Left and regardless of the power in its past, could not be counted on regularly to produce the kind of people we knew in our hearts it should produce. It was not producing the kind of people that we knew life demanded and that we ourselves longed to be.

We knew the way of living we saw was shallow. In Paul Scherer's priceless phrase, it was simply "too trivial to be true." It was not adequate to life and indeed did not even take life—our lives, the ordinary minutes and hours of our days—seriously in the process of redemption.

This is the setting from which we began to reach out to the disciplines, because we somehow realized they had a ring of authenticity about them. They suggested *how,* through concrete steps, we might "redeem the time" relentlessly flowing past and how by strenuous engagement we might "be redeemed from fire by fire." The disciplines promised to give our lives a form that would serve as a receptacle for the substance of the Christ-life in God's present Kingdom. To undertake the disciplines was to take our activities— our lives—seriously and to suppose that the following of Christ was at least as big a challenge as playing the violin or jogging.

And so it was, more than anything else, the religious *seriousness* the spiritual disciplines injected into the whole of our lives that made them attractive. They became meaningful because most of us were viewing them within a context of religious routine and ideology grown insipid and powerless—unalleviated for most Protestants even by rich liturgy that might have been able to keep some profound historical tradition alive, if nothing else.

STILL LACKING: THE THEOLOGICAL BASIS

But an important problem remains. Our tangible need and hunger for the spiritual disciplines do not by themselves make clear *why* we need them and *how* they fit into God's creative and redemptive action upon and within human life. And above all, they do not show how the practice of the disciplines is to be integrated with the great truth recovered with Protestantism—that we are saved by grace through faith, not by works or merit. It is precisely obscurity and confusion here that led to the abuses of the disciplines history reveals and ultimately to today's exclusion of them from the mainstream of Protestant religious life.

What do I mean? Centuries ago, disciplines such as fasting, service, and giving were confused with meritorious works, as well as with a useless and destructive "penance." So what resulted was a general failure to understand or accept the wonderful, positive functions of those disciplines as part of the course of the human personality's full redemption. We've all heard of "cheap grace." But "cheap grace" as a concept didn't just come merely from our wanting to have God's mercy and bounty at bargain basement prices. I believe that the misunderstanding of the spiritual disciplines' place in life has been responsible for Protestantism's adopting "cheap grace" as the dominant mode of its recent existence.

So what is needed, then, is a *theology of the disciplines for the spiritual life*. We need a foundation, a practical, workable theology of them. We must understand why the disciplines are integral to meaningful life in Christ. We must be clear about the essential part they play in the full and effective presentation of the gospel and the truth about life in God's Kingdom. The chapters that follow are an attempt to make such a theology accessible to every Christian.

We shouldn't be frightened of the word "theology." Admittedly, it has kept some pretty dry and dreary company, and we may be tempted to leave it to "the experts." But it stands for something far too important to each of our individual lives and to the communities in which we live for us to shy away from it. Theology *is* a part of our lives. It's unavoidable. And as we said earlier, a thoughtless theology guides our lives with just as much force as a thoughtful and informed one.

Such an informed theology must eventually be in the service of the ordinary lives of ordinary people, and when it is, it will have a great impact for good. Every Christian must strive to arrive at beliefs about God that faithfully reflect the realities of his or her life and experience, so that each may know how to live effectively before him in his world. That's theology!

One very insightful author wrote at the turn of the century:

One must hold it to be the chief business of the theology of any given age or year or hour, to help save men from "evasion of life's proof," to deliver them from shame of their best selves, to point out the conditions upon which the spiritual life may be made indubitably real.[9]

This is exactly what we must do now. Yet this book isn't one of directly practical advice on how to enter and carry through with specific disciplines. Other excellent books of a more practical application are available, most especially Foster's *Celebration of Discipline,* along with many profound writings from other ages. Instead, we will establish, strengthen, and elaborate on this one insight: *Full participation in the life of God's Kingdom and in the vivid companionship of Christ comes to us only through appropriate exercise in the disciplines for life in the spirit.*

Those disciplines alone can become for average Christians "the conditions upon which the spiritual life is made indubitably real." It's true. And if this point can be made as convincingly as its truth and its importance deserves, the practical effects will be stunning. There will be a life-giving revolution in our personal lives and in our world.

NOTES

Epigraph 1. William Law, *A Serious Call to a Devout and Holy Life,* Ch. III (London: Griffith Farran & Co., n.d.) 27.
Epigraph 2. H. D. Thoreau, "Life Without Principle," in *Thoreau: Walden and Other Writings,* Joseph Wood Krutch, ed. (New York: Bantam Books, 1962), 359.

1. Leo Tolstoy, *The Kingdom of God Is Within You,* Trans. Aylmer Maude (London: Oxford University Press 1936), 136.
2. John Wesley, sermon on "Causes of the Inefficacy of Christianity," in his *Sermons on Several Occasions,* 2 vols. (New York: Waugh & Mason, 1836), 1:437.
3. Among these are Derek Prince, *Shaping History Through Prayer and Fasting,* (Old Tappan, NJ: Fleming H. Revell Co., 1973); David R. Smith, *Fasting: A Neglected Discipline* (Fort Washington, PA.: Christian Literature Crusade, 1969); and Arthur Wallis, *God's Chosen Fast* (Fort Washington, PA.: Christian Literature Crusade, 1975). Older treatments of fasting should not be forgotten: John Wesley, Sermon 27 in Vol. I of his *Sermons on Several Occasions,* (New York: Waugh and Mason, 1836); William Law, *Christian Perfection,* Paul Rudolph, ed. (Carol Stream, IL: Creation House, 1975); and Jeremy Taylor, *Holy Living and Dying* (London: Henry G. Bohn, 1858).
4. Neil Q. Hamilton has recently published a striking analysis of the degeneration and failure of both groups in their current form in his *Recovery of the Protestant Adventure* (New York: Seabury, 1981), especially part 1.
5. Donald E. Miller, *The Case of Liberal Christianity* (New York: Harper & Row, 1981), 70.
6. Flora Wuellner, *Prayer and the Living Christ* (Nashville, TN: Abingdon, 1969), 12.
7. See my "Discipleship: For Super-Christians Only?" in Appendix II.
8. William Iverson, *"Christianity Today"* (June 6, 1980): 33.
9. Henry Churchill King, *The Seeming Unreality of the Spritual Life* (New York: Macmillan, 1908), 5.

3. Salvation Is a Life

> God has given to us eternal life, and this life is in his Son. He that has the Son has life.
>
> 1 JOHN 5:11–12

> I am come that they might have life, and that they might have it more abundantly.
>
> JOHN 10:10

> For if, when we were enemies, we were reconciled to God by the death of his Son, much more, being reconciled, we shall be saved by his life.
>
> ROMANS 5:10

Why is it that we look upon our salvation as a moment that began our religious life instead of the daily life we receive from God? We're encouraged somehow today to remove the essence of faith from the particulars of daily human life and relocate it in special times, places, and states of mind.

More and more, we are realizing the enormity of this problem. Upon occasion, we exhort Christians to "take Christ into the workplace" or "bring Christ into the home." But doesn't this only point to the deadly assumption that Christians normally leave Christ at the church?

Where does such an idea begin? More than anyplace else it originates from failure to recognize the part our body plays in our spiritual life—and this is, of course, where the disciplines enter the discussion.

Earlier, we suggested that the secret of the easy yoke is immersing and persisting in the overall style of life that characterized Jesus. We said that if we did this, the highest ideals of the "Christian Way" for our human personalities would be realized.

A close look at Jesus' "great acts" of humility, faith, and compassion recorded in the Gospel narratives finds them to be moments in a life more pervasively and deeply characterized by solitude, fasting, prayer, and service. Surely, then, the lives of his followers must be just as deeply characterized by those same practices.

The pervasive practices of our Lord form the core of those very activities that through the centuries have stood as disciplines for the spiritual life. It would seem only logical to emulate his daily actions since he was a great master of the spiritual life. So isn't it reasonable then to see in those disciplines the specific factors leading to the easy yoke, the light burden, and the abundance of life and power?

Without suggesting any mechanical "formula for success" in the spiritual life—for such things are always out of place—we want to answer that question with an unmistakable yes. Even of Jesus it is true that "he learned obedience through the things which he suffered," as Hebrews 5:8 states. Obedience, even for him, was something to be *learned*. Certainly we cannot reasonably hope to do his deeds without adopting his form of life. And we cannot adopt his form of life without engaging in his disciplines—maybe even more than he did and surely adding others demanded by our much more troubled condition.

But this connection between the disciplines and the easy yoke, with its abundant life, rests upon the nature of human personality. The fact that he was human just as we are ensures that we must likewise share the disciplines with him—not because he was sinful and in need of redemption, as we are, but because he had a body just as we do. His understanding with his Father was: "Sacrifice and offering thou hast not desired, but a body hast thou prepared for me" (Heb. 10:5, RSV). He shared the human frame, and as for all human beings, his body was the focal point of his life.

It is precisely this appropriate recognition of the body and of its implications for theology that is missing in currently dominant views of Christian salvation or deliverance. The human body *is* the focal point of human existence. Jesus had one. We have one. Without the body in its proper place, the pieces of the puzzle of new life in Christ do not realistically fit together, and the idea of *really* following him and becoming like him remains a practical impossibility.

And that is exactly how the average Christian sees the idea to-day—*a practical impossibility*. And where does this thinking come from? I believe it springs from the inability of the believer to think of Christ himself as *really* having a body, with all the normal functions attached to our own bodies. In fact, many feel it almost blasphemous to suppose that he was really like us in all the normal bodily details and functions.

Docetism is the ancient heresy that Christ did not in fact have a real body at all but only seemed to have one. This thinking remains alive and well today in the hearts and minds of many who say he was human as well as divine but in fact do not believe and cannot even imagine that he had a full-fledged human body. They cannot do so because we tend to think of the body and its functions as only a hindrance to our spiritual calling, with no positive role in our redemption or in our participation in the government of God.

So long as such a view of the body is held, the easy yoke will remain a lovely dream and discipleship a part-time diversion. One of our most important tasks here will be to make clear how and why the use of our body for positive spiritual ends is a large part of our share in the process of redemption.

RESULT: FAITH REMOVED FROM THE REALM OF REAL LIFE

No one denies, of course, that the foundational facts and teaching of the Christian religion essentially concern the human body. The incarnation, the crucifixion, and the resurrection of Christ are bodily events. The broken body and the spilled blood of our Lord are celebrated perpetually in the meetings of his people. The gift of himself to us is inseparable from the presence of his body upon the earth and the giving up of it to death upon the cross.

But we seem hard put to understand that what is true of the foundations is no less true of the superstructure. The surrender of myself to him is inseparable from the giving up of my body to him in such a way that it can serve both him and me as a common abode, as John 14:23, 1 Corinthians 6:15–20, and Ephesians 2:22 testify. The vitality and power of Christianity is lost when we fail to integrate our bodies into its practice by intelligent, conscious choice and steadfast intent. It is with our *bodies* we receive the new life that comes as we enter his Kingdom.

It can't be any other way. If salvation is to affect our lives, it can do so only by affecting our bodies. If we are to participate in the reign of God, it can only be by our actions. And our actions are physical—we live only in the processes of our bodies. *To withhold our bodies from religion is to exclude religion from our lives.* Our life is a bodily life, even though that life is one that can be fulfilled solely in union with God.

Spirituality in human beings is not an extra or "superior" mode of existence. It's not a hidden stream of separate reality, a separate life running parallel to our bodily existence. It does not consist of special "inward" acts even though it has an inner aspect. It is, rather, a relationship of our embodied selves to God that has the natural and irrepressable effect of making us alive to the Kingdom of God—here and now in the material world.

When our presentation of the gospel fails to do justice to this basic truth about the nature of human personality, Christianity inevitably becomes alienated from our actual everyday existence. All that remains for it are a few "special" acts to be engaged in on rare occasions. The church then is forced to occupy itself only with these special acts and occasions. Through what is in reality an astonishing lack of faith, the church removes itself from the substance of life. Powerless over life, then, it stands to one side, and God is left without a dwelling place through which he could effectively occupy the world in the manner he intends.

This disengagment from the concrete, embodied existence of ordinary human beings explains why we so rarely find within Christianity the tangible substance of that one, as John 1:4 states, "in whom was life: and the life was the light of men." The deficiency is there, and it cannot be successfully explained away. Think of how we exclaim over and mark as rarities those who seem truly to have the power and spirit of Christ about them. The very way the bright exceptions stand out proves the rule that the guidance given by the church is not even counted on by the *church itself* to produce the kinds of people we know it should produce.

No one is surprised, though we sometimes complain, when faithful church members do not grow to maturity in Christ. With steady regularity we fail to realize the "abundance of life" the gospel clearly promises. We know this to be painfully true. Experience has taught us this, though we may bravely try to ignore it.

This failure has nothing to do with the usual divisions between Christians, such as that between Protestant and Catholic or between liberal and conservative or between charismatic and noncharismatic, for the failure is shared on all sides. It stems from something the various parties must have in common. They all fail to foster those bodily behaviors of faith that would make concrete human existence vitally complete—taking them as a part of the total life in the Kingdom of God. Just as we mentioned in the opening of this chapter, we've somehow encouraged a separation of our faith from everyday life. We've relegated God's life in us to special times and places and states of mind. And we've become so used to this style of life, we are hardly aware of it. When we think of "taking Christ into the workplace" or "keeping Christ in the home," we are making our faith into a set of *special* acts. The "specialness" of such acts just underscores the point—that being a Christian, being Christ's, isn't thought of as a normal part of life.

I don't mean to say that special efforts should simply be ruled out. They can do much good. But we must cut to the root of the poisonous assumption that normal acts are excluded from our life in God. How can we do this? How can we come to grips with such a pervasive and powerful tendency in Christian thought and practice that actually removes our saving relationship with God from all of the little events that make up our lives?

SALVATION IS NOT JUST FORGIVENESS, BUT A NEW ORDER OF LIFE

We must, in fact, do nothing less than engage in a radical rethinking of the Christian conception of salvation. What does it mean to be "saved?" What do people understand when they hear "salvation," "redemption," and other New Testament terms used to refer to God's action in restoring women and men to their intended place in his world? Is it possible that we've been robbed of the words' true and coherent concepts? Is it possible that, through historical process and the drift of language use to reflect special theological interests, we've lost touch with the root meanings of concepts that would make grace and human personality fit like hand in glove when it comes to the process of Christian discipleship? I believe that is exactly what's happened.

We vigorously reject shallow thinking and erroneous conceptualization on the part of a computer analyst or a bridge designer or brain surgeon. For some strange reason, though, we find it easy to put our minds away when it comes to religion, when it comes to bringing the same type of care to our faith as we would to other subjects. But, in reality, we need to be even *more* careful with our religious teachers and theologians. The religion teacher's subject matter is at least as inaccessible as that of other professionals and, of course, it is much more important.

One specific errant concept has done inestimable harm to the church and God's purposes with us—and that is the concept that has restricted the Christian idea of salvation to *mere forgiveness of sins.* Yet it is so much more. Salvation as conceived today is far removed from what it was in the beginnings of Christianity and only by correcting it can God's grace in salvation be returned to the concrete, embodied existence of our human personalities walking with Jesus in his easy yoke.

Once salvation is relegated to mere forgiveness of sin, though, the discussions of salvation's nature are limited to debates about the death of Christ, about which arrangements involving Christ's death make forgiveness possible and actual. Such debates yield "theories of the atonement." And yet through these theories the connection between salvation and *life*—both his life and ours—becomes unintelligible. And it remains unintelligible to everyone who attempts to understand salvation through those theories alone. Why? It is because they are of no use in helping us, as the apostle Paul puts it, to understand how, being reconciled to God by the death of his Son, we are then "saved by his life." (Rom. 5:10) How can we be saved by his life when we believe salvation comes from his death alone? So if we concentrate on such theories exclusively, *the body and therefore the concrete life we find ourselves in are lost to the redemption process.* And when that happens, how else could we see the disciplines for the spiritual life but as historical oddities, the quaint but misguided practices of troubled people in far-off and benighted times?

WHY THE LATE EMERGENCE OF THE CROSS?

An interesting, maybe enlightening point about this confusion is the fact that aside from the New Testament teachings themselves, there are clear historical indications that forgiveness as the all-in-all of salvation is not part of the earliest Christian outlook. For instance, the late emergence of the cross as a Christian symbol is a very interesting development. In his magnificent television series and book called *Civilization,* Kenneth Clark remarks on how late the cross emerged as a significant symbol in Christian religion, art, and culture:

We have grown so used to the idea that the Crucifixion is the supreme symbol of Christianity that it is a shock to realize how late in the history of Christian art its power is recognized. In the first art of Christianity it hardly appears; and the earliest example, on the doors of Santa Sabina (built A.D. 430) in Rome, is stuck away in a corner almost out of sight. The simple fact is that the early church needed converts, and from this point of view the Crucifixion was not an encouraging subject. So, early Christian art is concerned with miracles, healings, and with hopeful aspects of the faith like the Ascension and the Resurrection.[1]

But what a strange and unusual reading of the state of mind of the early Christians! In view of all else we know about the period—the widespread and often deadly persecution that automatically greeted most converts—it is very hard to believe that there was an effort to avoid the subject of the cross and of death.

Tertullian's (A.D. 160–230) well-known words in the conclusion to his *Apology* seem much more representative of the practice of the early believers. To his provincial governors under the Roman Empire he wrote:

Proceed in your career of cruelty, but do not suppose that you will thus accomplish your purpose of extinguishing the hated sect [the Christians]. We are like the grass, which grows the more luxuriantly the oftener it is mown. The blood of Christians is the seed of Christianity. Your philosophers taught men to despise pain and death by words; but how few their converts compared with those of the Christians, who teach by example! The very obstinacy for which you upbraid us is the great propagator of our doctrines. For who can behold it, and not inquire into the nature of that faith which inspires such supernatural courage? Who can inquire into that faith, and not embrace it, and not desire himself to undergo the same sufferings in order that he may thus secure a participation in the fulness of divine favour?[2]

Thus, Clark's interpretation of the late emergence of the cross into general culture does not really fit with the actual attitude of the early Christians toward death. For them from the beginning, "to die is gain," as Philippians 1:21 attests. But also, and much more importantly, Clark misses the simple fact that it wasn't Christ's death that gave rise to this courageous early church—but his *life!*

As the pages of the Gospels amply show, Christ's transcendent life in the present Kingdom of heaven is what drew the disciples together around Jesus prior to his death. And then resurrection and postresurrection events proved that life to be indestructible. They verified that all of Jesus' teachings about life in the Kingdom were true. The cross, which was always present in their thought and experience, came to the center because the force of the higher life was allowed to dissipate as the generations passed by. Eyewitnesses—the people who had seen and felt the transcendent life—were no longer there to convey it and tell of it first hand. That "hands on" viewpoint was replaced with another. The church's understanding of salvation then slowly narrowed down to a mere forgiveness of sins, leading to heaven beyond this life. And Christ's death came to be regarded as *only* the merit-supplying means to that forgiveness, not as the point where his life was most fully displayed and triumphant, forever breaking the power of sin over concrete human existence.

So the emergence of the cross signifies what we today would call a "paradigm shift" in the human understanding of the person and work of Christ; that is, the basic structure of the redemptive relationship between us and God came to be pictured in a way radically different from its previous New Testament conception.[3] The cross act was first narrowly interpreted as mere vicarious suffering and then mistaken for the whole of the redemptive action of God. Christ's life and teaching were therefore nonessential to the work of redemption and were regarded as just poignant decorations for his cross, since his only saving function was conceived to be that of a blood sacrifice to purchase our forgiveness.

The effect of this shift is incalculably vast and profound for the history of the church and for the realities of the Christian's walk. They are well-illustrated in a story—probably apocryphal—that is told about one of the great thinkers of the Roman Catholic church, St. Thomas Aquinas. The story goes that, while walking amid the splendors of Rome, a friend said to St. Thomas, "We Christians certainly no longer have to say to the world, 'Silver and gold have we none.'" To this St. Thomas replied: "But neither can we say to the lame man, 'In the name of Jesus of Nazareth rise up and walk.'" As the shift settled in, the power diminished, just as St. Thomas Aquinas saw it. The church of his time could profess to dispense forgiveness but could not command a healing life force.

WHAT THE RESURRECTION MEANT TO THE FRIENDS OF JESUS

The message of Jesus himself and of the early disciples was not just one of the forgiveness of sins, but rather was one of newness of life—which of course involved forgiveness as well as his death for our sins. And yet that newness of life also involved much more beside. To be "saved" was to be "delivered from the power of darkness and translated into the Kingdom of his dear Son," as Colossians 1:13 says. We who are saved are to have a different order of life from that of the unsaved. We are to live in a different "world."

It is because this was the sort of salvation to be accomplished that the resurrection, not the death of Christ, was the central fact in the gospel of the early believers. As we've already suggested, the resurrection had the meaning it did to those early believers just because it proved that the new life that had already been present among them in the person of Jesus could not be quenched by killing the body.

The resurrection was a cosmic event only because it validated the reality and the indestructibility of what Jesus had preached and exemplified *before* his death—the enduring reality and openness of God's Kingdom. It meant that the Kingdom, with the communal form his disciples had come to know and hope in, would go on. The "gates of the grave" would not prevail against it, as Matthew 16:18 states. That, and the fact that Jesus was not dead after all— and that when *we* die, we won't stay dead—is what made the resurrection earthshaking, transforming good news.

With all of this clearly in view, it becomes understandable why the simple and wholly adequate word for salvation in the New Testament is "life." "I am come that they might have life and that they might have it more abundantly," says John 10:10. "He that hath the Son hath life," says 1 John 5:12. "Even when we were dead through our trespasses, God made us alive together with Christ," says Ephesians 2:5.

Once we forsake or cloud this meaning of "salvation" (or "redemption" or "regeneration") and substitute for it mere atonement or mere forgiveness of sins, we'll never be able to achieve a coherent return to concrete human existence. We'll never be able to make clear just exactly what it *is* that our lives have to do with our "salvation." Futile efforts of believers through the centuries somehow to tack obedience—or "works" or "law"—onto grace, or to insist that Christ cannot be our Savior without also being our Lord, are a historical proof of this point.[4]

But the idea of redemption as the *impartation of a life* provides a totally different framework of understanding. God's seminal redemptive act toward us is the communication of a new kind of life, as the seed—one of our Lord's most favored symbols—carries a new life into the enfolding soil. Turning from old ways with faith and hope in Christ stands forth as the natural first expression of the new life imparted.[5] That life will be poised to become a life of the same quality as Christ's, because it indeed *is* Christ's. He really does live on in us. The incarnation continues.

Obedience, "works," effectual lordship are then natural parts of such salvation, of this kind of life. They come as God's continuing gifts within our interactive relationship to him—not as something outside it that perhaps limps along behind at a distance or disappears totally. Like blossoms from that seed, they sprout from the life itself. The seventeenth-century Puritan writer Walter Marshall wrote: "Holiness . . . [as love of God and humankind] is considered, not as a means, but as a part, a distinguished part; or rather as the very central point in which all the means of grace, and all the ordinances of religion, terminate."[6]

FAITH AND WORKS—HOW DO THEY INTERACT?

The distinction between what is a natural part of salvation and what may be just an accompaniment also aids us in understanding the scripture, "faith without works is dead," a statement from the Epistle of James that has troubled many post-Reformation believers. "Works" are simply a natural part of faith. James's statement is about the inherent *nature* of faith, about what makes it up. It concerns what believing something really amounts to. It is not an exhortation to *prove* that one has faith or to work to *keep one's faith alive*.

It is well known that Martin Luther had severe problems with the Epistle of James, even suggesting that it should be eliminated from the New Testament. Ironically, however, he clearly understood James's point about the nature of faith and forcefully expresses it in his own language. In the preface to his commentary on

Romans, he asserts, through an appropriate comparison, that it is "impossible to separate works from faith—yea, just as impossible as to separate burning and shining from fire."

This is because faith is in its very nature a power and a life. Here is Luther's description:

O, this faith is a living, busy, active, powerful thing! It is impossible that it should not be ceaselessly doing that which is good. It does not even ask whether good works should be done; but before the question can be asked, it has done them, and it is constantly engaged in doing them. But he who does not do such works, is a man without faith. He gropes and casts about him to find faith and good works, not knowing what either of them is, and yet prattles and idly multiplies words about faith and good works.

Luther adds comments on the interior character of faith:

[Faith] is a living well-founded confidence in the grace of God, so perfectly certain that it would die a thousand times rather than surrender its conviction. Such confidence and personal knowledge of divine grace makes its possessor joyful, bold, and full of warm affection toward God and all created things—all of which the Holy Spirit works in faith. Hence, such a man becomes without constraint willing and eager to do good to everyone, to serve everyone, to suffer all manner of ills, in order to please and glorify God, who has shown toward him such grace.[7]

Kierkegaard's biting comments on how history has twisted Luther's teaching of salvation by faith express deep insight into our own situation today. He noted how there is always a certain worldliness that desires to seem Christian, but as cheaply as possible. This worldliness took note of Luther, listened closely to him, and found something it could make excellent use of. So all comes by faith alone! Wonderful! "We are free from all works. Long live Luther! 'Who loves not women, wine, and song remains a fool his whole life long!' This is the significance of the life of Luther, this man of God who, suited to the times, reformed Christianity."[8]

Once we have come to understand that faith is the powerful life force described by Luther, we can then recognize it as it displays itself on the pages of the New Testament in three major dimensions:

1. The presence of a new power *within* the individual, erupting into a break with the past through turning in repentance and the release of forgiveness. The old leaf automatically falls from the branch as the new leaf emerges. Thus we have the biblical representation of repentance, as well as of forgiveness, as something *given* to us by God in Psalms 80:3; 85:4; Acts 5:31; Romans 2:4; and 2 Timothy 2:25.

2. An immediate but also a developing transformation of the individual character and personality (2 Cor. 5:17, Rom. 5:1–5, 2 Pet. 1:4–11).

3. A significant, extrahuman power over the evils of this present age and world, exercised both by individuals and by the collective church ("All power is given to me in heaven and in earth. Go ye therefore . . .," Matt. 28:18).

To enjoy this three-dimensional life is just what it means to be "translated" into the Kingdom of God's dear Son, as Colossians 1:13 explains, or to "have our citizenship in heaven." (Phil. 3:20, NIV)

THE "VILE" BODY

Looking back over our discussions to this point, we have connected the reality of the easy yoke with the practice of the spiritual disciplines. These in turn have led us to the body's role in redemption. Although we call the disciplines "spiritual"—and although they must never be undertaken apart from a constant, inward interaction with God and his gracious Kingdom—they never fail to require specific acts and dispositions of our body as we engage in them. We are finite, limited to our bodies. So the disciplines cannot be carried out except as our body and its parts are surrendered in precise ways and definite actions to God.

Here we find the positive role of the body in the process of redemption, as we choose those uses of our body that advance the spiritual life. Only as we correctly appreciate that role can we understand the New Testament view of salvation as a life, for a life is, of course, something we live, and we live only in the actions and dispositions of our body.

This runs directly counter to the view of faith as an interior act of mind that secures forgiveness alone and has no necessary connection with the world of action in which normal human existence runs its course. But the New Testament knows nothing of such a purely mental "faith." The faith of the New Testament is a distinctive life force that originates in the impact of God's word upon the soul, as we see in Romans 10:17, and then exercises a determinating influence upon all aspects of our existence, including the body and its social and political environment.

This idea is the most convincing line of interpretation of faith and life in Christ's companionship as pictured in the New Testament. It is also one that opens the door to the use of the New Testament as a practical guide to Christian experience and aspiration. That is a very strong recommendation for it and one not really shared by the "mere forgiveness" view of salvation. However, I must admit that even those who find it convincing may still feel an overwhelming impression that the body just *could not* be more than a hindrance to our redemption. Our actual experience with the human body, especially our own, may reinforce the idea that the most we can ever hope for is to reach a standoff with it, barely managing by the grace of God to keep it from spiritually defeating us until we are rid of it.

After all, doesn't the Bible refer to it as a *vile* body in Philippians 3:21, and as earthy and corruptible in 1 Corinthians 15:48–50? Doesn't Christ himself indicate that evil things pour forth from it to defile humankind in Mark's Gospel (7:20–23)? Doesn't Romans chapter three characterize it as having a throat like an open grave, a tongue and lips full of deceit and poison, a mouth full of cursing and bitterness, feet in hurry to shed blood? Doesn't it leave behind it a path of destruction and misery?

It's true that our bodies can overwhelm us with their impulses and terrify us with their vulnerability. What can we do against their demands and needs for food and drink, security and comfort, power and love? We speak of the troubles of Job. The events he had to endure that drove him to spiritual despair were all events of the body—either his body or those for whom he cared. How could this vile, dangerous thing possibly be of benefit in realizing our deliverance?

The answer, of course, is that it cannot if we take it merely to be what we find it to be in this world set against God. And certainly it does not contain in itself alone the resources of redemption. But still, I must insist that it was not made to be what we find it to be in its alienation from God.

The body's sad condition is a sure indication that it does not now exist in its true element. We would not judge the possibilities of automobiles merely by a survey of those we find in the junk yard or the possibilities of plant life by considering only plants that have been starved of necessary nutrients.

The human body was made to be the vehicle of human personality ruling the earth for God and through his power. Withdrawn from that function by loss of its connection with God, the body is caught in the inevitable state of corruption in which we find it now. To readjust our view of the possibilities of our body and the spiritual life the body can experience, the next three chapters are devoted to an explanation, from the biblical viewpoint, of who we are and what spiritual life is. (Those who have less interest in the theological basis for the disciplines of the spiritual life may wish to skip those chapters and proceed directly to chapter 7, returning to read chapters 4–6 last.)

NOTES

1. Kenneth Clark, *Civilization: A Personal View* (New York: Harper & Row, 1969), 29.
2. Quoted in John, Bishop of Bristol, *The Ecclesiastical History of the Second and Third Centuries* (London: Griffith Farran Browne, n.d.), 66.
3. On the very useful conception of a "paradigm shift," see Thomas S. Kuhn, *The Structure of Scientific Revolutions*, 2d ed. (Chicago: University of Chicago Press, 1973), chap. 5, "The Priority of Paradigms."
4. Daniel P. Fuller's recent excellent study *Gospel and Law: Contrast or Continuum?* (Grand Rapids, MI: Eerdmans, 1980) has much to contribute toward a proper

understanding of the relationship between faith and law from the viewpoint of recent evangelical theology.

5. I believe that this was the understanding of "faith" accepted by the leaders of the Protestant Reformation. See the discussion, with lengthy quotations, of Melancthon, Luther, Calvin, and Latimer in Horatius Bonar, *God's Way of Holiness* (Chicago: Moody, n.d.), chap. 2.

6. Walter Marshall, *The Gospel Mystery of Sanctification* (1692; reprint, Grand Rapids, MI: Zondervan, 1954), 258.

7. *Great Voices of the Reformation: An Anthology* Martin Luther, quoted in Harry Emerson Fosdick, ed., (New York: Modern Library, 1954), 121–22.

8. Søren Kierkegaard. *For Self-examination: Recommended for the Times,* trans. Edna and Howard Hong (Minneapolis, MN: Augsburg, 1940), 10. I have translated the portion in single quotation marks, which was left in German in the edition quoted. It should never be forgotten, of course, that forgiveness can be *experienced* in such a way that the result is faith as just described by Luther. Indeed, I would not hesitate to equate salvation with forgiveness so experienced *for practical purposes.* The fine discussion of these matters in John Owen's (1616–1683) *The Forgiveness of Sins, Illustrated in Psalm CXXX* (various editions) has never been surpassed; see especially chap. 6, "Support from Forgiveness."

4. "Little Less Than a God"

> When I look up at thy heavens, the work of thy fingers, the moon and the stars set in their place by thee, what is man that thou shouldst remember him, mortal man that thou shouldst care for him? Yet thou hast made him little less than a god, crowning him with glory and honour. Thou makest him master over all thy creatures; thou has put everything under his feet.
>
> PSALM 8:3–6, NEB

> Then God said, "Let us make man in our image and likeness to rule the fish in the sea, the birds of heaven, the cattle, all wild animals on earth, and all reptiles that crawl upon the earth." So God created man in his own image.
>
> GENESIS 1:26–27, NEB

Who are we humans? What are we supposed to do? Surely life is for more than just surviving, or mastering nature and other human beings. Why are we here?

The inability to answer such questions is one of the most striking and troublesome quandaries of being a human. Questions like these usually do not seize us so long as we are immersed in the life of a strong family, tribe, nation, or other social unit. In such groups we feel sure of who we are and what we are to do. At least we think we are sure. But these ties can be broken by education, by social disruption, by emotional alienation, and a myriad of other reasons today. And then, the individual human being finds that it is no longer enough to know that he or she is a Smith or a Jones, a lawyer or an engineer, a Hopi or a Southerner, or a German or a Briton. And the questions begin. What is the purpose of our existence? How should we view ourselves as living beings?

Some of us may find relief from the *Angst* through identifying with sports teams, rock stars, or social movements of one kind or another. Some may resort to the dogmatisms of politics, science, or religion. Our bumper stickers and T-shirts may bear symbols and slogans intended to inform others as well as ourselves that we are very sure, thank you, of who we are and what we are doing and how we feel about the whole idea of being on this planet. But it's all empty bravado, a nervous whistling in the dark of our ignorance and uncertainty about our real nature and our real task in life.

The questions of who we are and what we are here for are not easy ones, of course. And for those who must rely solely upon a strictly secular viewpoint for insight, such questions are especially tough. Why? Because we *do* in fact live in a world in ruins. We do not exist now in the element for which we were designed. So, in light of that truth, it's essentially impossible to determine our nature by *observation* alone, because we are only seen in a perpetually unnatural posture. Oh, we can learn many exciting things from observing the normal course of human existence, but not what we most want to know: what our own nature is, and what the possibilities of our life are.

Without an understanding of our nature and purpose, we cannot have a proper understanding of redemption. You may wonder, what does all this really have to do with our salvation. Do we really need to know so much about our own nature before we understand how that nature can change through salvation? Yes, we do. What "salvation" is depends upon what is being saved. Before something can be saved it must face the risk of being lost. And, essentially, it is the *nature* of what is being saved that determines how it can be at risk and at loss. For example, "saving" an investment is a different kind of project from saving a life, a reputation, or an injured pet, because investments, lives, reputations, and pets are different kinds of things. So, if we want to know what it is to save a human being, to redeem the human soul or personality, we cannot find a better way to begin than by asking: *what* did God make when he made us, and how could creatures such as we be at risk and at loss?

BETWEEN THE DUST HEAP AND THE HEAVENS

An initial clue to guide our understanding of our nature may be found in our aspirations taken in their sharp and obvious contrast with our physical being. The poets as well as the writers of Scripture were vividly aware of this contrast. Humankind aspires to beauty and power, to purity and dignity, to knowledge and endless love. And yet we are wandering heaps of protoplasm—bits of "portable plumbing," as the poet Stephen Spender says. The dogmatic naturalist, sometimes under the guise of the latest "scientific thought," will insist that the human creature is only that—nothing more, nothing less. Plato, with tongue firmly implanted in cheek, defined humans as featherless bipeds to distinguish them from the birds. The sober truth is that we *are* made of dust, even if we do aspire to the heavens. And though the glow of youth will conceal that truth for a time, all of us will, if time allows, realize as the poet Yeats did in "Sailing to Byzantium" that "an aged man is but a paltry thing, a tattered coat upon a stick . . ."

When Job was discontent with the lot God had let befall him, he was scolded by Eliphaz the Temanite for his presumptiousness: "God cannot even trust his angels! How much less those who live in houses of clay, who are founded in dust? They are crushed as easily as a moth. One day is enough to grind them to powder." (Job 4:18–19, JB).

Clay, dust, powder—yes. But then there is the other side. What a splendor to it! Shakespeare makes Hamlet exclaim:

What a piece of work is man! how noble in reason! how infinite in faculty! in form and moving how express and admirable! in action how like an angel! in apprehension how like a god! the beauty of the world! the paragon of animals!

But for all this, Hamlet still concludes:

And yet, to me what is this quintessence of dust? Man delights not me.

The distance between the aspirations and the physical realities of humanity can be the stuff of the ridiculous, the cynical, and the tragic but at the same time be filled with compassion, faithfulness, heroism, and creativity. In short, that distance is life as we know it.

Yet, as creatures go, we *are* different. We *are* made for higher things. Our aspirations hint of such a truth. The age-old distinction between the body—the physique—and the person—the soul, spirit, mind—is rooted in the contrast between the unconscious physical facts of our lives, which sometimes shock or shame us, and our "conscious" life, our experiences, interests, meanings, thoughts, intents, and values. And it is the nature of our conscious life that separates us from other creatures, putting an odd distance between our innermost being and the dust heap we also truly are.

When God made us he made creatures capable of astonishing presumption. We humans can *almost* forget that we are dust. Perhaps we *must* in some measure forget it in order to carry on. Yet, as we breathe and eat and sleep, we also think and aspire—and that is amazing. In that paradox, that puzzle in which the pieces do not truly fit together, we can either applaud ourselves for such a rare and amazing accomplishment or we can begin to understand that we are touched by powers beyond ourselves. We are creatures given such diverse possibilities that they can actually lead us to heaven or to hell.

THE BIBLICAL PERSPECTIVE ON HUMANITY

An indication of our greatness, for all our dustiness, is found precisely in the fact that God pays attention to us, meets us, and gives us work to do. There must be something important about human beings that is not apparent, if this is so. As the psalmist said, "what is man that thou shouldst remember him, mortal man that thou shouldst care for him? Yet thou hast made him little less than a god. . ." (Ps. 8:4–5).

As we've seen, the poets secular and sacred alike see human nature and its power stretched between the sublime and the ridiculously crude and low. But the Judeo-Christian vision of the creation of humankind provides, in the *work* assigned to us at the creation, a clue to the unity and purpose of our many-sided nature. What were we originally put here to do?

In a classic writing of Orthodox spirituality, *The Way of a Pilgrim,* the story is told of a rosary that had belonged to a saintly man that turned a wolf away from the traveler carrying it. The following explanation is then given of how people have power over animals through the holy:

You remember that when our father Adam was still in a state of holy innocence all the animals were obedient to him. They approached him in fear and received from him their names. The old man to whom this rosary had belonged was a saint. Now what is the meaning of sanctity? For the sinner it means nothing else than a return through effort and discipline to the state of innocence of the first man. When the soul is made holy the body becomes holy also. The rosary had always been in the hands of a sanctified person; the effect of the contact of his hands and the exhalation of his body was to inoculate it with holy power—the power of the first man's innocence. That is the mystery of spiritual nature! All animals in natural succession down to the present time have experienced this power.[1]

Is this too fantastic? It will certainly seem less so to Christians who take seriously the account of human creation in the book of Genesis.

The biblical perception of the simultaneous magnificence and triviality of the human creature comes squarely and firmly to rest in the Bible's account of our origin. People were, for all their physical dimensions, made to be like God, and in that likeness they were made to exercise lordship, care, and supervision over the zoological creation. As Genesis 1:26 explains, "And God said, Let us make man in our image, after our likeness, and let them have dominion over the fish of the sea, and over the fowl of the air, and over the cattle, and over all the earth, and over every creeping thing that creepeth upon the earth."

So humankind's job description is clearly stated. We were *not* designed just to live in mystic communion with our Maker, as so often suggested.[2] Rather, we were created *to govern the earth* with all its living things—and to that specific end we were made in the divine likeness.

Perhaps we can for the moment lay aside the many controversies that hover over the first pages of the Bible and catch there a glimpse of the basis of our astonishing possibilities (and presumptions). If we can, we will see the nature and possibilities that were intended for us in the beginning—and are there now to be redeemed.

In the Genesis narrative life emerges in the form of plants during the third creative period or "day". At the command of God, it emerges from the previously created substance, "dry land" in 1:11. In the fifth period, after light is consolidated into the specific lights of sun, moon, and stars, the water is commanded to bring forth "the moving creature that hath life," both fish and fowl (1:20). In the sixth and final day of creation, the earth or dry land is commanded, once again, to bring forth "the beasts of the earth after his kind, and cattle after their kind, and everything that creepeth upon the earth after his kind."

And here, also in the sixth creative period, humanity is brought into being. But our creation process is strikingly different from all that preceded. Here for the first time, in 1:26, readers are informed of God's purposes in his creative activity. Up to this point, no reason has been given why God did what he did. But here, the Scriptures give us a reason. Humans are made to govern—to rule over the zoological realm as God rules over all things. The *imago Dei*, the likeness to God, consists, accordingly, of all those powers and activities required for fulfilling this job description, this rule to which we are appointed. And of course it includes the very rule itself.

But surely this has no bearing on our lives today! Wasn't this just a job description for the first man, Adam? No, it was not. The word "man," or "Adam," is a collective noun, and may be taken as referring both to the individual, Adam, and to humankind, the community of "governors" over all life higher than the plants. And to accomplish this task, humans were given the abilities appropriate to the task: powers of perception, conceptualization, valuation, and action. That curious scene in Genesis 2:19–20, for instance, where the animals were brought before Adam for names was, then, not just an occasion where labels were pinned on the animals like identification numbers. It represents—as "names" were understood in ancient times—Adam's (humankind's) insight into the natures of the various creatures, an insight needed to make his governing possible.

But in light of the immensity of the task, God also gave humankind another very important ability—the ability to live in right relationships to God and to other human beings. Only in those relationships, in the communication needed to keep those relationships healthy and thriving, could everything be found that was required to succeed at the work assigned.

It is still true today that the greatest and most admirable power of humans over animals is not found in those who slaughter or abuse them, but in those who can govern their behavior by speaking to them—by communicating with them. The "pen" is mightier than the sword because it teaches the deeper dimensions of us and our world. Anyone with a gun can blow the head off a cobra, but to charm it into quiescence with a flute is quite another thing. Since the Gospel narratives, the Genesis account, and other parts of the Bible indicate that God rules by speaking, we see once again how the presence of the *imago Dei* is active in our job description. In the same manner as God—by speaking, by communicating—we are to rule over our "subjects." And in our relationship with other people, the same manner holds true. Governance by a *person,* whether over other people or animals, is at its best when the outcome is harmony, understanding, and love, and at its best then the governed experience that "rule" as merely doing what they would want to do anyway. Laotse, a wise man of ancient China, observed: "When the work of the best rulers is done, their task accomplished, the people all remark, 'We have done it ourselves.'"[3]

CORPORATE HUMANKIND TO RULE THE EARTH WITH GOD

Certainly we must concede that the scope of the task assigned to humankind in the Genesis account is staggering. Even believing that there was originally only one unified land mass surrounded by the waters of the globe, which is the current earth science hypothesis, we can still hardly comprehend what it would mean to govern the animal kingdom over the entire earth.

But Adam, it is to be noted, was charged to initiate the *process:* "Be fruitful, multiply, fill the earth and conquer it. Be masters of the fish of the sea, the birds of heaven and all living animals on the earth" (1:28, JB). We have every reason to suppose that the task is one that in the best of circumstances was planned to take hundreds or thousands of generations.

Even though it would be vastly different because of the absence of evil and its effects, perhaps the process originally intended would not be *wholly* dissimilar to human history as we know it. Perhaps our present tendency to have pets and zoos, to be fond of living creatures and domesticate them, and our amazing powers to train and control other creatures on the planet are but dim reflections of the divine intention for us.

Our care about the extinction of species and our general feeling of responsibility and concern for the fate of animals, plants, and even the earth also speaks of this divine intention. Scientists talk easily and often of our responsibility to care for the oceans and forests and wild, living things. This urge toward such responsibility is, I think, only a manifestation of the *imago Dei* originally implanted in humankind and still not wholly destroyed.

For peace in the animal world, though, there would have to be complete harmony and understanding between people, their governors. Otherwise animals would be used to make war—which of course we've done for millennia. And there must be unity with God, upon whom all life forms ultimately depend. I believe that, as things were intended, humanity would have "spoken" to the animals, directed their lives as needed, in cooperation with the rest of humankind and with the sovereign action of God, and that such direction would have been sometimes carried out through natural law and sometimes through acts of divine cooperation. The world of peace and cooperation of which humanity now only fitfully dreams would have been a reality.

But we know that paradise was lost. The disruption of the harmony between God and humankind, and then between humans, were in fact earth-shattering, cosmic events that made impossible the exercise of that rule to which humankind was appointed.

Creation is now the unwilling subject of human vanity and folly, as we can see in Romans 8:20, just because it wasn't governed by a humanity in loving and intelligent harmony with itself and with

God. It is in its present state due to the fact that humanity is at *war* with itself and with its God. Animal sacrifice in religious ritual signals the effects of our failure to do what we were meant to do—whatever else its point. The poor animal "pays" with its life for humanity's sin. In the most graphic way imaginable, this portrays our failure through history to serve God in the appointed fashion.

THE HUMAN BODY AS PART OF THE *IMAGO DEI*

But the Genesis account of our creation tells us more than just God's intention for our place in nature. We are different than the rest of creation for another reason beyond our dominion over it. The *manner* of our creation was different from the rest of creation too. Before humankind, preexisting substance is simply *commanded* to bring forth a life form. In the case of humans, however, God imparts something of himself to an earthen form specially shaped to receive it. Genesis 2:7 states, "Then the Lord God formed man of dust from the ground, and breathed into his nostrils the breath of life; and man became a living being" (ASV).

Our earthly form seems from this wording to have come "alive" only in conjunction with the giving of God's "breath" or spirit to it. The term "living being" occurs in 1:24 and again in 2:19, referring to creatures with the power of *movement* in the air, waters, or earth. These earlier living beings had come forth from dust or water at God's command. Now, in humans, the "living being" emerges from shaped dust as a result of the influx of God's spirit.

Whatever the precise details of the process—and we must beware of filling them out in a manner that would be blasphemous of the nature of God—the human too becomes a "living being," with an animal nature, but with a vast difference—we have a nature that is suitably adapted to be the vehicle of God's likeness.

The two sides of the great human contradiction, dust and divinity, then, are set in place. Human creatures, like all living beings, have a life of their own. But though that life is mortal and short, it is still a life in which we alone among living beings can stand in opposition to God—in order that we may also choose to stand *with* God.

If it were not for this ability, we could not fill our part in God's plan, because we would just be puppets. And no puppet could bear his likeness or be his child. The human body itself then is part of the *imago Dei,* for it is the vehicle through which we can effectively acquire the limited self-subsistent power we must have to be truly in the image and likeness of God.

And herein lies the the pivotal concept about our nature we need to understand when we begin talk of redemption. Let us try to make this point as clear as possible since everything turns upon it in practical theology.

In creating human beings in his likeness so that we could govern in his manner, God gave us a measure of *independent* power. Without such power, we absolutely could not resemble God in the close manner he intended, nor could we be God's co-workers. *The locus or depository of this necessary power is the human body.* This explains, in theological terms, why we have a body at all. *That body is our primary area of power, freedom, and—therefore—responsibility.*

From the strictly physical point of view, we now know that bodily mass is in fact a storehouse of immense energy. Albert Einstein's formula $E = MC^2$—the energy potentially present in a bit of matter is equal to its mass times the square of the speed of light—is a striking revelation of the nature of matter. And matter, of course, is what our body is composed of. And its nature is *power.* The splitting of a uranium atom releases something like six million times the amount of power it exerts upon its surroundings before fission occurs. The power exerted when a pile of wood is burned, releasing the energy potentially present in it, is immensely greater than what it exerts before the burning, as is immediately clear from what happens to its surroundings when it catches on fire.

In us some small part of the potential power in our body stands at the disposal of our conscious thought, intention, and choice. In essence, an individual's *character* is nothing but the pattern of habitual ways in which that person comports his or her body—whether conforming to the conscious intentions of the individual or not.

With this explanation before us, then, we can come to a correct understanding of a term absolutely central to our understanding of the psychology of redemption—the term "flesh." This essential biblical term applies to the natural physical substance of a person (which we'll have more to say about at a later point), and it refers to the reservoir of finite independent *powers* inherent in the human body as a "living being" among other living beings. In Eden, one of those specifically *human* powers was the power to interact, not only with the organic, the other living beings such as the creatures of the air, earth, and water, or even with the inorganic, the nonliving matter, but also with God and *his* powers. But the death that befell Adam and Eve in the moment of their initial sin was also the death of this interactive relationship with God, the loss of this central closeness as a constant factor in their experience (Gen. 3). And with this loss came the loss of the power required to fulfill their role as God's rulers over the earth.

This original job description for humanity hints at a power far beyond what it now possesses independently of God's Kingdom order. I believe men and women were designed by God, in the very constitution of their human personalities, to carry out his rule by meshing the relatively little power resident in their own bodies with the power inherent in the infinite Rule or Kingdom of God.

We now have developed robots that move about their work area until their batteries run low. Then they internally sense their need for more power and go plug themselves into an electrical outlet and recharge their batteries. Similarly, so long as men and women remained in touch and harmony with God, they could tap the resources of God's power to carry out the vast, impossible function assigned to them. Their dominion would be complete and effective within the range God intended because their power was used in conjunction with God's. Their rule was indeed their rule—their understanding, their desire, their choice—but it was exercised by means of a power greater than their own bodies could muster, a power conveyed through a personal relation with the Creator of all things.

But to understand how such power is possible for us within the limitations of our finite bodily being, we must look more deeply into the nature of *life,* and especially at its surprising abilities to transcend itself—to pursue its course by means of a substance that lies beyond it. We are a little less than a god only because our life is of such a nature that it can draw upon the infinite resources of God.

NOTES

1. *The Way of the Pilgrim and The Pilgrim Continues His Way,* trans. R. M. French (New York: Seabury, 1965), 45.
2. See, for example, the famous statement from the Westminister Confession, according to which the purpose of human beings is to love God and enjoy him forever. See also *The Spiritual Exercises of St. Ignatius,* (Garden City, NY: Doubleday, Image Books, 1964), 47: "Man is created to praise, reverence, and serve God our Lord, and by this means to save his soul. All other things on the face of the earth are created for man to help him fulfill the end for which he is created." It might be possible to read these and similar statements in a way conforming to the interpretation here given of our vocation, according to which we were at least as much created for the rest of creation as it for us. This would allow us to connect our created nature with Jesus' teaching that the greatest is the servant of all (Matt. 20:26–27). But they have in fact not been so read as a rule in Western history. For a view of mysticism that might allow it to consist in a right care of the earth, see Evelyn Underhill, *Mysticism* (New York: New American Library, 1974), 81ff.
3. Quoted in Lin Yutang, ed., *The Wisdom of China and India* (New York: Modern Library, 1942), 591–92.

5. The Nature of Life

For anyone who wants to save his life will lose it; but anyone who loses his life for my sake, that man will save it. What gain, then, is it for a man to have won the whole world and to have lost or ruined his very self?

LUKE 9:24–25, JB

A grain of wheat remains a solitary grain unless it falls into the ground and dies; but if it dies, it bears a rich harvest.

JOHN 12:25, NEB

The sayings of Jesus above are most often taken as expressions of some ethereal truth for especially religious people. Instead, they are mere observations about how life actually works. As is so often the case with the statements of Jesus, they say nothing about what we ought to do. They simply state how things are. Anything with life in it can flourish only if it abandons itself to what lies beyond it, eventually to be lost as a *separate* being, though continuing to live on in relation to others. Life is inner power to reach and live "beyond."

Human life cannot flourish as God intended it to, in a divinely inspired and upheld corporate rule over this grand globe, if we see ourselves as "on our own"—and especially if we struggle to preserve ourselves that way. When we are in isolation from God and not in the proper social bonds with others, we cannot rule the earth for good—the idea is simply absurd. Our struggle for ascendency over others, the problem of who shall govern and who shall say what is to be done, is hardly manageable on a national scale. Most countries maintain a stable government only by great effort and at a great cost in blood and money. At the international level, this problem is strictly without acceptable solution apart from a global return to the government of God—not to be confused with any form of "one-world" *human* government. In the concrete texture of human existence, one look at family or community life shows the resentment, hatred, and violence that results when one member's isolated will is forced upon the rest.

Things do not have to be that way, but deep reflection upon the nature of life generally—and then upon human life and spiritual life—is required to make that clear. Men and women have the option of living under God and among other human beings in a cooperative relationship that fulfills their nature and makes the corporate rule of the earth the natural expression of who they are. This possibility is rooted in the amazing nature of life itself and of human life in particular.

To penetrate to the ultimate essence of life would, of course, be as difficult as to lay bare the ultimate natures of consciousness or matter. Maybe it would be absolutely impossible. But doing so, fortunately, is not necessary here. A correct description of the basic phenomenon of life will allow us to recognize its presence and to distinguish its various kinds, such as plant or animal—or *spiritual*.

LIFE IS POWER TO RELATE AND TO ASSIMILATE

Life is always and everywhere an inner power to relate to other things in certain specific ways. The living thing has an inherent power that contacts what is beyond it, drawing from this "beyond" to enhance and extend its own being and influence. For instance, the seed sends forth its root. The baby moves to its mother. The mind is improved for greater accomplishments by what it learns as knowledge or experience makes more knowledge or experience possible. Those who reach out in love find strength and love and understanding to carry on. It is another of Jesus' "laws of how things are" that those who give are given unto, as it says in Luke 6:38.

In such cases we see life—whatever its ultimate metaphysical nature and explanation—to be the ability to contact and selectively take in from the surroundings whatever supports its own survival, extension, and enhancement. In fact, the linguistic root of the word "life" in the Indo-European languages reflects this, having the general sense of *continuing, enduring,* or *persisting* through an interactive course of specific change.

A grain of wheat in the ground takes in heat energy and moisture and, by means of that and its specific inner force, extends tendrils to find further nourishment in the soil around it. If it finds that nourishment, it will continue its specific course of development to an end that makes it wheat, not corn or an oak tree. Then it will provide the means of "reproducing" itself "after its kind" (Gen. 1:12), and more wheat arises.

In animal life the powers to move about in space and to perceive things are added. It adds them not as an exterior attachment to its lower powers shared with plants, but as something on which those very powers of nourishment and procreation themselves depend. Thus, motion is very prominent in the Genesis description of those "living creatures" over which man was to have dominion. (1:20–25)

And then, of course, to the animals' motion and perceptual consciousness in humans are added the powers of thought, valuation, and choice, and these mold and make possible the continuance and success of our "lower" powers of perception, motion, nourishment, and procreation.

THE PHYSICIST AND THE PHILOSOPHER ON THE NATURE OF LIFE

Why are we discussing this? We must have a firm grasp upon the general nature of life to understand spirituality and the spiritual life. And it will aid us if we consider how these commonsense observations about the phenomenon of life agree with the deeper reflections of scientists and philosophers.

Erwin Schrodinger, Nobel Prize winning physicist, writes:

What is the characteristic feature of life? When is a piece of matter said to be alive? When it goes on "doing something," moving, exchanging material with its environment, and so forth, and that for a much longer period than we would expect an inanimate piece of matter to "keep going" under similar circumstances. When a system that is not alive is isolated or placed in a uniform environment, all motion usually comes to a standstill very soon as a result of various kinds of friction.[1]

Elsewhere he asks:

How does the living organism avoid decay? The obvious answer is: By eating, drinking, breathing and (in the case of plants) assimilating. The technical term is *metabolism*. The Greek word (*metaballein*) means change or exchange.[2]

Over half a century before Schrodinger wrote these words, the English philosopher and critic John Ruskin had said this of the human:

His true life is like that of lower organic beings, the independent force by which he moulds and governs external things; it is a force of assimilation which converts everything around him into food, or into instruments; and which, however humbly or obediently it may listen to or follow the guidance of superior intelligence, never forfeits its own authority as a judging principle and as a will capable of either obeying or rebelling.[3]

Ruskin proceeds to contrast this "true" life with the "false" life that is possible, and too often reality, for human beings: a false life of custom and accident "in which we do what we have not purposed, and speak what we do not mean, and assent to what we do not understand; that life which is overlaid by the weight of things external to it, and is moulded by them instead of assimilating them."[4] How often do we feel like this in our day-to-day life, doing and saying things we don't mean just to get along with the world around us?

INDIVIDUALITY AND LIFE

Once I counseled a sensitive and intelligent young woman who was quite miserable in her job at a department store. She told me that on the weekends she felt as if she had been "dug up" from being "buried" during the week. This graphically expressed the sense that her activities at work were not really *hers,* that she therefore was dead ("buried") during that time, only to come to life (be "dug up") on the weekends when her activities originated from within herself.

What constitutes the *individuality* and uniqueness that make living things precious? It is their inner source of activity. One brick or board may be as good as another since it has no inner life. But to treat one person as replaceable by another is not to treat them as *persons* at all. It denies the inner source, the originative power that is a *human* life. And that is why doing so is regarded as *de*humanizing.

Some persons may indeed try to abdicate their life, disown their spontaneity, seek security by "conforming" to what is outside of them. But they don't actually escape life or their responsibility for it. They only succeed in appearing "wooden," unlively. We may know what to expect from them, but we have as little delight in them as they do in themselves.

Ever wonder why we love the frankness, the audacity of the little child? It's because a child presents life in an unblushing directness that permits no mistake about its originality and therefore its individuality.

It's the same reason we delight in the frolics of a puppy or the lollings about of a panda. These are so utterly gratuitous that they could, we think, only be evidences of an inward life completely unrestrained. And we love them for it.

"TO HIM THAT HATH SHALL BE GIVEN"

Individual growth, though, must include internal growth—internal complexity. As a life unfolds, it develops this *internal complexity* as well as an *external scope* that multiplies the effect of its inherent powers. Once again, Ruskin states his opinion on the matter:

The power which causes the several portions of the plant to help each other, we call life. Much more is this so in the animal. We may take away the branch of a tree without much harm to it; but not the animal's limb. Thus, intensity of life is also intensity of helpfulness—completeness of depending of each part on all the rest. The ceasing of this help is what we call corruption.[5]

The expansion of *internal* parts and powers in the orderly "helpful" way proper to the living thing's nature then serves as foundation for it to extend its powers into its *external* surroundings. It is a law of life: "To him that hath shall be given, and from him that hath not shall be taken away what he hath" (Mark 4:25). The larger and stronger plant or animal crowds out the others and appropriates resources to become stronger still, limited only by the life cycle of its kind.

So what does this say about the human being?

THE RANGE OF HUMAN LIFE

The astonishing human power to *use* what is beyond ourselves is one of the main clues to who and what we are. Due to our intelligence and social organization alone (we shall return to the spiritual dimension later), we extend our powers over the earth and its inhabitants to a degree both awe-inspiring and terrifying, promising to heal the agony of human history or threatening utterly to destroy the planet. The more power we get, the more power we *can* get—for good or evil! Such is human life in its current condition. In our spiritual disintegration we may not be able to rule the earth, but we now have the power several times over to ruin it utterly.

We not only make "tools" to extend our power and life, but we also live in relationships of such vast and pervasive effect on ourselves and the cosmos as to far transcend the category of mere instrumentality. Those relationships enter into the very substance of our life. They are the most powerful of our cultural and social relations and structures—the artistic, the commercial, the scientific, and the military—and they are the ones seen in action in the major phases of human society and history.

This range of powers is so great that it seems to underscore humankind's original "job description" quoted earlier from the book of Genesis. We seem to have the potentiality to tap into the inexhaustible powers of all creation. For instance, by his unaided energies a man can leap a barrier about his own height, if he is in good physical condition; but with practice and the right kind of pole he can vault triple that height or more. Unaided he can swim a broad river, but in the right social and technological setting he can effortlessly cross oceans or fly above the highest mountains. Without the assistance of appropriate tools he may find it difficult to number a flock of sheep, but with his computers he can plot the trajectory of a rocket to other planets and beyond or analyze unimaginably complex economic data.

It is the amazing *extent* of our ability to utilize power outside ourselves that we must consider when we ask what the human being is. The limits of our power to transcend ourselves utilizing powers not located in us—including, of course, the spiritual—are yet to be fully known. Philosophers of other ages used to say that God had hidden from humans the glory of their own soul, that we might not be overwhelmed with pride.

Looking at men and women reclaimed by the spiritual rule of God in Christ, John the apostle exclaimed (1 John 3:2, JB):

My dear people, we are already the children of God, but what we are to be in the future has not yet been revealed; all we know is, that when it is revealed we shall be like Him, because we shall see Him as he really is.

Because of his personal experience with spiritual powers brought to him in Christ, John sensed an unimaginable greatness in our destiny.

LIFE DEFORMED

We humans, though, *on our own*—manipulating the natural powers around us, whether of the atom or of social processes—are truly a terrifying phenomenon. We easily appear to be completely out of control today, careening madly toward the edge of the cosmic cliff. Candid observers quickly come to the conclusion that *there is some pervasive and basic lack in human life.*

Life in general can carry on within limits even though some of its specific needs are not adequately met. A plant or animal without the appropriate food, light, or space may lead a weakened and deformed existence, but one that is still a life. Human life is not what it could be, though it is still here, still going on. But the question is, *what* is human life being cut off from to leave it in such a sad and depleted condition?

In the hierarchy of abilities, any disruption or malfunctioning of the higher powers deforms and weakens the lower ones, not the other way around. An animal that is unable to perceive or move—its highest powers—is distorted in its other powers—taking in nourishment, for example. Personality disorders in humans often have physical symptoms—in fact, the person in whom thought or feeling malfunctions is deformed throughout the rest of his or her living powers. "If you have bad eyesight, your whole body is in the dark," as Matthew 6:23 states.

Yet there is a life higher than natural thought and feeling for which the "living being" in human nature was made. It is the spiritual. Disruption of that higher life wrecks our thinking and valuation, thereby corrupting our entire history and being, down to the most physical of levels. It is this pervasive distortion and disruption of human existence from the top down that the Bible refers to as sin (not sins)—the general posture of fallen humankind. Humans are not only wrong, they are also *wrung,* twisted out of proper shape and proportion.

The philosopher Jacob Needleman points out that "there is an innate element in human nature . . . that can grow and develop through impressions of truth received in the organism like a special nourishing energy."[6] In other words, robbed of a vital nutrient, the whole plant sickens. Robbed of spiritual truth and reality—of right relationship to the spiritual Kingdom of God—the social, psychological, and even the *physical* life of humankind is disordered and, in Ruskin's strictly descriptive sense, corrupt.

The evil that we do in our present condition is a reflection of a weakness caused by spiritual starvation. When Jesus prayed on the cross, "Father forgive them, for they know not what they do," he was not just being generous to his killers; he was expressing the facts of the case. They really did not know what they were doing. As St. Augustine so clearly saw, the deranged condition of humankind is not, at bottom, a positive fact, but a deprivation. It is one that results in vast positive evils, of course, yet depravity is no less a horror because it stems from a deficiency, and people are no less responsible for it and its consequences.

In this condition of fundamental lack and disconnection we are described by St. Paul as being *dead,* "dead in trespasses and sins" (Eph. 2:1). It is a condition that can be displaced only when by a new relationship to God we become "alive unto him." The light bulb is dead when disconnected from the electrical current, even though it still exists. But when connected to the current, it radiates and affects its surroundings with a power and substance that is *in* it but not *of* it.

WHAT IS SPIRIT?

If the missing element in the present human order is that of the spirit, what then is spirit? Very simply, *spirit* is *unembodied personal power.*[7] Ultimately it is God, who *is* Spirit (John 4:24). Electricity, magnetism, and gravity, by contrast, are embodied nonpersonal powers.

The idea of spirit as nonbodily power—though capable of interacting with, influencing, and in some manner even inhabiting a body—is a common heritage of the human race. Drawing upon that heritage Leonardo da Vinci (1452–1519) could, quite naturally, even describe the force associated with *physical* objects as a "spiritual" capacity, on the grounds that it is invisible and impalpable.[8] He omitted the personal element in the spiritual, however. But anything without physical being is held up to question—especially in scientific theory. Some decades after Da Vinci, the force of gravitation was scientifically described by Sir Isaac Newton. But it was regarded as "occult" and rejected by many of his contemporaries just *because* it was held to act without physical contact and thus to extend, in a "disembodied" fashion, beyond the bodies that nevertheless fell under its sway.

No doubt the distinction between the physical and the spiritual is not easy to draw in a clear and philosophically sound fashion, and we must not place too much weight upon the common ideas about it. But we may be sure, at least, that the *biblical* conception of the spiritual is that of an *ordered realm of personal power* founded in the God who is himself spirit and not a localizable physical body.

The biblical worldview also regards the spiritual as a realm fundamental to the existence and behavior of *all* natural or physical reality (see especially John 1:1–14; Col. 1:17; Heb. 1:2; 11:3). And it is one in which people may participate by engaging it through the active life tendency called "faith," as we see in Hebrews 11:3, 27. Its integrity in our minds is sternly guarded by the second of the Ten Commandments: "You shall not make a carved image for yourself, nor the likeness of anything in the heavens above, or in the earth below, or in the waters under the earth" (Exod. 20:4).

What is it that is missing in our deformed condition? From a biblical perspective, there can be no doubt that *it is the appropriate relation to the spiritual Kingdom of God that is the missing "nutriment" in the human system.* Without it our life is left mutilated, stunted, weakened, and deformed in various stages of disintegration and corruption.

DRINKING IN THE DIVINE "STREAM OF ORDER"

What happens when people get these missing spiritual nutrients? Returning to Schrodinger:

The device by which an organism maintains itself stationary at a fairly high level of orderliness . . . really consists in continually sucking orderliness from its environment.[9]

For human beings, this extends to their spiritual capabilities. When the human organism is brought into a willing, personal relationship with the spiritual Kingdom of God, "sucking in orderliness" from *that* particular part of the human environment, it becomes pervasively transformed, as a corn stalk in drought is transformed by the onset of drenching rain—the contact with the water transforms the plant inwardly and then extends it outwardly.

In the same way, people are transformed by contact with God. In creation the human organism was endowed with astonishing capacities to interact—through individual, social, and historical development—with the realities around it, including the spiritual. People of course can be alive at the merely physical level, oblivious to the realms of knowledge, social relations, and artistic creativity, which are, all the while, there for others who are willing and able to claim them. Or they can claim these too and yet remain dead to God and the world of the spiritual and to the cosmic vocation for which they were initially created.

In the Genesis account of human origin, God told Adam and Eve—as they lived in "Eden," which means "delight" or "enjoyment"—that if they ate of the tree of knowledge of good and evil they would "surely die" (2:17). When Eve through mistrust of God (3:6) took the fatal step, she and Adam did not cease to be "living beings." But they nevertheless died, as God said they would. They ceased to relate to and function in harmony with that spiritual reality that is at the foundation of all things and of whose glory the universe is an expression. They were dead to God.

The small reservoir of independent powers that was resident in their bodies continued to function as it does in "living beings" generally, but the connection to God through which those powers would have been properly ordered and fulfilled was broken. Men and women no longer had the life they were primarily made for. What was previously done for them, or by their word as representatives of God, was now done with pain and labor and blood (3:16–21).

Between spirit and flesh, then, there was a constant warfare (6:3). Robbed of their highest unifying principle—their relation to God—humans were no longer beings with integrity or coherent wholeness. Their lower powers set themselves against the Spirit, and the Spirit against them. "They are in conflict with one another so that what you will to do you cannot do" (Gal. 5:17, NEB). The very idea of a spiritual *life* for human beings was lost and could be regained only through millennia of grinding history in which God nevertheless refused to abandon his original purpose in human creation.

"SPIRITUAL LIFE" AND ITS "DISCIPLINES"—
A DEFINITION

With an understanding of such basic concepts, we are now in a position to explain the terms most central to our study in this book and to an understanding of Christ's gospel of life in the Kingdom of God. A "spiritual life" consists in that range of activities in which people cooperatively interact with God—and with the spiritual order deriving from God's personality and action. And what is the result? A new overall quality of human existence with corresponding new powers.

A person is a "spiritual person" to the degree that his or her life is correctly integrated into and dominated by God's spiritual Kingdom. Thus, as Gustavo Gutierrez explains, "Spirituality, in the strict and profound sense of the word, is the dominion of the spirit."[10] The "babe in Christ" in 1 Corinthians 3:1 has spiritual life, but in a largely incipient form. Much in his embodied and concretely socialized personality is not under the effective direction of the Spirit and the reintegration of the self under God is not yet achieved.

Spirituality is a matter of *another reality*. It is absolutely indispensible to keep before us the fact that it is not a "commitment" and it is not a "life-style," even though a commitment and a life-style will come from it. Above all it is not a social or political stance. It is, today, in great danger of being "politicized." In a way, it is natural that it should be, for in the "other reality" there is the death knell of this world's orders. Seeing Jesus' power, those around him naturally tried to set up a government with him as the "king."

But the essence and aim of spirituality is not to correct social and political injustices. That will be its effect—though never exactly in ways we imagine as we come to it with our preexisting political concerns. That is not its use, and all thought of *using* it violates its nature.

Those who worry that unless we act against authority structures our spirituality will accomplish nothing simply do not understand what spirituality is. On the other hand, the authorities will always find the spirituality of Jesus and his followers impossible to deal with, for it stands beyond their manipulation and control.

So, now that we know what "spiritual life" is, what are "the disciplines for the spiritual life"? The disciplines are activities of mind and body purposefully undertaken, to bring our personality and total being into effective cooperation with the divine order. They enable us more and more to live in a power that is, strictly speaking, beyond us, deriving from the spiritual realm itself, as we "yield ourselves to God, as those that are alive from the dead, and our members as instruments of righteousness unto God," as Romans 6:13 puts it.

The necessity for such disciplines comes from the very nature of the self in the image of God, discussed earlier. Once the individual has through divine initiative become alive to God and his Kingdom, the extent of integration of his or her *total* being into that Kingdom order significantly depends upon the individual's initiative.

Of course we all know that the human personality is an incredibly complex, dynamic structure, with physical, social, psychological and—Christians would add—spiritual dimensions. Our *conscious* understanding and good intentions focused at the outset of the spiritual life constitute an important, even crucial, part of us. We soon learn by sad experience, however, that there is much more in us than what we can consciously command. We find how hard it is to discern and to harmonize the *whole* self with the will and personality of God. Yet even as we reach for more grace to this end, we also learn by experience that the harmonization of our total self with God will not be done *for* us. *We* must act.

THE PROBLEM OF METHOD

But what are we to do? How are the deeper reaches of the self to be discerned and dealt with? Depending on our religious background, we may think of regular church attendance and faithfulness to commonly recognized religious duties, of individual or social "experiences," of decisions or commitments of various kinds, as means of radical transformation of the self. Good effects often come from these. They are to be used and not despised. But their track record as means for actual transformation of individuals into Christlikeness is not impressive.

The contemporary world would generally think of some form of psychological counseling or psychotherapy in answer to this question instead of "spiritual disciplines." Carl Jung, for example, writes that "the self can be defined as an inner guiding factor that is different from the conscious personality and that can be grasped only through the investigation of one's own dreams."[11]

I would not deny that insight gained from dream analysis or other forms of psychotherapy may be of aid in the transformation of the self, and in certain cases it may even be necessary. We do not have to accept the worldview of psychoanalysis in any of its forms to admit this. Dreams belonged to the prophets for millennia before the psychotherapist showed up. But there is much else available to us that can directly illuminate the depths of the total personality—the ultimate subject of *full* salvation—and provide guidelines for our action leading to transformation. Not least among these other sources is of course the Bible, with its many portrayals of lives in transformation and of the essential activities involved therein.

How do such Bible stories help? Upon a realistic, critical, adult reading, by those prepared to be honest with their experience, the Bible incisively lays bare the depths and obscurities of the human heart. This is why it continues to play the decisive role it does in human history and culture and why it is fitted to be the perpetual instrument of the Spirit of God for human transformation, as 2 Timothy 3:16–17 indicates.

But the Bible also informs us that there are certain *practices*—solitude, prayer, fasting, celebration, and so forth—we can undertake, in cooperation with grace, to raise the level of our lives toward godliness. Further help along the same lines is available from the writings of the saints and moralists throughout the ages, of course, who also are very wise to the hidden ways of the human soul. And when all of these resources are well used, especially in the spiritually enlivened church, they bolster common sense in such a way that it alone can often function as an immediate and reliable guide in spiritual matters.

NO QUICK FIX

But the one lesson we learn from all available sources is that there is no "quick fix" for the human condition. The approach to wholeness is for humankind a process of great length and difficulty that engages all our own powers to their fullest extent over a long course of experience. But we don't like to hear this. We are somewhat misled by the reports of experiences by many great spiritual leaders, and we assign their greatness to these great moments they were given, neglecting the years of slow progress they endured before them. Francis de Sales wisely counsels us not to expect transformation in a moment, though it is possible for God to give it.

The ordinary purification and healing, whether of the body or of the mind, takes place only little by little, by passing from one degree to another with labor and patience. The angels upon Jacob's ladder had wings; yet they flew not, but ascended and descended in order from one step to another. The soul that rises from sin to devotion may be compared to the dawning of the day, which at its approach does not expel the darkness instantaneously but only little by little.[12]

Thus it is necessary to say that conversion, as understood in Christian circles, is *not* the same thing as *the required transformation of the self.* The fact that a long course of experience is needed for the transformation is not set aside when we are touched by the new life from above. Some well-known scenes from the life of one of Jesus' closest friends, Simon Peter—the "rock" who upon occasion more resembled a pile of shifting sand—illustrates this fact well.

STAGES ON THE SPIRITUAL WAY: THE CASE OF SIMON PETER

As the time of the cross approached, Jesus informed his closest friends that he was to be taken and killed. Looking deeply into their hearts he told them that when the sword fell upon him they would desert him, they would *run*. This was not to scold them, I think, but to help them in the moment of their failure and afterward, by letting them know that he all along understood what was happening to them and accepted them nonetheless.

Simon Peter, of course, insisted that he would not desert Jesus, even if everyone else did. Once again, to prepare Peter by letting him know that his Lord knew *exactly* what was happening, Jesus assured him that he would deny him, three times, before the crow of the cock. Peter stood his ground, affirming even more aggressively: "Though I should die with thee, yet will I not deny thee. Likewise also said all the disciples" (Matt. 26:35).

Hours pass. Peter was confused and worried by his Lord's words and behavior and by the turn events were obviously taking. They all wandered from the upper room out into the Garden of Gethsemane. Called upon by Jesus simply to "watch with me"—to just stay awake and be with him—Peter and the others were found "sleeping for sorrow" (Luke 22:45).

Jesus then analyzed their case with surgical precision: "The spirit is willing, but the flesh is weak" (Matt. 26:41). He did justice to that element in them that *was* genuinely turned to God, "the spirit." But the natural powers of their bodies, those of "the flesh," were not at that time aligned with their spirits, and hence the flesh was weak in that toward which their spirit was truly and rightly directed.

When the soldiers came with the betrayer to get his Lord, Peter awoke, grabbed a sword, and, acting where his flesh was strong, chopped off some poor fellow's ear. Jesus rebuked him for doing the only thing he really knew how to do in such circumstances, so he (and the others) did exactly what Jesus had predicted: "All the disciples forsook him and fled" (Matt. 26:56).

But Peter fled only a little way. He really was stronger than the others, it seems, for he turned and followed at a distance, even into the palace of the high priest "to see the end" (Matt. 26:58). But it soon became clear that at this point the Spirit had more control of his legs than of his mouth. There on three occasions, as the group sat around and waited for what would happen, he was charged with being a companion of Jesus. Each time he denied it, culminating in a great act of profane emphasis: "Then began he to curse and to swear, saying, I know not the man" (26:74). The tirade was punctuated by the crowing of a cock. "And Peter remembered. . . . And he went out and wept bitterly." (26:75).

All his most sincere and good intentions, even though specifically alerted by Jesus' prediction and warning of a few hours earlier, were not able to withstand *the automatic tendencies ingrained in his flesh* and activated by the circumstances. What a firsthand knowledge Peter gained this night of "the motions of sins, which work in our members to bring forth fruit unto death" (Rom. 7:5)!

But God was not done with Simon Peter. He would make a "rock" of him yet. In the hours and days that followed, Peter was subjected to experiences that synthesized what he had gathered from his years of companionship with Jesus on the road and drove it deep into the governing tendencies of his body.

He beheld the death and the manner of dying of his great friend whom he had confessed as Messiah. He encountered Christ yet alive beyond that death, and during a forty-day period of postresurrection fellowship he received anew the commission to lead the little group of believers: to "feed my sheep" and "follow me" (John 21:17, 19, 22). He now understood that he and the church were to exercise a transcendent power that did not depend upon having a kingdom or government in any human sense, for it was literally a "God government" in which they were participants (Acts 1:6–8).

That power would be sent upon them in a special way as they waited in Jerusalem and sent to them precisely "from heaven," into which Jesus had visibly ascended. Ten days they waited in an "upper room" with the other apostles, with mother Mary and the Lord's brothers, and with the faithful women who had been brought to spiritual life by the ministrations of Jesus (Acts 1:13–14).

If one but fully dwells in imagination upon this sequence of events, one begins to sense what an impact it would have had on the total personality of Peter and that of the others. Think of how a comparable process would affect your life or mine even now!

That old hand that automatically reached for the sword to kill, the legs that spontaneously took flight, the detestable tongue that forgot its inspired confession of the Messiah and, as with a life of its own, denied all relationship to Jesus, cursing God to "prove it!"—now all were of an entirely different character.

"Peter stood up in the midst of the disciples," the little band of outlaws, to take leadership (Acts 1:15). And as the promised power poured in "from heaven," filling the room (Acts 2:2) and bursting upon the city of Jerusalem itself (2:6), it found Peter with both legs and mouth strong for the spirit. "*Standing* up with the eleven" (2:14) he "lifted up his *voice*" and, as Jesus had foretold (John 14:12), did a greater work than he himself had ever done in that place:

They were convinced by his arguments, and they accepted what he said and were baptized. That very day about three thousand were added to their number. These remained faithful to the teaching of the apostles, to the brotherhood, to the breaking of bread and to prayers. The many miracles and signs worked through the apostles made a deep impression on everyone. The faithful all lived together and owned everything in common; they sold their goods and possessions and shared out of the proceeds among themselves according to what each one needed. They went as a body to the temple every day but met in their houses for the breaking of bread; they shared their food gladly and generously; they praised God and were looked up to by everyone. Day by day the Lord added to their community those destined to be saved (Acts 2:41–47, JB).

And now he *is* a "rock." *Petros*. Shall we call him "Rocky"? That would be our equivalent to what Jesus meant by his new name.

Living in dynamic interaction with God and his Kingdom through the Holy Spirit, the new church could not but conflict with those who thought *they* were in charge of the world. Persecution broke out as a matter of course and blood ran in the streets. The church was scattered, "except the apostles" (Acts 8:1).

Public attack, beatings, imprisonment, and threat of death did not move Peter from his course. He was still not entirely untroubled in his walk of faith, as we see in places such as Galatians 2:11–14, but on the whole and with very little exception his flesh remained strong on behalf of the Spirit. And when he finally met his cross in Rome, tradition tells us, he requested to be nailed to it upside down, because he did not regard himself worthy of taking the same posture in death as his old friend and Lord, Jesus Christ.

It is in Peter and his kind that we begin to get a glimpse of what is *really* possible for human life. We can see what the grand restoration of human life to its proper center in the spiritual life could mean for humankinds' divine calling to have dominion over the glorious earth for its good and for the pleasure and glory of God.

NOTES

1. Erwin Schrodinger, *What Is Life? and Other Scientific Essays,* (Garden City, NY: Doubleday, Anchor Books, 1965), 69.
2. *Ibid.,* 73.
3. John Ruskin, *The Seven Lamps of Architecture* (London: Dent, 1969), 152. See also chap. 3 of Ruskin's *Ethics of the Dust,* numerous editions.
4. Ruskin, *Seven Lamps,* 152–53.
5. Ruskin, *Modern Painters,* vol. 7 of *The Complete Works of John Ruskin* (London: Allen, 1905), 205.
6. Jacob Needleman, *Lost Christianity* (New York: Bantam, 1982), 57.
7. With this brief statement I try to draw together the results of an extensive literature concerning the nature of spirit. A useful introduction to philosophical problems having to do with spirit and to the literature on the subject is Edgar Sheffield Brightman's *The Spiritual Life* (New York: Abingdon-Cokesbury, 1942). See also Henry Churchill King, *The Seeming Unreality of the Spiritual Life* (New York: Macmillan, 1908) and B. H. Streeter, ed., *The Spirit* (London: Macmillan, 1919).
8. Will Durant, *The Renaissance,* vol. 5 in *The History of Civilization,* (New York: Simon & Schuster, 1958), 223.
9. Schrodinger, *What is Life?,* 73, 75.
10. Gustavo Gutierrez. *A Theology of Liberation,* trans. Caridad Inda and John Eagleson (New York: Orbis, 1973), 203.
11. Carl G. Jung, *Man and His Symbols* (New York: Dell, 1975), 163. See also the profound remarks about the self in Josef Goldbrunner, *Holiness Is Wholeness and Other Essays* (Notre Dame, IN: University of Notre Dame Press, 1964), 12–21.
12. Francis de Sales, *Introduction to the Devout Life,* trans. John K. Ryan (Garden City, NY: Doubleday, Image Books, 1957), 43–44.

6. Spiritual Life: The Body's Fulfillment

Low lie the bounding heart, the teeming brain
'Til, sent from God, they mount to God again.

HENRY MONTAGUE BUTLER

The body as well as the spirit now yearns to tread the way of redemption that leads to Calvary. It too wants to expose itself to the scorching sun of God's holiness. Formerly spiritualization was the goal, now it is rather the moulding of the whole human life. The meaning of Christ's incarnation for the Christian life on earth is being understood in a new light.

JOSEF GOLDBRUNNER

Given our history and cultural context, it is all too easy to believe that the spiritual life may be a life *opposed* to the body or even, at its "best," a totally disembodied mode of existence. So the idea is widespread that you can only be *really* spiritual after you are dead. Spirituality, it has been said, is for the very old and the very dead. This is where the popular idea that the spiritual frustrates or even harms the body originates. This view is found throughout Western history. But in our discussions thus far concerning the spiritual life and the spiritual person, nothing has been said about the suppression of the body. That omission is no accident. It is absolutely central to the meaning of the gospel and its relation to human nature.

Volumes could be written on the harm done to human personality and to the practice of Christianity by the "repressionist" view of spirituality. The spiritual and the bodily are by no means opposed in human life—they are complementary. We here explicitly disown and condemn any suggestion to the contrary, because it is the spiritual life alone that makes possible fulfillment of bodily existence—and hence human existence.

How does this fulfillment take place? It comes through interaction of our powers *as* bodily beings with God and his Kingdom—an interaction for which our bodies were specifically designed. Such bodies have the health and wholeness appropriate to them when we through thought, worship, and action draw upon the spiritual realm that encompasses and underlies them along with the rest of creation.

Thus the apostle Paul boldly asserts that "the body is for the Lord, and the Lord for the body" (1 Cor 6:13), and that our bodies are "members of Christ." (6:15) Later chapters will be devoted to interpretation of Paul's view of the body both as the subject of and as an instrument in the process of redemption. But we must proceed no further without some brief elaboration of the truth that the body is fulfilled in the spiritual life. There is an essential continuity and union between the person and the body. In an important sense to be explained, a person *is* his or her body.

THE SPIRITUAL AND BIOLOGICAL TOGETHER IN PSYCHOLOGY

Recently, there has been an attempt by humanistic psychology, a distinctive group within the field of professional psychology, to integrate the "spiritual" and the biological. Although I cannot agree with the entirety of humanist Abraham Maslow's views on the "spiritual" life—especially not with his view that it is attainable by *unaided* human effort—it is possible to understand in a wholly biblical way his statement:

. . . the so-called spiritual or "higher" life is on the same continuum (is the same kind of quality or thing) with the life of the flesh, or of the body, i.e., the animal life, the "lower" life. The spiritual life is part of our biological life. It is the "highest" part of it, but yet part of it. The spiritual life is part of the human essence. It is a defining characteristic of human nature without which human nature is not full human nature. It is part of the real self, of one's identity, of one's inner core, of one's specieshood, of full humanness.[1]

Of course. This simply *must* be so. Certainly such a statement must, from the Christian point of view, be carefully guarded against interpretations compatible with *naturalistic reductionism*—which insists that everything human must be explainable by the laws of Physics, Chemistry, and Biology, the "Natural" Sciences. But, on the other hand, only if we are able to understand the sense in which it is and must be true will we be able to avoid the exclusion of spirituality from our "real" life. That exclusion would reject the complete humanity of Christ himself and leave our lives largely beyond redemption.

The key to such an understanding is the recognition of what we have already learned in our discussion of human creation—that the physical human frame as created was designed for interaction with the spiritual realm and that this interaction can be resumed at the initiative of God. Then, *through the disciplines for the spiritual life*, that interaction can be developed by joint efforts of both God and the person alive in the dynamism of the Spirit. Given this understanding, all that Maslow says in his statement can, and indeed must, be accepted.

"TRUE SPIRITUALITY"

Once it is so accepted, we are secured against the idea that actual spirituality in people alienated from God is possible. But we must also guard against the view of spirituality as something "wholly inward" or something to be kept just between the individual and God.

Spirituality is simply the holistic quality of human life as it was meant to be, at the center of which is our relation to God. Concerning "true spirituality" Francis Schaeffer acutely observes:

Sweeping out of the inward positive reality, there is to be a positive manifestation externally. It is not just that we are dead to certain things, but we are to love God, we are to be alive to Him, we are to be in communion with Him, *in this present moment of history*. And we are to love men, to be alive to men as men, and to be in communication on a true personal level with men, *in this present moment of history*.[2]

But the "are to be" clauses in this statement change from exhortation to prophecy and description only if we understand that the "inward positive reality" and the "external positive manifestation" are not two separate things, but *one* unified process in which those who are alive in God are caught up in their embodied, socialized totality. Such a *life*-affirming view of spirituality as Schaeffer here and elsewhere asserts cannot be maintained among thoughtful people, though, unless it is understood that the spiritual is a homogeneous aspect, part and parcel of the biological (and therefore social) nature of human beings.

We must not allow atheistically biased ideologies, such as the secular humanism currently so widespread, to veil the fact that *bios* (in "biology") is simply a general term for life, one that carries no physical or materialistic account of life in it.

What life is can only be decided as the cosmos and our understanding of it develops. The dimensions and powers of matter and life in the case of any specific type of living organism are something that can only be ascertained by bold and imaginative experimentation and observation as free from prejudgment as possible. The belief that people cannot live in constant union with the spiritual God throughout their daily life shall one day appear as odd as the belief that metal bodies cannot float on water or fly through the air. We must simply observe the living subject under all possible conditions to understand it deeply. For the matters at issue, that means that we human beings must lead our lives before God in an open, adventurous, and reflective manner. Only then shall we find what is actually possible for us as physical organisms. The wise words of Archbishop William Temple are: "We only know what matter is when spirit dwells in it; we only know what man is when God dwells in him."[3]

SPIRITUALITY AND PLAY

Yet hardly anyone needs to be told how badly the relationship of spirituality to the physical life has been misunderstood. A recent movie of the life of Christ scandalized many people because it contained a scene in which Christ was engaged in a ball game with a number of other men. He was actually leaping around and catching the ball and jostling others with his body!

"Spiritual people do not play." That is the usual view. For one thing, they are too serious ever to play. It is a test of their spirituality that they never let up from their special spiritual activities. For another, play might be pleasureable. And while spiritual people can have *joy*, they probably should stay away from just plain pleasure. While it is not in itself bad, it might ensnare them. Or so we seem to think.

Spirituality has thus come to be regarded by the world as those futile, self-torturing excesses of strange men and women who lived in far-off, benighted places and times. Accordingly, the One who came to give abundance of life is commonly thought of as a cosmic stuffed shirt, whose excessive "spirituality" probably did not allow him normal bodily functions and certainly would not permit him to throw a frisbee or tackle someone in a football game.

But God is not opposed to natural life with all of its pleasures and pains and is even very favorably disposed toward it. Yet we find that hard to believe even though many well-known Christian teachers have laid great emphasis upon the point. In his book *He That Is Spiritual*, Lewis Sperry Chafer remarks that it is a morbid human consciousness that has misled us into the view that to be spiritual one must avoid play, diversion, and helpful amusement. This view, however, is not only opposed to scriptural teaching, but is a device of Satan to make the blessed life in God distasteful to young people overflowing with physical energy. Overemphasis on negatives, Chafer points out, leaves the impression that spirituality is contrary to pleasure, liberty, and spontaneous expression.

Spirituality is not a pious pose. It is not a "Thou shalt *not*"; it is "Thou shalt." It flings open the doors into the eternal blessedness, energies and resources of God. It is a serious thing to remove the element of relaxation and play from any life. We cannot be normal physically, mentally or spiritually if we neglect this vital factor in human life. God has provided that our joy shall be full.

Chafer concludes this passage with a penetrating observation on the *manner* in which the spiritual dimension asserts its priority:

It is also to be noted that one of the characteristics of true spirituality is that it supercedes lesser desires and issues. The Biblical, as well as practical, cure for "worldliness" among Christians is so to fill the heart and life with the eternal blessings of God that there will be a joyous preoccupation and absentmindedness to unspiritual things. . . . A dead leaf cannot remain where a new bud is springing, nor can worldliness remain where the blessings of the Spirit are flowing.[4]

By "unspiritual" we do *not* mean simply the physical or bodily. We mean whatever is taken without regard to its place in the spiritual rule of God through his creation. *Nothing* is in itself unspiritual, as "spiritual" has been explained in our previous chapter, for all things finally rest upon the spiritual realm. That explanation enables us to understand why and how "To the pure all things *are* pure, but to those who are defiled and faithless, *nothing* is pure" (Titus 1:15).

Still, just because we succeed in overiding our "lesser" desires as is appropriate, that does not necessarily mean that they will be omitted or even neglected. It does mean they are in subordination to the overall economy of life in God. This certainly will, on some occasions, lead to their being either opposed or left unsatisfied, but never with the attitude that what is vital to our life is therefore lost or that we have been damaged in any serious way. The "joyous preoccupation and absentmindedness" of which Chafer speaks will see to that.

THE CENTRALITY OF THE SHADOW SIDE

It is extremely important for us to realize that what we are discussing here is no mere matter of fine philosophical speculation or psychological theory. It deeply concerns Christian *practice* and its effects upon others. How many people are radically and permanently repelled from The Way by Christians who are unfeeling, stiff, unapproachable, boringly lifeless, obsessive, and dissatisfied? Yet such Christians are everywhere, and what they are missing is the wholesome liveliness springing from a balanced vitality within the freedom of God's loving rule.

Such failure to attain a deeply satisfying life always has the effect of making sinful actions seem good. Here lies the strength of temptation. This is no less true if the failure is caused by our efforts to be what we regard as "spiritual." Normally, our success in overcoming temptation will be easier if we are basically happy in our lives. To cut off the joys and pleasures associated with our bodily and social existence as "unspiritual," then, can actually have the effect of *weakening* us in our efforts to do what is right. It makes it impossible for us to see and draw strength from the goodness of rightness.

Christians who fail in the area of sex and love are among the more "colorful" sinners commonly encountered. It has become almost proverbial how the minister may fall in love with the church organist or other associate and leave an offended community and a floundering church group behind to wonder why. Frequently in such cases, as Agnes Sanford says so well, the minister "did not remember that he was dust . . . as God most mercifully does!" The minister failed to take into account his "shadow side," as she calls it, which for a while "wanted to forget all about God and play golf." This side too is holy in God's sight and was given to humankind "to make and keep him whole, lest he lose his balance while walking on the tightrope of his divine-human life."[5]

It is in this connection that the wise man warns us: "Do not be excessively righteous, and do not be overly wise. Why should you ruin yourself?" (Eccles. 7:16, NAS). "Spirituality" wrongly understood or pursued is a major source of human misery and rebellion against God.

HOW IS A PERSON THE SAME AS HIS OR HER BODY?

Our soul is not something we can separate from the body and hold pure without regard to the body to which it belongs.

A priest once said to Meister Eckhart: "I wish that your soul were in my body." To which he replied: "You would really be foolish. That would get you nowhere—it would accomplish as little as for your soul to be in my body. No soul can really do anything except through the body to which it is attached."[6]

The union of spirituality with the fullness of human life finds its deepest ground in the identification of the person with his or her body. This is a very difficult topic to treat in a popular way, and it is subject to many misinterpretations. But only if we can achieve some appreciation of it will we be able to grasp firmly the body's place in our redemption.

The materialist or behaviorist who asserts such an identification intends to *deny* that there is anything more to a person than the "physical facts" that any physical or chemical analysis finds in the human body. Such a denial obviously cannot be accepted from the Christian viewpoint, which insists upon a spiritual dimension of the human self.

But others such as the phenomenological and existentialist writers of the recent past use this identification as a way of denying that the body is "just physical," just some more or less *mechanical* device incidentally associated with a purely spiritual mind or self. That is, they use the identification to deny materialism's account of the human body. The possibilities of their view for a Christian understanding of our nature are much more promising.

This is especially true when they are brought into conjunction with much recent biblical scholarship, which also insists upon the bodily character of human nature. This biblical scholarship even goes so far as to reject the idea of a purely spiritual "immortality" of the soul in the afterlife, regarding it as a Platonic imposition upon the biblical view of personality. Instead, resurrection is insisted upon as the true form of human existence beyond death. The works of H. Wheeler Robinson and Oscar Cullman seem quite decisive on this point.[7]

But what is really meant by saying that the person *is* his or her body? This claim may seem quite paradoxical, but a basis for understanding can be laid by considering experiences that happen to everyone.

For instance, we do not have any knowledge or experience that is totally free from involvement with our bodies. Our experience of others and of ourselves is always directed in part toward an embodied condition. When I see a table, the location of my body in relation to it is stamped on how it appears to me. I cannot see the bottom side of the table because my head is above it, and I can only infer the relative position of my body from how things appear to me at any given moment. My perceptual consciousness is always marked by the specific state of my body. It is the same for every human being—that's part of our essence.

It may be less obvious, but even our abstract thought rarely if ever is separate from all physical artifacts, images, and symbolisms associated with our bodies. Our ten fingers are abstractly mirrored in an arithmetic based on powers of ten, and very little calculating of any kind can be done without bodily behaviors of some sort.

Emotions and feelings also inhabit distinct parts of our bodies: face, stomach, genitals, legs, arms, heart, shoulders. The famous "James/Lange Theory of the Emotions," which is studied in introductory psychology, attempts to do justice to this fact by insisting that the emotions we feel are only awarenesses of the appropriately excited conditions of our body.[8]

Even our decisions, choices, and actions issue from our sense of the position and posture of our bodies in our physical and our social world. Loss of balance or dizziness is essentially the loss of our grip upon our posture in relation to the surrounding physical environment. "Disorientation" is a more general term for the inability to grasp our *place* in our experienced surroundings, physical or social.

It should be emphasized that this does not just apply to our experience of ourselves. Our experience of others is also inescapably an experience of *their* embodied existence.

The novelist Pearl Buck was a child of missionaries in China. She recalls how her infant brother took fever and died, as happened with so many missionary children. When friends attempted to comfort her mother by saying, "It is only his body that is gone," the mother practically flew at them for it, crying out in her distress that she had conceived and born this little body, dressed and fed and cared for it, and that she loved *this body!*

Only someone hopelessly alienated from an authentic sense of embodied human existence can fail to understand what this grief-stricken mother was saying. Her baby was not a disembodied spirit. Whatever further qualifications and explanations must be added, you cannot in the final analysis love another person in the normal human sense and not also love his or her body; and you cannot love or really care about that body and not love the person also.

It is clear from all of this that nothing we can recognize as human experience and personality is separable from the meanings and orientations and habits embedded in the flesh of a particular human body. When we wish to get a grip on someone's life we ask such questions as: "Where do you come from? When were you born? Who are your parents? How tall are you? Where did you go to school?"—all questions about our bodies!

Human personality is not separable in our consciousness from the human body. And that fact is expressed by asserting the IDENTITY of the person as his or her body. This fact is what makes it necessary for us to make our bodies, through the disciplines for the spiritual life, our primary focus of effort in *our* part in the process of redemption.

The additional fact that we are unable to understand human behavior or society and culture using only chemical and mechanical principles indicates that this body of ours is no mere physical mechanism. As the physicist Schrodinger, once again, remarks: "From all we have learnt about the structure of living matter, we must be prepared to find it working in a manner that cannot be reduced to the ordinary laws of Physics."[9]

Here we must leave the more ultimate questions about these facts to be pursued in other contexts.[10]

THE BODY AS BATTLEFIELD

But while the human being is to be identified with his or her body, within the embodied self there are diverse and powerful forces that turn the individual personality into a battlefield. Sometimes, as it did for Simon Peter, it often appears as if the body has a life of its own capable of action to some degree independent of, or in conflict with, our conscious thoughts and intentions.

Everyone knows, of course, that the vital functions of our body—heartbeat, respiration, digestion, general metabolism, and so forth—normally lie beyond the direct control of our consciousness. All of us have also experienced the conflict between the basic drives for food, sleep, and sex, for example, and our intentions to behave in certain ways. This is elemental and universal. In extreme cases the struggle between the forces within the embodied self may manifest themselves as mental illness. The self may project its unacceptable elements or experiences onto its body, which it then refuses to accept as its own, and the person loses touch with the real world.

The influential psychoanalyst Alexander Lowen writes:

The complete loss of body contact characterizes the schizophrenic state. Broadly speaking, the schizophrenic doesn't know who he is, and is so much out of touch with reality that he cannot even phrase the question. On the other hand, the schizoid individual knows that he has a body and is, therefore, oriented in time and space. But since his ego is not identified with his body and does not perceive it in an alive way, he feels unrelated to the world and to people. Similarly, his conscious sense of identity is unrelated to the way he feels about himself. This conflict does not exist in a healthy person whose ego is identified with his body and in whom the knowledge of his identity stems from the feeling of the body.[11]

I believe that this is one of those places where the findings of psychotherapy strikingly illuminate religious truth. In the full redemption of life by Christ the embodied human personality is accepted and made truly whole.

From the viewpoint of the Christian religion, of course, the primary struggle within human nature first appears as the struggle between the individual and God. This makes perfect sense once we understand human nature in relation to the purpose for us in Creation, as explained earlier. We were made able to serve God in freedom, but we rebelled and in rebellion we used our independent power (in our body) against God.

Upon conversion, however, we have peace with God (Rom. 5:1). But the problem of reconciliation then shifts to the self and to those two components the New Testament refers to as "the flesh" and "the spirit." How? After conversion our will and conscious intent are for God or "the spiritual," as we've seen with Simon Peter. But the layer upon layer of life experience that is embedded in our bodies, as living organisms born and bred in a world set against or without God, doesn't directly and immediately follow the shift of our conscious will. It largely retains the tendencies in which it has so long lived.

In this condition, "the flesh lusteth against the Spirit, and the Spirit against the flesh: and these are contrary the one to the other, so that ye cannot do the things ye would" (Gal. 5:17). Here we have from the analytical mind of St. Paul a precise description of the experience of Peter—up to the point where his flesh was aligned with the spirit to such a degree that he indeed could do the things that he, as a converted person, wanted to do.

The conflict between flesh and spirit is the experience of all who begin the spiritual life by the influx of God's life-giving word. Sometimes the conflict is long, sometimes short. This is where the spiritual disciplines come in. *The disciplines for the spiritual life,* rightly understood, are time-tested activities consciously undertaken by us as new men or women to allow our spirit ever-increasing sway over our embodied selves. They help by assisting the ways of God's Kingdom to take the place of the habits of sin embedded in our bodies.

IN PRAISE OF THE FLESH, A STEPPING STONE TO GOD

It is now time to put in a good word for flesh, which has been badly misunderstood and falsely accused. "Flesh" in its biblical usage seldom means the mere physical substance that makes up the parts of the body. The term is sometimes used as the equivalent of "meat" to designate a passive material that might be cut up or eaten. (see Exod. 12; 16; Lev. 7; Ps. 78:20–21; Mic. 3:2–3; Rom. 14:21; 1 Cor. 8:13). But flesh is generally spoken of in the Bible as something *active,* a specific power or range of powers that is embedded in a body of a specific type, able or likely to do only certain kinds of things.

Thus it is said that the animals "went in unto Noah into the ark, two and two of all flesh, wherein is the breath of life. And they that went in, went in male and female of all flesh, as God had commanded him: and the Lord shut him up" (Gen. 7:15). Also: "I will not fear what flesh can do unto me" (Ps. 56:4). Yet again: "Now the Egyptians are men and not God; and their horses flesh and not spirit" (Isa. 31:3). And: "But he who was of the bondswoman was born after the flesh," without assistance from the "promise" of God who is spirit (Gal. 4:23).

These passages among many others illustrate the basic scriptural sense of the term "flesh." They do not presuppose that flesh must be something inherently evil, even though it is a finite power with some degree of independence from direct support by God.

Nicolas Berdyaev describes the flesh with great accuracy:

This lower nature, when it occupies its proper place in the hierarchy of the universe, is not in itself evil, for it belongs to the divine world. It is only when it usurps the place of something higher that it becomes untrue to itself and an evil. Animal nature certainly has its place in the scale of values and an eternal destiny; but when it takes possession of man, when man submits his spirit to the control of the lower element, then it does indeed become an evil thing. For evil is a question of the direction pursued by the spirit, not of the constitution of nature itself.[12]

The points about flesh to be emphasized for our discussion are its specific tendencies toward action and the limitations of its independent powers—what it can and cannot do. The tendencies and limitations of course vary from one kind of "living being" to another. Human flesh is characterized by its astonishing range of social and intellectual possibilities, as well as its capacity for God. It can be the locus of ingrained evil or of ingrained righteousness (Ezek. 11:19–20). It can totally give place to another kind of substance in the overall makeup of the body, providing the individual with a "heavenly" body. The person of corruptible flesh can thus put on incorruption. This is the teaching of the New Testament. (1 Cor. 15)

THE INCORRUPTIBLE BODY

In his Letters, Paul the apostle takes up distinctions we have seen emerge in the first chapters of Genesis. In his most elaborate discussion of the final stages in the process of redemption he remarks: "All flesh is not the same flesh: but there is one kind of flesh of men, another flesh of beasts, another of fishes and another of birds" (1 Cor. 15:39). But then to such distinctions between "fleshes" the apostle adds a further distinction: one profoundly rooted in the experience of humankind with God in the Old and New Testaments, but also rooted in the scientific or Aristotelian outlook in the Greco-Roman culture.

This is the distinction between kinds of bodies: "There are also celestial *bodies,* and bodies terrestrial" (1 Cor. 15:40). Here is, in fact, a commonplace of Aristotelian science. But it was given vast new dimensions of meaning for the Christian community by the transfiguration and the postresurrection appearances of Christ. That in turn made possible certain intriguing reinterpretations of remarkable events of the Old Testament as also being manifestations of Christ (1 Cor. 10:1–4).

The human "living being," "the first man Adam," possessed as his bodily substance the highest and most potent form of flesh. He was therefore "the quintessence of dust."[13] Being the highest form of dust, he was also one that proves, in the vision of Paul, to be capable of transmigration from one form of body (the "terrestrial") to another (the "celestial")—that of the "glorious" body of Jesus after his resurrection (Phil. 3:21).

Thus in the final analysis it is true that "flesh and blood cannot inherit the Kingdom of God" (1 Cor. 15:50). But the flesh and blood *person* can inherit it. At the initiative and guidance of the spiritual word of God (John 6:63), a person's finite energies can be meshed with God's in such a way that progressively—and, eventually, totally—he or she can "put on incorruption" (1 Cor. 15:54: cf. 1 Pet. 1:4 and Phil. 3:11)

The flesh and blood person can also, of course, restrict his or her thinking and action to the flesh alone and die. That person can place his or her thought and hope solely on the natural powers resident in the human body apart from God and will then "reap corruption." There is a choice to be made and a discipline to be followed.

SOWING TO THE SPIRIT

Paul himself formulates this haunting fact in such well-known passages as the following:

Those who live on the level of our lower nature have their outlook formed by it, and that spells death; but those who live on the level of the spirit have the spiritual outlook, and that is life and peace. For the outlook of the lower nature is enmity with God; it is not subject to the law of God; indeed it cannot be: those who live on such a level cannot possibly please God (Rom. 8:5–8, NEB).

Make no mistake about this: God is not to be fooled; a man reaps what he sows. If he sows seed in the field of his lower nature, he will reap from it a harvest of corruption, but if he sows in the field of the Spirit, the Spirit will bring him a harvest of eternal life. So let us never tire of doing good, for if we do not slacken our efforts we shall in due time reap our harvest (Gal. 6:7–9, NEB).[14]

The choice is a very grave one in its outcome, and we must be as careful as possible in understanding what the alternatives mean. It is my aim in these pages to help us see that our choices concern *specific life processes of spiritual growth or decay* and that we will not be exempted from the law of those processes by God's actions on our behalf.

I especially hope that our discussions will have made it clear that we badly err in thinking of flesh as essentially degraded or bad or sinful; the biblical view of grace and human nature does not see it that way. This mistake must be avoided if we are to take seriously our task of "yielding our members servants to righteousness unto holiness" (Rom. 6:19; cf. 6:12–22). Otherwise we will despise our bodies and not take them to be the resource for the spiritual life that God made them to be.

FLESH—NOT "FALLEN" HUMAN NATURE

But there are several other facts about the body we must add to our understanding. The body cannot be the resource for the Christian life it was intended to be if we equate its flesh with "fallen human nature." It is not true to say that "flesh" simply "stands for human nature as the fall of the first man affected it, crippled, disordered, no longer answering naturally to reasonable control, and therefore ever afterwards a source of rebellion, a thing which the unaided human will is unable to dominate. Left to itself this fallen human nature is a source of sin."[15]

Certainly it is true that in the unredeemed the flesh, both as the material stuff of the body and as the natural powers that that stuff exhibits, now serves as primary host to sin. Nevertheless, not *it* but its *deformed condition* is "fallen human nature." *In this condition* the flesh opposes the spirit, does that which is evil, and must be crucified to restrain it (Gal. 5:16, 19f.).

Unfortunately, very few throughout the ages of the church have seen the fallacies in treating the flesh as identical with *fallen* human nature. George Fox, who founded the Friends or Quaker movement, was such a one, and his insight frequently brought him into bitter conflict with his contemporaries. Of one such conflict he says:

Then these professors said the outward body was the body of death and sin. I shewed them their mistake in that also; for Adam and Eve had each of them an outward body, before the body of death and sin got into them; and that man and woman will have bodies when the body of sin and death is put off again; when they are renewed up into the image of God again by Jesus Christ, which they were in before they fell.[16]

Fox clearly saw that the "body of the sins of the flesh" (Col. 2:11) and "the old man" (Eph. 4:22) we are commanded to "put off" could not be the mere natural body of our fleshly existence, since we cannot put it off—short of suicide.

So far as we can tell, the first human beings had fleshly bodies *before* they sinned, and hence the flesh is not the same thing as fallen human nature. So, the biblical correlate of fallen human nature is, rather, *the world,* as described in 1 John 2:16: "For all that is in the world, the lust of the flesh, and the lust of the eyes, and the pride of life, is not of the Father, but is of the world." Fallen human nature is a certain manner in which the good powers deposited at creation in our human flesh are twisted and organized against God. This comes about through processes that are social and historical as well as individual.

The true effect of the Fall was to lead us to trust in the flesh alone, to "not see fit to acknowledge God any longer" (Rom. 1:28) because we now suppose (like mother Eve) that, since there is no God to be counted on in the living of our lives, we must take things into our own hands. This is what it is to be carnally minded. It is the carnal mind—not the flesh—that is at enmity with God and incapable of subjection to his law.

By contrast, the promise of old was that spirit would be poured out *upon flesh* (Joel 2:28; Acts 2:17). The flesh also can long for God (Ps. 63:1), come to God (Ps. 65:2), cry out for God (Ps. 84:2), bless his holy name (Ps. 145:21), and even, along the lines suggested above, "not see corruption" (Acts 2:31). Nothing comparable, of course, is ever said of "the world."

THE ROLE OF THE DISCIPLINES IN THE FULL REDEMPTION OF THE PERSON

So, through our long course of reflection, we come to see how the easy yoke of Christ is inescapably bound up with the disciplines for the spiritual life. Redemption as it is portrayed in the New Testament is comprehensible only when placed into careful relation with embodied human nature and God's purposes in our creation. It could not have been otherwise.

God in creation placed in the fleshly human organism abilities to serve as the vehicle of our vocation—including the capacity for voluntary interaction with his spiritual Kingdom in ruling the zo-ological realm on earth. The human body is the primary field of independent power and freedom given by God to people. Put sim-ply—no body, no power. People have a body for one reason—that we might have at our disposal the resources that would allow us to be persons in fellowship and cooperation with a personal God.

Our bodies are shaped into a specific character and laden with specific skills and tendencies by our experiences, including those we voluntarily undertake. There is some latitude within which our character is formed by ourselves. Through the instrumentality of his life-giving word, God in regeneration renews our original ca-pacity for divine interaction. But our body's substance is only to be transformed totally by actions and events in which we choose to participate from day to day.

In other words, grace alone does not ensure we'll undertake the proper actions toward that life. We do have a part in our body's transformation. The body God has given to us is one that is "plas-tic," in the primary sense of being pliable and capable of being formed in various ways. In the fine wording of the physiologist, psychologist, and philosopher William James,

Plasticity . . . means the possession of a structure weak enough to yield to an influence, but strong enough not to yield all at once. Each relatively stable phase of equilibrium in such a structure is marked by what we may call a new set of habits. Organic matter, especially nervous tissue, seems endowed with a very extraordinary degree of plasticity of this sort; so that we may without hesitation lay down . . . that the phenomena of habit in living beings are due to the plasticity of the organic materials of which their bodies are composed.[17]

The very substance of our bodies is shaped by our actions, as well as by grace, into pathways of good and evil.

What then is the specific role of the spiritual disciplines? Their role rests upon the nature of the embodied human self—they are to *mold* and *shape* it. And our part in our redemption is, through specific and appropriate activities, to "yield" the plastic substance of which we are made to the ways of that new life which is im-parted to us by the "quickening spirit."

We are to take this task with the utmost seriousness and in the most literal of senses, since *no one,* not even God himself, *will do it for us*. That is the meaning of our freedom and of our responsibility. Then and only then shall we be able to enter with intelligence, steadfastness, and success into the exercises, the disciplines, that are profitable unto all things, "having promise of the life that now is, and of that which is to come" (1 Tim. 4:8).

NOTES

Epigraph 1. Henry Montague Butler, "Lift Up Your Hearts," #258 in *The Hymnal* (Philadelphia: Presbyterian Board of Christian Education, 1936).

Epigraph 2. Josef Goldbrunner, *Holiness Is Wholeness and Other Essays* (Notre Dame, IN: University of Notre Dame Press, 1964), 7.

1. Abraham H. Maslow, "The Good Life of the Self-Actualizing Person," *The Humanist* (July–August, 1967): 139. Consider also the statements on related points in Alasdair MacIntyre, "Theology, Ethics, and the Ethics of Medicine and Health Care," *The Journal of Medicine and Philosophy,* vol. 4 (1979): 435–43, especially this: "On the biblical view, God commands us to do and be that which He created us to do and be: in obeying the commandments our created human nature is being true to itself, not to a set of external commandments. Moreover, . . . this relationship of human nature to the divine is of the essence of human nature, not something superadded, let alone imposed" (p. 436).

2. Francis A. Schaeffer, *True Spirituality* (Wheaton, IL: Tyndale, 1971), 17.

3. William Temple, "The Divinity of Christ," in B. H. Streeter, ed., *Foundations* (London: Macmillan, 1920), 259.

4. Lewis Sperry Chafer, *He That Is Spiritual* (Findlay, OH: Dunham, 1918), 69–71.

5. Agnes Sanford, *The Healing Gifts of the Spirit* (New York: Lippincott, 1966), 154.

6. Eckhart *Meister Eckhart,* trans. Raymond Blakney (New York: Harper, 1941), 253.

7. See chap. 1 of H. Wheeler Robinson, *The Christian Doctrine of Man 3rd edition, (Edinburgh: T.&T. Clark, 1926),* and Oscar Cullmann, "Immortality of the Soul or Resurrection of the Dead," in Krister Stendhal, ed., *Immortality and Resurrection* (New York: Macmillan, 1965), 9–53. The literature is reviewed in John A. T. Robinson, *The Body: A Study in Pauline Theology* (London: SCM, 1952).

8. See the classical discussion in William James, *The Principles of Psychology* (New York: Holt, 1890), chap. 25.

9. Erwin Schrodinger, *What Is Life? and Other Scientific Essays* (Garden City, NY: Doubleday, Anchor Books, 1965), 74.

10. For further study of the existential, phenomenological viewpoint on the nature of the body, see Richard Zaner, *The Problem of Embodiment,* 2d ed. (The Hague: Nijhoff, 1971).

11. Alexander Lowen, *The Betrayal of the Body* (New York: Collier, 1971), 2–3.

12. Nicolas Berdyaev, *Freedom and the Spirit* (London: Bles, 1935), 169.

13. The word "quintessence" in this Shakespearian phrase refers to the fifth and highest form of bodily reality in the Aristotelian scheme of the cosmos. See Aristotle's book on the nature of the soul, *De Anima,* p. 418b, lines 7–9 of the Bekker pagination.

14. The *New English Bible* very helpfully translates *sarx* in these passages as "lower nature," instead of "flesh." Even the phrase "lower nature" has its dangers, however, as it may be taken to mean "worse nature." The "lower" here, if our interpretation is correct, must be understood on analogy with the "lower" floors of a building, for example: as that which supports and finds it completion in the higher, but is not necessarily "worse" than the higher—just different in a specific manner.

15. Philip Hughes, *A History of the Church,* 2 vols. (New York: Sheed and Ward, 1935), 1:170.

16. George Fox, *Journal of George Fox,* ed. Norman Penney (London: Dent, 1948), 91. See also James Gilchrist Lawson's discussion of Fox in his *Deeper Experiences of Famous Christians* (Anderson, IN: Warner, 1970), 100.

    For scholarly analysis of biblical terms for *flesh* and related concepts, see Robert Jewett, *Paul's Anthropological Terms: A Study of Their Use in Conflict Settings* (Leiden: Brill, 1971) and Ernest De Witt Burton, *A Critical and Exegetical Commentary on the Epistle to the Galatians* (Edinburgh: Clark, 1952), 492–95.

17. James, *The Principles of Psychology,* chap. 4.

7. St. Paul's Psychology of Redemption—The Example

You know (do you not?) that at the sports all the runners run the race, though only one wins the prize. Like them, run to win! But every athlete goes into strict training. They do it to win a fading wreath; we, a wreath that never fades. For my part, I run with a clear goal before me; I am like a boxer who does not beat the air; I bruise my own body and make it know its master, for fear that after preaching to others I should find myself rejected.

1 COR. 9:24–27, NEB

In Paul, for the first time since Aristotle, Greek philosophy made a real step forward.

SIR WILLIAM RAMSEY

Is there a life we can examine that would give us insight into the disciplined life?

The spiritual disciplines are in a real sense an "exercise unto godliness." This is St. Paul's language (1 Tim. 4:7), expressing a fundamental theme of his life and belief. Surely, then, an indispensible test of what we have said about life in Christ's easy yoke would be the manner in which his great apostle to the Gentiles walked with him. Was "exercise unto godliness" just a lofty concept with no definite meaning in Paul's mouth? Or does it indicate a precise course of action he understood in definite terms, carefully followed himself, and called others to share?

Of course it was the latter. So obviously so, for him and the readers of his own day, that he would feel no need to write a book on the disciplines for the spiritual life that explained systematically what he had in mind.

But quite a bit of time has passed—and many abuses have occurred in the name of spiritual disciplines. History has so conditioned us today, as discussed in the next chapter, that we don't easily understand either Paul's practice or the teachings about "mortification of the body" that he practiced. Let's look closely at Paul's way of Christian living.

PAUL, THE ENIGMA

The apostle Paul stands among those few gigantic figures who have shaped the history of the world and made the human mind and spirit what it is. Yet he is an enigma to anyone who sees him only from a modern perspective. That is true even, or perhaps especially, for those who look to him for guidance in their spiritual life.

The contemptuous description of Paul by Frederich Nietzsche, though extreme, expresses the attitude of many secular thinkers in today's world. According to Nietzsche, Paul was, "one of the most ambitious of men, whose superstition was only equalled by his cunning; a much tortured, much to be pitied man, an exceedingly unpleasant person both to himself and to others."[1] I leave it to you to decide whether that statement tells us more about Nietzsche or about Paul.

Christian scholars, on the other hand, are unable to agree on whether the genius of Paul was as a systematic theologian, ecclesiastical organizer, an ethical thinker, a mystical visionary, or an ascetic saint. Perhaps he is most commonly thought of as a dogmatic system builder—which James S. Stewart calls "history's greatest injustice to its greatest saint."[2]

But Stewart's remarkable book on Paul, *A Man in Christ,* makes it clear that the heart of Paul and of his message lies in one area— in the continuous appropriation of the "real presence" of Christ himself within the experiential life of the believer. Stewart's book, as helpful as it is, though, shares a basic omission with all of the major discussions of Paul in recent centuries. It is an omission that leaves Paul's experiences of the Christ-life, so well described in its substance and effect by Stewart, largely inaccessible in practice to those who wish to follow Paul as he followed Christ, as 1 Corinthians 4:16 and 11:1 indicate.

In Chapter 2, we spoke of how the modern church seems unable to learn from the Christian past or from the Bible itself how to foster a true "growth in grace and knowledge of our Lord and Savior Jesus Christ." We simply seem not to see *what was in fact done* by Jesus himself, as well as by those who at his invitation rose up to seize and enter into the Kingdom of God as described in Luke 16:16 and Matthew 11:12. We are somehow blind to the information that should guide us. It's invisible and just does not fall within our mental horizons. This peculiar blindness causes us to reject from our lives what Jesus and Paul actually did, what they chose to live through or experience.

"Reject" is not too strong a term, but it is not quite accurate. To reject something, one must first consider or analyze it. But the details of Jesus' and Paul's daily lives, as opposed to their commands or instructions, we don't even seem to consider, so we don't feel called upon to accept *or* reject them. Such details somehow are irrelevent to any actual choices we have to make. So we say, "What does the long period of fasting and solitude that Jesus entered after his baptism have to do with us? We aren't Jesus, are we? And Paul's forceful subjugation of his body may have been necessary for *his* work, but I am doing quite well without it, you see."

What happens, then, is that all talk of following Jesus—or of Paul's example of following him—is emptied of *practical* meaning. It does not express an actual strategy of living our day-to-day existence but at most concerns only certain special moments or articles of faith. This in turn makes it impossible for us to share their experiences and consistently carry through with behavior like theirs. That behavior rested, after all, upon their experiences. And the experiences in turn resulted from how they arranged their lives. Since we do not share their behaviors, we are left with much talk *about* them and an occasional application of some of their language to our experience. The only way to overcome this alienation from their sort of life is by entering into the actual *practices* of Jesus and Paul as something essential to *our* life in Christ.

SPIRITUAL EXERCISES ASSUMED NECESSARY IN PAUL'S WORLD

The context in which Paul uses the words "exercise unto godliness" is an intensely practical one. He is telling Timothy, his son in the faith, how to succeed in leading God's people. In speaking of exercise or training he uses the term *gumnaze*, from which we get our term "gymnasium." Instead of spending time dwelling on godless myths and legends, Paul tells his young friend, he is to be at work in the "spiritual gymnasium:" "Train *(gumnaze)* yourself unto godliness; for while bodily training *(gumnasia)* is of some value, godliness is of value in every way, as it holds promise for the present life and also for the life to come" (1 Tim. 4:7–8, RSV).

Physical exercise was something Paul and others in the Aegean world understood very well. For long centuries before Timothy was left to shepherd the church in Ephesus, people of the time recognized the physical trainer with his charges as a very familiar of sight. Everyone knew what was involved in training for the enhancement of our physical powers. In his advice to Timothy, Paul's points out that there is a precisely parallel phenomenon in the spiritual realm and draws upon that parallelism in his statement. And it's a very workable analogy. Because just as with the physical, there is a specific round of activities we must do to establish, maintain, and enhance our spiritual powers. One must *train* as well as *try*. An athlete may have all the enthusiasm in the world; he may "talk a good game." But talk will not win the race. Zeal without knowledge or without appropriate practice is never enough. Plus, one must train *wisely* as well as intensely for spiritual attainment.

Paul did not have to explain or argue for this assumption. It was commonplace to the developing Christian church, as well in the surrounding culture, whether Jewish, Hellenistic, or Roman. That point cannot be too strongly emphasized.

Why? It is almost impossible in the thought climate of today's Western world to appreciate just *how* utterly unnecessary it was for

Paul to say explicitly, in the world in which *he* lived, that Christians should fast, be alone, study, give, and so forth as regular disciplines for the spiritual life. We of course tend to think of ascetic practices as oddities of human history, prominent only in "pagan India," perhaps, or in the spiritually degraded "Dark Ages" of Western Europe. But such thinking is far from the truth. It's an illusion created in part by our own conviction that our unrestrained natural impulse is in itself a good thing and that we have an unquestionable right to fulfill our natural impulses so long as "no one gets hurt."

But thoughtful and religiously devout people of the classical and Hellenistic world, from the Ganges to the Tiber, knew that the mind and body of the human being had to be rigorously disciplined to achieve a decent individual and social existence. This is not something St. Paul had to prove or even explicitly state to his readers—but it also was not something that he overlooked, leaving it to be thought up by crazed monks in the Dark Ages. It is, rather, a wisdom gleaned from millennia of collective human experience. There is nothing especially religious about it, though every religion of historical significance has accepted and inculcated it in one way or another. It has a special importance in religion, but it also is just good sense about human nature.

Where have we gotten this idea about "doing what feels good"? The unrestrained hedonism of our own day comes historically from the 18th-century idealization of happiness and is filtered through the 19th-century English ideology of pleasure as *the* good for people. Finally it emerges in the form of our present "feel good" society—tragically pandered to by the popular culture and much of popular religion as well.

Think about it. Isn't the most generally applied standard of success for a religious service whether or not people feel good in it and after it? The preeminence of the "feel good" mentality in our world is what makes it impossible for many people now even to imagine what Paul and his contemporaries accepted as a fact of life. Our communities and our churches are thickly populated with people who are neurotic or paralyzed by their devotion and willing bondage to how they feel. Drug dependence and addiction is epidemic because of the cultural imperative to "feel good."

THE PRACTICE OF THE EARLY CHURCH

If this early, generally accepted assumption about the necessity of disciplining one's desires and feelings needed any detailing for Paul's hearers, it could have been amply provided by his own practice and that of other leaders in the young church. In addition, the persons and ministries of John the Baptist and of Jesus himself, both rich in the practice of activities designed to strengthen the spirit, were held constantly before them. So, wherever early Christians looked they saw examples of the practice of solitude, fasting, prayer, private study, communal study, worship, and sacrificial service and giving—to mention only some of the more obvious disciplines for spiritual life.

These early Christians really did arrange their lives *very* differently from their non-Christian neighbors, as well as from the vast majority of those of us called Christians today. We are speaking of their overall style of life, not just what they did under pressure, which frequently was also astonishingly different. This behavior is a *fact* and can be confirmed by a casual reading of the biblical literature, as well as other written records of the time. When one reads through a Letter like that of Paul to the Ephesians or the Philippians, for example, and takes the Letters to mean what they say, there arises the irresistible impression that the writer really is living from within another order of things. Extrabiblical works, such as Eusebius' (A.D. 263–339) *History of the Church from Christ to Constantine,* strongly confirm this impression.

THE USE OF SOLITUDE

To illustrate how disciplinary practices were constantly before the early Christians, consider how Jesus and his initial followers made extensive use of solitude. As will be seen in a later chapter, solitude is the most radical of the disciplines for life in the spirit. In penal institutions, solitary confinement is used to break the strongest of wills. It is capable of this because it excludes interactions with others upon which fallen human personality completely depends. The life alienated from God collapses when deprived of its support from the sin-laden world. But the life in tune with God is actually nurtured by time spent alone.

John the Baptist, like many of his forerunners in the prophetic line, was much alone in the deserted places of his land. Jesus constantly sought solitude from the time of his baptism up to the Garden of Gethsemane, when he even went apart from those he took there to watch with him (Matt. 26:38–42). It is solitude and solitude alone that opens the possibility of a radical relationship to God that can withstand all external events up to and beyond death.

Retirement is the laboratory of the spirit; interior solitude and silence are its two wings. All great works are prepared in the desert, including the redemption of the world. The precursors, the followers, the Master Himself, all obeyed or have to obey one and the same law. Prophets, apostles, preachers, martyrs, pioneers of knowledge, inspired artists in every art, ordinary men and the Man-God, all pay tribute to loneliness, to the life of silence, to the night.[3]

JESUS STRENGTHENED BY SOLITUDE

Today, sustained withdrawal from society into solitude seems to indicate weakness, suffering, flight, or failure rather than great strength, joy, and effectiveness. Believing that, we, for instance, thoroughly misunderstand the context of Jesus' temptations after his baptism (Matt. 4). The Spirit, we are told, led him into the wilderness to be tempted by the devil. Was this not to put Jesus in the weakest possible position before Satan, starving and alone in the wilds? Most to whom I have spoken about this matter are shocked at the suggestion that the "wilderness," the place of solitude and deprivation, was actually *the place of strength and strengthening* for our Lord and that the Spirit led him there—as he would lead *us* there—to ensure that Christ was in the best possible condition for the trial.

In that desert solitude, Jesus fasted for more than a month. *Then,* and not before, Satan was allowed to approach him with his glittering proposals of bread, notoriety, and power. Only then was Jesus at the height of his strength. The desert was his fortress, his place of power. Throughout his life he sought the solitary place as an indirect submission of *his* own physical body to righteousness (e.g., Mark 1:35, 3:13, 6:31, 46). That is, he sought it not as an activity done for its own sake, but one done to give him power for good. All of those who followed Jesus knew of his practice of solitude, and it was greatly imitated in the centuries after his death.

PAUL'S PRACTICE: SOLITUDE, FASTING, PRAYER

The lessons I taught you, the tradition I have passed on, all that you heard me say or saw me do, put into practice; and the God of peace will be with you (Phil. 4:9, NEB).

Paul, of course, was one of those followers. But at the time of his conversion Paul was already a person far advanced beyond the ordinary in the Jewish religion, "being more exceedingly zealous," he tells us, "of the traditions of my fathers" (Gal. 1:14). As he elsewhere says, he was, "touching the righteousness which is in the law, blameless" (Phil. 3:6). Remember the self-righteous Pharisee in the Gospel of Luke? If that man fasted twice a week and gave tithes of all he possessed, we may be sure that the zealous Saul did even more in the way of ascetic and disciplinary behaviors.

So, even before following Christ, Paul was most certainly a person of great self-control and discipline, and that didn't disappear upon his conversion. His discipline was just given a new meaning and was no longer regarded as constituting his righteousness before God (Phil. 3:7–8). The emphasis upon self-control, which is only attained by extensive disciplined experience, is a constant drumbeat in his life and writings. For instance, it is mentioned five times in the first two chapters of the Epistle to Titus alone.

Think about Paul's encounter with Christ. Immediately after the Damascus road event, he prayed and fasted, neither eating nor drinking for three days (Acts 9:9, 11). A short while later, he fled to the Arabian desert for a lengthy period of time, not "consulting with flesh and blood." In the desert isolation of the Sinaitic peninsula[4] he continued the interchange with his Lord until he was ready to return to Damascus, to Jerusalem, and finally to his hometown of Tarsus in Asia Minor.

John Pollock provides an intriguing picture of those "hidden years" in and around Tarsus. Pollock locates the five beatings by the Jews ("forty stripes save one") of 2 Corinthians 11:24 during this time, as the local synagogue tried to save their erring brother and avoid excommunicating him. All to no avail, however, for Paul remained steadfast in his testimony to the risen Christ, his companion and Messiah. Then, according to Pollock,

Cast out of home, comforts and position, Paul disappeared into the wild country of the Taurus foothills and here, in A.D. 41 or 42, possibly in the cave that used to be shown as "St. Paul's Cave," he had a "vision and revelation of the Lord" so sacred that he never referred to it for over fourteen years and then in guarded terms in the third person: "I know a man in Christ who was caught up to the third heaven—whether in the body or out of the body I do not know, God knows."[5]

Then some fifteen or so years after Paul met Christ on the road, and after he ministered for a while in the church at Syrian Antioch, the leaders of that church were directed by the Holy Spirit to dedicate him and Barnabas for special efforts in missionary evangelism. Having fasted and prayed, they laid their hands on them and sent them away (Acts 13:2). Through the following months, many groups of converts emerged under the ministry of Paul and Barnabas in a number of cities in central Asia Minor. And as they returned through those cities on their way back to Antioch, they ordained leaders in every group with fasting and prayer (Acts 14:23). Paul's effectiveness is simply inconceivable without its extensive use of fasting, solitude, and prayer.

SERVING OTHERS

But his life and work were also characterized by great self-sacrifice, simplicity, and frugality. He worked to support himself through much of the time that he was founding and developing Christian communities. He declined the "perks" of apostleship to which he had every right (1 Cor. 9:12) and which were richly enjoyed by others, such as Peter and Jesus' brothers (1 Cor. 9:5).

His aim in living this way makes perfect sense once we see the parallelism between physical and spiritual training. That aim stands out clearly once again in his remarkable testimony about his treatment of his body. Those who would follow Paul as Paul followed Christ should see in how he actually lived precisely what he meant when he said "I beat my body and make it my slave" (1 Cor. 9:27, NIV). They will then also know how, exactly, they are to do as he did in this respect.

Consider Paul's testimony as he took his final leave of Ephesus, the field of some of his most significant and fruitful labors: "You know how, from the day that I first set foot in the province of Asia, for the whole time that I was with you, I served the Lord in all humility amid the sorrows and trials that came upon me. . . . I have not wanted anyone's money or clothes for myself; you all know that these hands of mine earned enough for the needs of me and my companions. I showed you that it is our duty to help the weak in this way, by hard work, and that we should keep in mind the words of the Lord Jesus, who himself said, 'Happiness lies more in giving than in receiving'" (Acts 20: 18–19, 33–35, NEB).

The one chosen by God to lay the foundations of the gentile church chose to support himself and others by his own labor during the very time he was carrying out a ministry of unsurpassed significance (1 Thess. 2:8–9; 2 Thess. 3:8–9). It was Paul's genius to understand that there was no conflict in this arrangement, but, in fact, an empowerment. He knew the Master's secret that the greatest person is the one who is servant of all, and he put it into practice as a matter of principle (Matt. 20:26–27; 1 Cor. 9:19). His whole life was to be the servant of all, just like Jesus, and *that* is why such great work was trusted to him and not to others.

HIS PRACTICE INTERPRETS HIS STATEMENTS

So it is in the light of Paul's *practice,* the way he lived, that we must interpret the statements he makes about his experience and behavior and about what *we* are to do. When he elsewhere directs us to "mortify" the deeds of the body through the spirit (Rom. 6:13) or to mortify our members that are upon the earth (Col. 3:5), we are to interpret his words in the light of his acts. And when we do so there is no doubt that he is directing us to undertake the standard activities for training the natural desires toward godliness, ones that are readily recognized by anyone at all familiar with the history of religion. And these activities are solitude, fasting, "watching," silence, routines of prayer and study, the giving of one's time, energy, and goods in various kinds of service, worship, frugality, submission to the spiritual fellowship and its leaders, and so forth.

We today are accustomed to thinking of Jesus or Paul as being much like our ordinary minister or parish priest. We may therefore feel a great deal of resistance to any suggestion that they led such a rigorous style of life and called their disciples to do the same. "Doesn't this make Christianity sound more like an army than a church?" we may ask. "If *that* is what Paul meant in speaking of submitting the body to righteousness, why did he not come right out and *say* it?"

But he *did* come right out and say it. This is what he *is* saying in the passages we have quoted and cited above and many similar ones.

Paul says to us, "Follow my example as I follow the example of Christ" (1 Cor. 11:1, NIV). He says, "Whatever you have learned or received or heard from me, or seen in me—put it into practice. And the God of peace will be with you" (Phil. 4:9, NIV). We then, within our modern view of life, busily set to work explaining how, of course, we *are* following him as he follows his Lord. Don't we believe and say the same things he did? But our lives are not like his life at all. We do not do the things he did. Yet it is surely Paul's *practice* that alone explains his marvelously victorious life in the easy yoke of Christ, for he in faith adopted his Lord's *overall* style of life. And as he did, he experienced the upholding of God's grace in it. This is the key to the understanding of Paul's life, teachings, and effect on history.

ENIGMA RESOLVED

Now I have given up everything else—I have found it to be the only way to really know Christ and to experience the mighty power that brought him back to life again, and to find out what it means to suffer and die with him. So, whatever it takes, I will be one who lives in the fresh newness of life of those who are alive from the dead (Phil. 3:10–11, LB).

The key to understanding Paul is to know that, with all his "weaknesses" and failures and personality deficiencies, he gave himself solely to being like his Lord. He lived and practiced daily the things his Lord taught and practiced. He lived a life of abandonment; and it was his confidence in this path, and in the power that derived from the rich union with Christ it created, that enabled him to call others to do the same. His actions, his character, his motivations—and the astonishing world-changing power derived from his lowly life-style—can only be understood by keeping this fact in mind: *Paul followed Jesus by living as he lived*. And how did he do that? Through activities and ways of living that would train his whole personality to depend upon the risen Christ as Christ trained himself to depend upon the Father.

In other words, Paul and his Lord were people of immense power, who saw clearly the wayward ways the world considered natural. With calm premeditation and clear vision of a deeper order, they took their stand always among those "last who shall be first" mentioned repeatedly in the Gospels. With their feet planted in the deeper order of God, they lived lives of utter self-sacrifice and abandonment, seeing in such a life the highest possible personal attainment.

And through that way of living God gave them "the power of an indestructible life" (Heb. 7:16) to accomplish the work of their appointed ministry and to raise them above the power of death. During their lives, they both were men of lowly and plain origin and manner, when compared with the glittering and glamorous ones who dominated the world's attention. So most of their powerful contemporaries could not possibly have seen either of them for who they were. Nor can we, until we have begun in faith actually to live as they lived.

INSULATED AGAINST REAL CHANGE OF LIFE

But today we are insulated from such thinking. Our modern religious context assures us that such drastic action as we see in Jesus and Paul is not necessary for *our* Christianity—may not even be useful, may even be harmful. In any case, it certainly will be upsetting to those around us and especially to our religious associates, who often have no intention of changing their lives in such a radical way. So we pass off Paul's intensely practical directions and example as being only about attitude. Or possibly we see in them some fine theological point regarding God's attitude toward us. In some cultural contexts Paul's writings are read as telling us not to enjoy secular entertainments or bodily pleasures—or as commanding us to embrace whatever the current prudishness is. We take something out of our contemporary grab bag of ideas and assume that *that* is what he is saying. However, no sane, practical course of action that results in progress toward pervasive Christlikeness ever seems to emerge from such thinking.

Evelyn Christenson remarks on this mind-set:

Sometimes we take a perfectly good word from the Bible (such as "chastisement," "suffering," "submission," "healing," "God's justice"), dive immediately into our pool of "I thinks" and weave them subtly and securely around that word, leaving the impression that all of our "I thinks" about the word were included in the scriptural meaning of the word.[6]

But nowhere is this temptation greater, or more harmful, than when we read what our Lord says about the conditions of following him (Luke 14, for example) or when we read Paul's statements about how we are to deal with our body and the flesh in the course of spiritual development (Rom. 6:13, 19; 8:13; 1 Cor. 9:27; 2 Cor. 4:10; Gal. 2:20; 5:24; Phil. 1:20–22; Col. 3:5). Both the secular and the religious setting in which we live today is almost irresistibly biased toward an interpretation of these passages that condones a life more like that of decent people around us than like the life of Paul and his Lord. We talk about leading a different kind of life, but we also have ready explanations for not being really different. And with those explanations we have talked our way out of the very practices that alone would enable us to be citizens of another world.

THE REALISM OF PAUL'S LANGUAGE

When read carefully, the stern realism of Paul's language also helps underscore this point. We today rest upon many centuries of interpreting his words and the words of the other biblical writers in a fanciful, sentimental, or "spiritual" manner. His often quoted words, "I die daily," for example, have been turned into an expression of an attitude or spirit of self-sacrifice and humility. The context of this phrase, however, makes it amply clear that for him this wasn't an attitude but a daily fact of life—one in which he daily stared death in the face and accepted it for that day, as we can see in 1 Corinthians 15:30–32.

When Paul describes his life or the life of the Christian disciple he always uses language *realistically,* though of course not always literally. When he says, for example, that "those who belong to Christ Jesus have crucified the flesh with its passions and desires" (Gal. 5:24, RSV), he does not mean that the flesh is literally fastened to a cross. But he does refer to a real and definite action or type of action by believers through which the claims of normal feelings and desires are suspended and removed from control of their lives.

It is the same as what Jesus calls the denial of one's self and the taking up of the cross.

These events then are real events that have certain constant and definite properties that a believer can discover by living through them. They *can* be made a part of our plan for life in Christ. Paul's language expresses his own experience through the stern realism of concrete existence in the fellowship of the church. Paul was a summa cum laude graduate of the school of self-denial, and he knew from experience what he was talking about. His crucifixion of the flesh, and ours, is accomplished through those activities such as solitude, fasting, frugality, service, and so forth, which constitute the curriculum in the school of self-denial and place us on the front line of spiritual combat, as we read in Mark 8:34–36 and Luke 17:33.

What about some of the phrases Paul uses over and over? We're so familiar with them in a religious context that their true meaning—their "stern realism"—is not that familiar. Our use of the same or similar words today—when they are used at all—does not correspond to those actions and experiences that Paul had clearly before him. The Pauline ideas of spiritual death and life, crucifixion, putting off the old person and putting on the new, union with Christ, ministry with the spirit of God, mortification of the deeds of the flesh, being buried and raised with Christ, submitting our bodily members as instruments of righteousness, submitting our bodies as living sacrifices, and so forth correspond to little or nothing in our action or experience—individual or shared. So they are without force and substance. They no longer can serve as a basis around which *realistic plans* for becoming like Jesus can be framed.

That is not a problem for Paul's life and writings alone; it is possibly even more of one for John's. The great "union" passages in his Gospel, such as 14:10–20; 15:1–10; and 17:20–26, are explicitly about real interactions and personal conditions and their concrete results. But most of us find great difficulty in translating "abiding in Christ and his words abiding in us" into familiar events of our daily lives. Yet this is precisely what *must* be done. It is the central task for those who would guide us as ministers of the gospel. We are dealing here with the *essence* of the new life from above, not with just Paul's or John's language. Our most serious failure today is the inability to provide effective practical guidance as to how to live the life of Jesus. And I believe that is due to this very real loss of biblical realism for our lives.

BIBLICAL REALISM, PSYCHOLOGY, AND MODERN CHRISTIAN THINKING

The tendency to blunt or altogether lose the realism of biblical language about the human self is furthered by the ideology dominant in professional psychology during recent decades, as well as by much of the excellent literature produced by Christians since the Reformation. In its efforts to be what is regarded as scientific, psychology tends not to accept religious experience and behavior as realities to be investigated on a par with other psychological phenomena. Many practitioners in the psychoanalytic tradition deriving from Sigmund Freud still regard treatment as having failed if the client retains belief in God. Many Christian psychologists remain somewhat intimidated by the naturalistic bias of psychology. Therefore they are unable to approach Christian behavior and experience as realities to be investigated in their best experimental and theoretical manner.

The Freudian tradition remains very influential on the way in which psychology sees itself, even though it has many dissenters. It is to a large extent responsible for the fact that religious experience is rarely a serious topic of psychological research. As Merton P. Strommen, recipient of the 1983 William James Award in the psychology of religion observes: "Though most Americans view religion as important, scholars have largely ignored it as a factor in making a significant contribution to personal and national well-being. Most psychologists have treated this aspect of human behavior as non-consequential or as something to avoid."[7]

This attitude toward religious experience is unwittingly brought to the study of the Bible, even by devout Christians. And that makes impossible any thorough appreciation of Paul's understanding of redemption, because Paul understood redemption as a progressive sequence of real human and divine actions and events that resulted in the transformation of the body and the mind. For him these were actions—events—real experiences we humans have, real parts of our lives, so real we cannot ignore them. But the attitude that doesn't see them as such doesn't come just from modern psychology.

The church's gradual loss, over the centuries, of the reality of Paul's experience of Christ has also contributed to this attitude of our culture. And so the meaning of Paul's writings as he mapped out the terrain of the disciple's soul is also lost.

But some of the greatest literature in the English language has also contributed to the loss of biblical realism. The great works of writers such as Milton and Bunyan have had the effect of wholly allegorizing the battle between good and evil as well as the Christian's struggle to follow the Lord. This is true to such an extent that generations of readers have emerged with a head full of images, but no idea of what to *do* in their own individual "pilgrim's progress" or "paradise regained." Worse still, the impression is conveyed that this progress will somehow automatically take place through the normal course of life, if only the pilgrim holds on to certain beliefs.

Certainly I do not attack this literature in its own right as literature. But it has entered into a fatal combination with the general Protestant overreaction against ascetic or disciplinary practices. A "head trip" of mental assent to doctrine and the enjoyment of pleasant imagery and imagination is quietly substituted for a rigorous practice of discipleship that would bring a true transformation of character.

But the new life in Christ simply is not an inner life of belief and imagination, even if spiritually inspired. It is a life of the whole embodied person in the social context. Peter's great revelation of Jesus being the Christ was genuine. But subsequent events proved that it alone did not transform his life. What he *lived through* did that, as was also the case even with our Lord, who "learned obedience by the things he suffered" (Heb 5:8–9). An adequate psychology of redemption must make much of this crucial point, and St. Paul's writings, as well as the rest of the Bible, must be read in the light of it.

BIBLICAL PSYCHOLOGY IN THE EARLY CHURCH

In fact, that's exactly the way Paul's writings *were* read by the early Christians. Franz Delitzsch pointed out over a century ago that biblical psychology is "one of the oldest sciences of the church."[8] Already by the second century a Christian writer, Melito of Sardis, had composed a work, *Concerning the Soul, the Body and the Mind,* mentioned by subsequent Christian leaders such as Eusebius and Jerome. At the beginning of the third century Tertullian wrote his *De Anima,* intending to supercede the monumental works of Plato and Aristotle with a Christian treatment of the main psychological topics.

This concern to understand the fundamental parts and processes of the human self and its redemption—biblical psychology—remains an unrelenting preoccupation of the Christian community until well past the Protestant Reformation. But the extremely rich experimentation and analysis to which the early and later Christian experience was subjected is but a continuation of what is found in the inspired thought and writings of Paul.

We customarily think of Paul as a great theologian, not as a master psychologist. But he clearly perceived and explained the fundamental structures and processes of the human self related to its well-being, its corruption, and its redemption. His Letter to the Romans can never be fully appreciated unless it is read as, among other things, a treatise on social and individual psychology. The fact that he viewed his doctrine of redemption as a doctrine of the transformation of the self required him to be a psychologist. In fact, our ability to imagine that a great theologian would not at the same time be a profound psychologist, a profound theorist of human life, shows how far off-course our thinking is today. Only the fatal separation of salvation from life in modern thinking makes it possible to separate theology from psychology.

Our age fails to understand that Paul's teachings about salvation are unavoidably psychological—but none the less theological because of that. This has turned his most brilliant and profound passages, such as Romans 6–8; Colossians 2–3; and Galatians 2, 3, and 5, into a quagmire of theological speculation or into vaguely inspiring exortation with no power of practical guidance. We are then forced to try capturing Paul's thought and experience in abstract theological ideas merely about God's attitude toward us or about some arrangement God has made in heaven. But his words are really guideposts to direct us in our personal struggle to overcome the evil that reigns in our world. This evil—after Christ's life has touched us—is effectively being challenged right in our own body by the grace and truth of God that has entered our souls.

The early church fathers saw Paul's ideas for what they truly were. When we compare the works of the church fathers with the language of Paul, it becomes clear that in much of their work they are only developing statements found in many biblical writers' work, including Paul's. The church fathers construe the constant biblical references to the mind, the heart, the soul, and the body as if the writers were really referring to the embodied human personality—as they clearly *are*—and as if they had a definite meaning of essential importance to the understanding of life in Christ.

SPIRITUALITY AND HABIT: THE "LAWS IN OUR MEMBERS"

Paul's fundamental psycho-theological insight has to do with the nature of the human body as a bearer of active tendencies to evil and to good. In other words, it had to do with *spirituality and habit*.

In C. S. Lewis's *Screwtape Letters,* Uncle Screwtape reproaches the apprentice demon, Wormwood, for permitting his "patient" to become a Christian. Nevertheless, he says, "There is no need to despair; hundreds of these adult converts have been reclaimed after a brief sojourn in the enemy's camp and are now with us. All the *habits* of the patient, both mental and bodily, are still in our favour."[9] Uncle Screwtape has deep insight into the psychology of redemption. If a convert's habits remain the same they will realize little of the life in Christ.

Paul knew this. His inspiration as a Christian psychologist shines most brightly in Romans 6–7. There he deals with *how* our body and its members are to be transformed into servants of God through the replacement of habits of sin by habits of righteousness.

Habits are to be transformed by our interaction with God, of course, and thus by his grace. But exactly what form does this interaction take, and what is *our* part in it? The answer is given in Romans 6:13: "Neither yield ye your members as instruments of unrighteousness unto sin: but yield yourselves unto God as those that are alive from the dead, and your members as instruments of righteousness unto God." What does that mean? To understand this statement is to understand our part in changing our habits. Its context points out three stages of personal redemption as a real, psychological process.

STAGE 1: BAPTIZED INTO CHRIST

Paul opens Romans 6 with a question that anyone reading his explanation of sin and grace in Romans 1–5 might ask: "If grace is to abound more than sin, should we not increase sin and thereby increase grace?" He responds with the surprising claim that we cannot increase sin, because we are dead to it. To employ a crude mechanical metaphor, we can no longer run on sin because our engines have been switched over to another, superior type of fuel. We cannot run on that fuel *and* on the other at the same time. We cannot live from Christ *and* from sin.

We were baptized *into* Christ and brought to "experiential union" with him. What he experienced *then* we *now* also experience through our *communion* with him. And this also means that we share his death to the sin powers that run the world. As they were not what moved *him,* so they are also not what move us. We participate in the new form of life, the one in Jesus and the one so powerful it could overcome physical death. Remember, this is a matter of what we find in our conscious experience. This new form of life provides not only new powers for our human self, but also, as we grow, a new center of organization and orientation for all of the natural impulses of our bodily self.

These old impulses, as we discussed earlier, are not in themselves sinful. Sin has had them in its grip and has twisted them. To be dead to sin with Christ is not to be lacking in these natural desires, but to have a real alternative to sin and the world's sin system as the orientation and motivation for our natural impulses. In our new life, we are capable of standing *beyond* sin's reach as we choose what we will do and in that sense we are unattached from it, we are dead to it. It *is* still possible in the abstract for us to sin, but we see it as the uninteresting or disgusting thing it is. The psychological condition established in us by the influx of Christ's life—a psychological reality—allows us to rise above our "old person" for the motivation, organization, and direction of our physical existence.

Even if we waver and turn back to the "old person" upon occasion, we still are *able* to do otherwise. People without the new life have no choice. But we have a new force within us that gives us choice. In this sense we are free *from* sin even if not yet free *of* it. Doing what is good and right becomes increasingly easy, sweet, and sensible to us as grace grows in us.

STAGE 2: "RECKON"—A NEW ATTITUDE

The second stage in the process of the individual's full redemption is a specific act on our part that develops into an enduring attitude. In our new freedom we are to "reckon"—that is, consciously and purposefully regard ourselves as "dead to sin and alive to God in union with Jesus Christ" (Rom. 6:11, NEB). Note carefully the *psychological realism*. Whatever may have come before this point, this is something we *do*. It is something that will not be done for us. We are freely entering into this actual event in our lives. As Oswald Chambers writes, "We cannot grow *into* holiness, but we must grow *in* it."[10]

So we bring the "old person" before our minds and, with resolute consciousness, we disassociate ourselves from him or her. We say, with confidence in God and our new life: "*That* is not, and shall not be, me." And as for the remnants of sin still inhabiting me—those "automatic" tendencies to act and feel in ways that are wrong (the "law of sin which is in my members" [Rom. 7:23]), I recognize that "it is no more I, but sin that dwelleth in me" (7:17). Paul was enough of a psychologist to know that not all of the forces at work in the human self are expressions of our conscious will, and that we must effectually disassociate ourselves from our sinful tendencies or have our hopes for purity and health soundly defeated.

So, with his doctrine of "reckoning," Paul has capitalized upon the first effect of "the light of the glorious gospel of Christ" upon our personalities. This effect is that we now vividly see and are gripped by an alternative to sin. With the life imparted by this vision we love what we see and are drawn to it. In this vision and the power it provides lies our freedom to determine who we shall be.

And this is the standpoint from which the reign of sin over our bodies and lives can be broken. We have the simple power, communicated by the gospel, to think in a certain way and to count upon things being as we then think of them. Paul teaches us to think of ourselves as if the world's sinful motivational system were nothing to us, were dead to us, because of the vision of that alternative life present with us in Christ. When we so think, then his life enables us to live independently of the world's values. We can be dead to them.

The psychological power to direct how we think has its positive side in our living consciousness of Christ. But that power is largely one of dismissing thoughts originating from this old life's motivational structure. We know old habits are hard to break, but the decision to dwell or not to dwell in thought upon certain things is the freedom secured for us by our vision of Christ.

The Abba Evagrius (who died in 399) taught:

There are eight principal thoughts, from which all other thoughts stem. The first thought is of gluttony; the second, of fornication; the third, of love of money; the fourth, of discontent; the fifth, of anger; the sixth, of despondency; the seventh, of vainglory; the eighth, of pride. Whether these thoughts disturb the soul or not does not depend on us; but whether they linger in us or not and set passions in motion or not—does depend on us.[11]

In the mid-fourteenth century the anonymous Christian who wrote *The Cloud of Unknowing* advised his readers to weigh each thought and each "stirring" within themselves as soon as they appear. They should "travail busily to destroy the first stirring and thought" of those things they might sin in.[12] That is the only way to avoid following the thought into the deed.

Luther is reported to have said that you cannot stop the birds from flying over your head, but you can keep them from building a nest in your hair. The Pauline doctrine of *reckoning* reminds us we have the power to identify and dismiss wrong thoughts, to separate them from our "selves," and thus by grace to escape them.

STAGE 3: SUBMITTING OUR MEMBERS TO RIGHTEOUSNESS

This then brings us back to Romans 6:13 and the complete understanding of *our* part in the full redemption of our bodily, socialized selves. As we "reckon ourselves to be dead indeed unto sin, but alive unto God through Jesus Christ our Lord," as 6:11 states, we find that we no longer have to obey the directions of sin embedded in our distorted impulses. As those who have been through the experience of putting the "old person" to death and have found new life as a reliable fact beyond it, we are able to submit our body and its parts to God as instruments of righteousness.

So, in the third stage of personal redemption as a real, psychological process, we consciously direct our bodies in a manner that will ensure that it eventually will come "automatically" to serve righteousness as it previously served sin automatically.

Here, as in the preceding stage, we are facing something that will not be done for us, though in our effort we'll find gracious strength beyond ourselves. Oswald Chambers puts it so well. He states that if we've experienced regeneration, we must not only talk about it, but exercise it, working out what God has worked in. We must show it "in our fingertips, in our tongue, and in our bodily contact with other people, and as we obey God we'll find we have a wealth of power on the inside." It becomes a natural part of us, and practice is the key:

The question of forming habits on the basis of the grace of God is a very vital one. To ignore it is to fall into the snare of the Pharisee—the grace of God is praised, Jesus Christ is praised, the Redemption is praised, but the practical everyday life evades working it out. If we refuse to practice, it is not God's grace that fails when a crisis comes, but our own nature. When the crisis comes, we ask God to help us, but He cannot if we have not made our nature our ally. The practicing is ours, not God's. God regenerates us and puts us in contact with all His divine resources, but He cannot make us walk according to His will. [13]

He goes on to stress that when we obey the Spirit and practice through our physical life all that God has put in our hearts, then when crisis comes we will find we have not only God's grace to stand by us, "but our own nature also." The crisis passes without disaster, and our souls, instead of being devastated, can actually acquire a stronger attitude toward God.

The outcome of these three stages, including God's part and our our part, is expressed by Paul in these words in Romans 6:17–18: "God be thanked, you, who once were slaves to sin, have yielded whole-hearted obedience to the pattern of teaching to which you were made subject, and emancipated from sin, have become slaves of righteousness" (NEB). Habitual reliance upon God as we dedicate our bodies to righteous behavior and to all reasonable preparation for righteous behavior makes sin dispensable, even uninteresting and revolting—just as righteousness was revolting to us when our behavior was locked into the sin system. Our desires and delights are changed because our actions and attitude are based upon the reality of God's Kingdom.

PREPARATION FOR BIGGER THINGS

The "practice" that prepares us for righteous living includes not only putting our body through the motions of actions *directly* commanded by our Lord. It also involves engaging in whatever other activities may prepare us to carry out his commands—and not just carry them out, but carry them out with strength, effectiveness, and joy. And this is where the standard, well-recognized spiritual disciplines become involved.

These disciplines constitute the *indirect,* yet vitally necessary submission of our body and its members to righteousness. How? I submit my tongue as an instrument of righteousness when I *make* it bless them that curse me and pray for them who persecute me, even though it "automatically" tends to strike and wound those who have wounded me. I submit my legs to God as instruments of righteousness when I engage them in physical labor as service, perhaps carrying a burden the "second mile" for someone whom I would rather let my legs kick. I submit my body to righteousness when I do my good deeds without letting them be known, though my whole frame cries out to strut and crow. And when I do, I offer up my body as the place of God's action. I prepare myself for God's action in me just as Abraham prepared the sacrifice in Genesis 15 and would have no fire touch it but what God himself sent.

Of course, we do the righteous deed because of our redemption, not *for* our redemption. Our eyes and our life are fixed upon God who is our life and who sets us free from bondage to all that is less than himself, including the bondage of righteous deeds. This is how, in Paul's terminology, we "sow to the spirit" through doing "good to all men, especially unto them who are of the household of faith" (Gal. 6:9–19). Or again, in the words of this shameless do-gooder, we are "steadfast, unmoveable, always abounding in the work of the Lord, forasmuch as ye know that our labour is not in vain in the Lord" (1 Cor. 15:58). In such a life one constantly draws strength from the goodness of rightness in the Kingdom of God.

But such efforts, while disciplinary in effect, are more expressions *of* spiritual life than they are disciplines *for* it. Discipline, strictly speaking, is activity carried on to prepare us indirectly for some activity other than itself. We do not practice the piano to practice the piano well, but to play it well. The activities just discussed above as illustrations of submission to righteousness are the performance, not the practice—though performance also has the effect of practice.

However, we cannot always reliably and inexhaustibly submit our members to righteousness directly in performance. This is especially true of those whose brain, hands, tongue, legs, eyebrows, and the like are still clogged by dispositions imported from the world—by what Paul refers to as "the sin which is in our members"—and whose flesh is still weak in the cause for which their spirit may be ever so willing. Here, then, is where the *pure* disciplines for the spiritual life must be brought to bear.

In the hurly-burly of daily life I may not be able to speak the truth always. But, as a discipline, I can perhaps make myself return to those to whom I have lied and tell them I misled or deceived them. This, in turn, will marvelously enhance my ability to speak the truth on other occasions. I may be overly dependent upon food and unable not to eat, because when I try not to eat, food is all I think about. But perhaps I can train myself to pray for a specific person or circumstance whenever I am hungry or restless and thus escape from my obsession with food.

Then again, perhaps I cannot even do that. Then I need to go deeper to find the place where I do have freedom to submit myself to God: down into the radical, life-transforming activities of solitude, silence, fasting, study, or sacrifice. Whatever activity of this type may be required to free me up, I must undertake it. Now that new life is graciously visited upon me, my part in the redemptive process is to do just that. God will not do it for me any more than he did it for Moses or Elijah, for his son Jesus or his apostle Paul. And if I do not submit my actions through the disciplines that fit my personality, I will not enter into the powerful, virtuous new life in a psychologically real way.

Today, around every corner stands someone hawking wisdom and goodness on easy terms. But this is not what history and experience teach.[14] Such instant wisdom is just another expression of our modern, hedonistic ideology fueled by our constitutional right to pursue happiness. Somehow, we think that virtue should come easily. Experience teaches, to the contrary, that almost everything worth doing in human life is very difficult in its early stages and the good we are aiming at is never available at first, to strengthen us when we seem to need it most.

Think of all the projects, all the resolutions we begin and never finish. Starting is easy. Following through is hard. Few people get very far in most activities, even those at which we all long to excel. While this is obviously true in the arts and sports, it is just as true in activities such as communicating with people, making money, directing a group activity, or caring for honeybees. *And we are not exempted from this rule when we enter the Kingdom of grace.* So there's nothing left to do but accept this psychological fact about human personality and realize that the rigorous form of life mandatory for excellence is the only way in which we can, as Paul directs, "purge" ourselves into becoming a "vessel unto honor, sanctified, and meet for the Master's use, prepared unto every good work" (2 Tim. 2:21). We must accept it and submit ourselves to it, knowing that the rigors of discipline certainly lead to the easy yoke and the full joy of Christ.

THE BODY AS STOREHOUSE AND TRANSMITTER OF POWER

What is the disciplined body capable of doing? When we read the Scriptures, we can't help but wonder about the strange power Christ and his apostles displayed. We may be puzzled upon finding "the laying on of hands" listed along with repentance, faith, the resurrection of the dead, and eternal judgment as one of the principles or primary doctrines of Christ (Heb. 6:1–2). But if we have come to understand the psychological realism of biblical language, this will cease to be puzzling.

We pointed out in an earlier chapter that salvation as portrayed in the New Testament involves significant power over evil, both by individuals and by the church collectively. Life is everywhere inseparable from power, and new life means new powers. This power is, in the New Testament conception, *literally* located in the body of the redeemed or spiritually enlivened person. In the New Testament it is present to an even higher degree when that person is together with others in the *ecclesia,* or the community called of God, as in Matthew 18:18–20 and 1 Corinthians 5:4–5.

Localization of power in the body is nowhere clearer than in the Gospel stories. Jesus (and later the apostles) worked to a remarkable extent through bodily contact, or at least proximity. Fourteen of the miracles of Jesus recorded in the Gospels involve physical contact.

Most illustrative is the woman in Mark 5:25–30 "who had an issue of blood twelve years." She had steadily declined in health as she spent all her money on physicians; but when she heard of Jesus she said, "If I may touch but his clothes, I shall be whole". She slipped through the crowd and touched his garment, "and immediately she felt in her body that she was healed". On the other side of the transaction, Jesus immediately sensed "that power (*dunamin*) had gone out of him." Turning around he asked who it was that had touched him. Characteristically there was physical contact in the healing ministry of Jesus, and such contact continued to play a large role in the work of the apostolic church.

The practice of the laying on of hands is but another dimension of contact with a power-bearing body. Paul exhorts Timothy not to "neglect the spiritual gift within you, which was bestowed upon you through prophetic utterance with the laying on of hands by the presbytery" (1 Tim. 4:14). But he also admonishes him: "Do not lay hands on anyone too hastily and thus share responsibility for the sins of others" (1 Tim. 5:22). The thought behind both of these statements is that in the laying on of hands something that is *in* one person is transmitted to another, something that gives these people power to do what they could not otherwise do, but power they *may* either neglect or misuse.

Certainly Paul was conscious of such a power in himself and pleaded with those in Corinth to rectify themselves before he came to visit them, that he might not be required to use it on them (2 Cor. 13:10). This he said after telling them (13:2) that when he came he would not spare anyone still derelict. Recollection of what he had done to Elymas the sorcerer (Acts 13:8–12) perhaps gave weight to his threat.

He also minces no words in relationship to "Hymenaeus and Alexander, whom I have delivered unto Satan, that they may learn not to blaspheme" (1 Tim. 1:20). In the case of one in the church at Corinth who engaged in sexual relations with his stepmother, Paul instructs those in that fellowship that "being assembled in the name of our Lord Jesus, and I with you in spirit, with the power of our Lord Jesus over us, this man is to be consigned to Satan for the destruction of the body, so that his spirit may be saved in the day of our Lord" (1 Cor. 5:4–5, NEB).

Ananias and Sapphira found what it was like to fall across the flowing power of God (Acts 5:1–11); and it seems to have been commonly understood that sickness or death would come upon those in the *ecclesia* who sufficiently offended the ways of that power (1 Cor. 11:30; 1 John 5:16).

Such displays of power, emanating forth from the individual and collective bodies of Jesus, the apostles, and the early church are difficult to comprehend from the contemporary point of view. We have so little experience of or sensible teaching about such things. And in a world of a naturalistic outlook, where secularism takes many guises and even penetrates deeply into the substance of the "church visible," some will go to any lengths to explain away such manifestations—or at least to explain why they have nothing to do with *us*.

Hence we may be tempted to pass these scriptural reports off as myths. But we should remember that we are here dealing with a new kind of life, and that to deny the powers associated with it is really to deny the life. The myth falls to those who would have the new life in Christ *without* novel manifestations of power. That would be incomprehensible in any realistic terms. Those who take that course were already singled out by Paul as those "holding a form of religion, but denying the power of it. Avoid such people" (2 Tim. 3:5).

THE "BODY," NOT "THE BODY OF CHRIST"

When we lose the psychological realism of Paul's language, large and obviously important parts of his writings become unintelligible to practice as well as theory. But we also will then distort his views as a whole. In his work *The Body: A Study of Pauline Theology,* John A. T. Robinson states that "the body forms the keystone of Paul's theology."[15] He sees quite clearly that the modern ideals of human freedom and a free society can only find their realization in a proper treatment of the body, to which Paul's insights can show the way. Robinson's discussions of "flesh" and "body" in his first chapter are among the most useful a person can read on these topics. But as Robinson's work progresses we see the psychological realism of Paul replaced by an emphasis upon the body as the church, as the "body" of Christ.

For Robinson the problem of redemption is just that of breaking the crushing hold of mass society over the individual by immersing him or her into a new corporiety, the church. This is the central theme of the book. But that leaves unanswered the question of the means employed to that end. And in Paul's view the individual's relation to *his or her own body*—not just to the church—is a major and indispensible factor that makes possible the deliverance of persons through immersion in the body of Christ. The central statements of Paul about his own body and his directions on how each believer should relate to his or her own body cannot be understood or applied unless we understand that there is much more to his view of the body's role in the processes of sin and redemption than Robinson takes into consideration.

Robinson clearly assumes that the "faith and practice" of his own denominational communion is adequate to bring about immersion into Christ's body, resulting in that freedom and power in Christ that characterized Paul himself. This is the usual assumption from denomination to denomination. But the infrequency of people like Paul among our fellow church members should alert us that this hope is in vain. Much more is required—and it is supplied by the appropriate program of spiritual disciplines such as Paul himself practiced.

Certainly the social dimension of life is essential to spirituality. *Of course* I should not disregard social evils and should oppose them when it is strategically possible to make some difference. *Of course* I should not disregard the corporate body of Christ. I should sustain it and nourish myself within it and upon it. But how can I succeed in doing this? Concretely, the only place where I can "fight the good fight of faith, lay hold on eternal life" (1 Tim. 6:12), is in and through the management of my body, dealing rigorously and wisely with it and depending on God's help.

Today there's an almost universal failure to give good counsel on the specific steps to be taken to enter this life Paul so well knew. To suppose that the practical regimen now actually commended by any significant Christian denomination can reliably bring about deliverance from sin is simply contrary to observable fact. Moreover, it is bad theology, unscriptural, and involves a radically misconceived psychology. Such off-centered thinking explains the generally poor results of our teaching on human transformation.

The concluding statement from A. B. Bruce's book on *The Training of the Twelve* gives, by contrast, the effects of the course of experience through which Jesus led his earliest disciples. That training

. . . was fitted to make the disciples what they were required to be as the apostles of a spiritual and universal religion: enlightened in mind, endowed with a charity wide enough to embrace all mankind, having their conscience tremulously sensitive to all claims of duty, yet delivered from all superstitious scruples, emancipated from the fetters of custom, tradition, and the commandments of men, and possessing tempers purged from pride, self-will, impatience, angry passions, vindictiveness, and implacability. That they were slow to learn, and even when their master left them were far from perfect, we have frankly admitted; still they were men of such excellent stuff, that it might be confidently anticipated that having been so long with Jesus they would prove themselves exceptionally good and noble men when they came before the world as leaders in a great movement, called to act on their own responsibility."[16]

IGNORING THE GREAT LEADER'S LEAD

It would be amusing, if it were not so tragic, to contemplate how the followers of great religious leaders devise ways and rationalizations for *not* engaging in the practices their leaders and forerunners found necessary. People we admit to be far greater than we are—and, in the case of Jesus himself, even divine—found it necessary to practice disciplines and engage in activities with which we blithely dispense.

A John Wesley, a John Knox, a Martin Luther, a George Fox, as well as a Paul may be admired in word. But in reality we must think that they were a little fanatical or silly, for few of us think enough of the practices they found necessary to adopt them ourselves.

By and large these plus many others recognized for their greatness in The Way of Christ were simply being true to the psychological laws intertwined with spiritual life when they undertook such measures, even though they were often confused and blundering in their efforts. But they met God in their practices—and they are the result of the grace of God they met. And that result— even when far from perfect—speaks for itself to the ages.

The result of *not* practicing rigorously for the spiritual life, on the other hand, also speaks for itself. Who are the great ones in The Way, what are the significant movements in the history of the church that do *not* bear the deep and pervasive imprint of the disciplines for the spiritual life? If there are none, what leads us to believe that *we* might be an exception to the rule and might know the power of the Kingdom life without the appropriate disciplines? How could we be justified in doing anything less than practicing and teaching the disciplines Jesus Christ himself and the best of his followers found necessary?

It is easy to praise the great ones now passed on, because we can in their absence disregard the concrete reality of their practices. When those same practices are brought to life in someone walking next to us, we reach for stones to throw, just as Jesus said in Matthew 23. Why did they respond that way? Such persons reveal us for who we are. They expose our profession of being one with Christ without living as he lived, and their presence insists that we truly change and enter the Kingdom.

PAUL AS PHILOSOPHER

The gospel of Christ offers radical change for human existence. Sir William Ramsey's statement at the beginning of this chapter is correct. As a result of Paul's experience with Christ's Kingdom, Paul recaptured the ancient, prophetic vision of the world being governed by the people of God—governing through the light and power resident in them *as* God's earthly dwelling place.

In its original Jewish form that vision was rendered impotent because God's blessing was turned toward nationalistic and cultural ends. But Paul's all-encompassing vision of what human society could be when structured around men and women walking in the fullness of Christ solved the problems human government always fails to solve—the problems of any government which relies on force and the threat of death, invariably controlled by certain social or cultural groups within the society. This kind of government by human force, he saw, could be replaced by a kingdom of truth and love conducted by those indwelt by Christ. This *total vision* of human life, on its individual as well as corporate level, is what made Paul a philosopher.

Greek philosophy had failed at the point of producing people of practical power and wisdom who could govern and be governed. It simply had no workable answer to the question of how this could be done. The same inability of classical civilization to produce sufficient people capable of serving as the foundation of good government destroyed the Roman Empire. Early in human development, races of people are sufficiently under the duress of real needs to exhalt the virtues that can make them strong. But after they become strong they have no sustaining principle that will allow the further development of virtue to maintain their society. They lack the tension adequate to maintain character in their citizens. No stable society can, therefore, be long maintained if it is prosperous. A transcendental principle and tension is lacking, and that is what is abundantly supplied in the gospel of Jesus Christ and his Kingdom.

It is all very well to speak, with Thomas Jefferson, of "an aristocracy of virtue and talent" that can serve as the backbone of a society and make decent and free government possible. It is quite another to produce such people in sufficient number. Only the Kingdom of God and its disciplines, taken in the following of Christ, can do that. Paul's understanding of this assured him that "the saints shall judge the earth" (1 Cor. 6:2) and qualified him as a greater philosopher of human life than Aristotle. We shall return to this theme in our final chapter.

NOTES

Epigraph. William M. Ramsay, *The Cities of St. Paul: Their Influence on His Life and Thought* (New York: Hodder & Stoughton, 1907), 4. James S. Stewart remarks: "For sheer mental force, apart altogether from spiritual experience, Paul's place is with Plato and Socrates and the world's giants of thought" (*A Man In Christ* [New York: Harper, n. d.], 21).

1. Quoted in John Pollock, *The Man Who Shook the World* (Wheaton, IL: Victor, 1972), pref.

2. Stewart, *A Man in Christ,* 3.

3. A. G. Sertillanges, *The Intellectual Life* (Westminster, MD: Christian Classics, 1980), 48.

4. Gal. 1:16–17. On this passage see Ernest De Witt Burton, *A Critical and Exegetical Commentary on the Epistle to the Galatians* (Edinburgh: Clark, 1952), 55–58, for a discussion of Paul's activities during this period in Arabia. See also David Smith, *The Life and Letters of St. Paul* (New York: Harper, n. d.), 56n.

5. Stewart, *A Man in Christ,* 38.

6. Evelyn Christenson, *Lord, Change Me!* (Wheaton, IL: Victor, 1979), 143.

7. Reported in the *Los Angeles Times,* September 3, 1983, part 2, 4.

8. Franz Delitzsch, *A System of Biblical Psychology,* trans. Robert E. Wallis (Edinburgh: Clark, 1869), 3.

9. C. S. Lewis, *The Screwtape Letters and Screwtape Proposes a Toast* (New York: Macmillan, 1962), 11.

10. Oswald Chambers, *The Psychology of Redemption* (London: Simpkin Marshall, 1947), 51.
11. E. Kadloubovsky and G. E. H. Palmer, ed., *Early Fathers from the Philokalia* (London: Faber and Faber, 1963), 110. The remarkable insights of this fourth-century Christian teacher into the control of our actions through the control of our feelings through the control of our thoughts are upheld today in the writings of secular psychologists such as Michael J. Mahoney (*Cognition and Behavior Modification* [Cambridge, MA: Ballinger, 1974]) and David D. Burns (*Feeling Good: The New Mood Therapy* [New York: New American Library, 1981]). The corresponding mode of psychological treatment is called "cognitive therapy" or "cognitive behavior modification." Burns says: "The first principle of cognitive therapy is that *all* your moods are created by your 'cognitions' or thoughts" (p. 11).
12. *The Cloud of Unknowing*, ed. Dom Justin McCann (London: Burns Oates and Washbourne, 1943), 21.
13. Chambers, *The Psychology of Redemption*, 26–27.
14. On this see the wise words of O. Hardman, *The Ideals of Asceticism: An Essay in the Comparative Study of Religion* (New York: Macmillan, 1924), 158–59.
15. John A. T. Robinson, *The Body: A Study in Pauline Theology* (London: SCM, 1952), 9. For an exhaustive study of Paul's concept of body, see Robert Jewett, *Paul's Anthropological Terms: A Study of Their Use in Conflict Settings* (Leiden: Brill, 1971), chap. 5.
16. Alexander Balmain Bruce, *The Training of the Twelve* (Garden City, NY: Doubleday, Doran, 1928), 545.

8. History and the Meaning of the Disciplines

In the theological discourse of our time, the word "asceticism" has become one that collects everything we want to reject in ourselves and in historical Christian tradition. Theologies of embodiment, of play and of sexual identity celebrate the demise of asceticism. We lump together all historical asceticism and indicate our evaluation of it by labeling it "masochism." This method distorts and foreshortens historical phenomena and constructs a past that is nothing but caricature. But an even more unfortunate result of the cavalier treatment of historical asceticism is the loss of ascetic practices as tools for the present care and cure of our own bodies and souls.

MARGARET R. MILES

What we are beginning to learn is that asceticism is a valid part of religion or of any other important enterprise.

ELTON TRUEBLOOD

Where have we acquired our negative attitude toward the spiritual disciplines? The tenacles of history reach deeply into our brains and bodies, our teachings and our rituals. They cause us to "see" things as they "must be," rather than as they *are*. To understand the history of the disciplines will help us understand our modern attitude and approach to the disciplines.

THE "GOOD LIFE" NOW

Contemporary Westerners are nurtured on the faith that everyone has a *right* to do what they want when they want, to pursue happiness in all ways possible, to feel good, and to lead a "productive and successful life," understood largely in terms of self-contentment and material well-being. This vision of life has come, in the popular mind, to be identified with "the good life," and even with civilized existence. It is taught through the popular media, political rhetoric, and the educational system as the *natural* way for life to be.

Our commercialized environment takes this idea a step too far at times, frequently degrading the vision to its lowest possible level. An advertisement for an expensive automobile that ran for a long while in the *Los Angeles Times* urged readers to "Pursue happiness in a car that can catch it!" In the *Atlantic* for October 1983 there is a full-page advertisement for a certain brandy captioned: "Taste the Good Life!" On the west side of Los Angeles a paper is published under the name *The Good Life*. From the contents one sees that the good life has to do exclusively with weight loss, eating (paradoxically), hairstyling, entertainment, celebrities, fancy automobiles, and hot tubs. That's about it.

These cultural outtakes aptly characterize the giddy condition of much of our public life and private thinking. If for any reason we are not fully exercising and enjoying the right to "freedom" and "happiness" as popularly conceived, then we automatically assume that something is somewhere wrong. Either we have failed or circumstances (or other people) have treated us unfairly. If we ourselves refuse to work for this "happy and successful life," we may be quickly dismissed as not wholly sane and rational—or worse still, written off as "a saint."

Against the crushing social presence of this vision, the call to forsake all and to "hate one's own life also" (Luke 14:26), which stands at the threshold of discipleship to Christ, is incomprehensible. That is, most of us who hear the call, living as we do with our modern ideology, cannot relate it in any concrete or practical way to our own experience, education, and existence. We are not sure how it might be incorporated into our plans for living. The deep wisdom of Jesus—so fully congruent with all the great traditions of religion and ethical culture—that he who would save his life must lose it (Mark 8:35–36) just "does not compute." To the contrary, we are confidently told by the current wisdom that the age-old practices identified with the spiritual life cannot be regarded as desirable, "where men judge of things by their natural, unprejudiced reason, without the delusive glosses of superstition and false religion."[1]

A MAN OF "ENLIGHTENMENT"

The words of David Hume, an eighteenth-century Scottish writer and thinker, exemplify this modern worldview underlying the current version of "the good life":

Celibacy, fasting, penance, mortification, self-denial, humility, silence, solitude, and the whole train of monkish virtues:—for what reason are they everywhere rejected by men of sense, but because they serve to no manner of purpose; neither advance a man's fortune in the world, nor render him a more valuable member of society; neither qualify him for the entertainment of company, nor increase his power of self-enjoyment? We observe, on the contrary, that they cross all these desirable ends; stupify the understanding and harden the heart, obscure the fancy and sour the temper. . . . A gloomy, hair-brained enthusiast, after his death, may have a place in the Calendar; but will scarcely ever be admitted, when alive, into intimacy and society, except by those who are as delirious and dismal as himself."[1]

This statement requires only a little updating, a few references to hot tubs and such, and it could easily take its place in California's paper *The Good Life*. In fact this "man of reason"—like so many of those who speak from a similar perspective today—had no clear idea of what he was talking about. On the usefulness of the "monkish" practices, he himself was but a "man of prejudice." But it is not as if he were wholly free in adopting his attitude. He spoke from deep, historically conditioned prejudices. These prejudices were rooted primarily in the Protestant and Catholic struggles of the European past, but they also stemmed from the contrast assumed between the "Dark Ages" and the world of modern enlightenment. He would naturally take his views to be the clear-eyed vision of pure reason and good common sense.

Hume's outlook made it impossible for him to sort out what caused that attitude within the complex phenomena of social and religious history. As a result he could not see that spiritual discipline, informed by Christ's message and example, is in essence and reality *opposed* to the evils now historically associated with their abuses. He could not understand that those very evils were themselves attributable, not to the practice of the spiritual disciplines, but to the *failure* to practice them or to practice them rightly. So how could he see that such discipline *rightly practiced* is the absolutely indispensible condition of human life as it was meant to be?

THE PROTESTANT PRINCIPLE

The prejudice is even stronger today, two hundred years after Hume wrote. This is due to the further development of the idea that Protestantism, or just the progress of enlightenment, has refuted any view of Christian salvation requiring disciplines for the spiritual life. The Western world at large, not merely philosophers and scholars, is now firmly prejudiced against disciplinary activities as a part of the religious life.

What, we wonder, could possibly be the point of such discipline, if not the earning of merit or maybe forgiveness through self-denial and suffering? We are confidently informed that the fundamental principle of the Protestant movement—that salvation is secured by justification through faith and not through dead works—"struck at the root of monkery and mortification in general."[2] That's how the article on "asceticism" in the long-standard M'Clintock and Strong encyclopedia on religion expresses this accepted attitude of Protestant culture. Somehow, the fact that "mortification"—self-denial, the disciplining of one's natural impulses—happens to be a central teaching of the New Testament is conveniently ignored.

At the practical level of parish life, this attitude toward spiritual discipline has had a great effect on Catholics as well, since our Protestant culture is so pervasive. The result is our almost universal inability to understand what the disciplines for the spiritual life are. The biblical passages that exemplify or command "mortification" have had to be ignored, legalized, or spiritualized in one way or another, their practical point turned to suit the inclinations of the particular social group.

Of course almost everyone can name a few specific types of actions or practices they take to be "spiritual." We may, for example, think of poverty, celibacy, and obedience to a superior, which are parts of numerous orders in the Catholic church and familiar to the general public through literature and the other arts. Or our study of the Bible may have led us to think of fasting, giving to the poor, or the routine saying of prayers in this connection. However, my conversations with most Christians I meet show them to be quite mystified by these practices when it is suggested that they might be relevant to their lives.

DISCIPLINARY MALPRACTICE

It is easy to see why the disciplines for the spiritual life might make little sense in the prevailing secular worldview, even for the nominally religious, who are in fact governed by that view. But those who are more familiar with the Bible also know that all such activities may be done for various misguided reasons and motives. Under some circumstances they may even harm the spiritual life, or at least not work in its favor.

This fact is the main *religious* support for our modern disdain of spiritual discipline. Fasting and the rituals of worship, for example, are among the practices most commonly attacked by the Hebrew prophets as useless, or even harmful, exercises in religion (Isa. 58, 59; Matt. 23). We read these accounts and seem to overlook that the attack there is not upon the practices themselves, but upon their abuse. When such practices were conducted, as they often were, as expressions of fear and hatred of the material world or as attempts to manipulate or impress God and others, they were being abused. So instead of aiding life in vital interaction with the Kingdom of God, such activities became, and still become, exercises in human cleverness and superstition. They do nothing for the growth of our souls in godliness or the progress of God's cause in the world.

As he did on so many topics, Paul really said the last word on this matter in 1 Corinthians 13:3: "Though I bestow all my goods to feed the poor, and though I give my body to be burned, and have not love, it profiteth me nothing." A discipline of the spiritual life *cannot* be identified—either for acceptance or rejection—merely by the externals of the associated action. It, like circumcision among the Jews, is a matter of a meeting of external and internal conditions; that is, outward manifestation and inward motivation must both be right. Rejection of spiritual disciplines because of an identification of them with the outward acts alone simply does not go to the heart of the matter.

THE MISUNDERSTANDING ABOUT SUFFERING

One of the frequent misunderstandings of the spiritual disciplines involves the idea of self-inflicted pain or of accepting pain from the hand of another. And the historical context is real. It derives from certain actual practices of the Middle Ages. The phrase "the discipline" was for centuries used to refer to a whip of a certain kind that was used to chastise the body during acts of penance. In the earlier periods of this practice thorn branches, iron chains, or leather straps tipped with metal or bone were used, but the instrument was gradually modified over the years to consist of several strands of rope knotted at the ends. In the thirteenth century, flagellation came into practice for penitential processions of the laity as well as of the religious orders—continuing into the nineteenth century, and in some places even into the twentieth. It was frequently thought of as an act of imitating Christ's last hours, but it is practiced in non-Christian religions as well and may be observed in some Islamic processions. Such practices, needless to say, really have nothing to do with the following of Christ. He himself never engaged in them.

IS JUDAISM AN ASCETIC RELIGION?

To have an adequate perspective on the present, we must look at it through the past. And we must begin by clearing up a mistake that says Judaism is a nonascetic religion. There is no need to document the point, since any reading at all on the subject will constantly discover such pronouncements. But its legitimate meaning must be clarified, since the gospel of Christ arises within Judaism.

What is meant, perhaps, is that the branding of the body as evil and the infliction of pain upon it as its "just deserts," as punishment, or to gain merit—all the negative ideas attached to ascetic behavior we've been taught—are no part of the Hebrew tradition. And that is largely true. But when we look at the exemplars of Hebrew religion such as Abraham, Moses, David, Daniel, John the Baptist, Jesus, and St. Paul, we are looking at people who fast, pray, seek solitude, and give themselves up to humankind and God in ways that are readily recognizable as ascetic. They all serve as models for these practices.

What R. L. Nettleship said of Plato's views of the philosophical life can equally be said of these leaders and of Judaism generally— possibly excepting some of its modern variants:

If asceticism means the disciplined effort to attain an end which cannot be attained without giving up many things often considered desirable, the philosophical life (as Plato saw it) is ascetic; but, if it means giving up for the sake of giving up, there is no asceticism in Plato.[3]

Indeed, given what we have already seen about the nature of human life, *any* religion must be in some significant degree ascetic—admitted or not, consistent or not. Just think what it would mean if it were otherwise. It would mean that those conditions that constitute the nature of religious life are all attainable by "natural" growth, by external imposition, or by direct acts of will and that purpose-filled preparation and training and taking pains to learn are entirely irrelevant.

This, ironically enough, is where misunderstanding of the doctrine of salvation by grace through faith has brought many in the Protestant culture of this century. But it is contrary to all experience of life, including the spiritual life, and makes it impossible to have any practical direction in the conduct of that life. In fact no religion, including Judaism, accepts such a view, even though it is easy for some to drift into a posture that makes it seem as if they do.

WAS JESUS AN ASCETIC?

We have previously referred to the ascetic practices of Jesus, especially his use of solitude, fasting, and prayer. He was conscious of the public comparison of himself to John the Baptist: "For John came neither eating or drinking, and they say 'He has a demon!' The Son of Man came eating and drinking, and they say, 'Behold, a gluttonous man and a drunkard, a friend of tax gatherers and sinners!'" (Matt. 11:18–19).

In understanding these remarks a number of things must be kept in mind. First, there was a point to the comparison, for John's manner of life seems to have been ascetic in a manner more extreme and more recognizable *as* ascetic by the people of his time than was that of Jesus himself. Jesus' life was in its externals more of a "normal" existence, though it included long and regular periods of solitude, fasting, and prayer, as well as a voluntary homelessness, poverty, and chastity.

Second, the statements about himself and John the Baptist that Jesus quoted probably originated with those Pharisees whose legalistic sense of propriety he had offended. Certainly he was not a drunkard or a glutton, but he also was not fastidious about the eating and drinking legalisms treasured by the Pharisees. And he did keep the "wrong kind of company"—the oppressive tax gatherer and those who were loose sexually, and gluttonous, and alcoholic.

MASTER OF SPIRITUAL LIFE

But more than anything—and most important for our goal of understanding the disciplines for the spiritual life—we must recognize that Jesus *was* a master of life in the spirit. He showed us that spiritual strength is not manifested by great and extensive practice of the spiritual disciplines, *but by little need to practice them and still maintain full spiritual life.* To have misunderstood this point was the fundamental and devastating error of Christian asceticism in the Western church from the desert fathers up to the time of the Reformation. Yet when we look closely and continually at Jesus, we do not lose sight of this one fundamental, crucial point—the activities constituting the disciplines *have no value in themselves.* The aim and substance of spiritual life is not fasting, prayer, hymn singing, frugal living, and so forth. Rather, it is the effective and full enjoyment of active love of God and humankind in all the daily rounds of normal existence where we are placed. The spiritually advanced person is not the one who engages in lots and lots of disciplines, any more than the good child is the one who receives lots and lots of instruction or punishment.

People who think that they are spiritually superior *because* they make a practice of a discipline such as fasting or silence or frugality are entirely missing the point. The need for extensive practice of a given discipline is an indication of our *weakness,* not our strength. We can even lay it down as a rule of thumb that if it is *easy* for us to engage in a certain discipline, we probably don't need to practice it. The disciplines we need to practice are precisely the ones we are *not* "good at" and hence do not enjoy.

Baseball player Pete Rose, when asked to explain his phenomenal success as an athlete, said: "I practice what I'm not good at. Most folks practice what they're good at." The same is true for our success in our spiritual living.

Anyone who looks squarely at Jesus' manner of life must see that it was one of great rigor and discipline, but it was one clearly fitting the pattern of a *sensible* asceticism as described earlier. The same is true of Christ's followers, both during his life and after his death (See Matt. 8:18–22; 20:26–28; John 13:4–17; Mark 4:19; Luke 9:57–62; 10:3–8; 14:25–35).

If we but look into that "upper room" in Jerusalem (Acts 1:13) where his little band stayed between the ascension and Pentecost, we see first of all how much progress had been made. Those who earlier could not "watch and pray" with the Lord for one hour now guided the group in continuous prayer for a ten-day period. The various disciplines appropriate to the occassion were no doubt fully in use as they "tarried in Jerusalem until endued with power from on high" (Luke 24:49). And their pattern of life continued after Pentecost, to the end of the New Testament record, and then beyond the confines of that record onto the pages of history.

THE EMERGENCE OF MONASTICISM

Monasticism—nothing in the history of the Western world has done more harm to the present-day prospects of a sensible and necessary asceticism than the emergence of monasticism as a form of Christian life. It should go without saying that much of the *motivation* that gave rise to monasticism was praiseworthy, that many great Christians have served within the monastic orders, and many good things were accomplished by these great men. And no one capable of seeing what Jesus and his earliest followers did can fail to miss the substantial continuity between their lives and the great monastics such as Antony and Benedict. It is equally true, however, that within those orders spiritual discipline came over the years to be identified with confused, pointless, and even destructive excesses. These excesses were supported upon attitudes of body hatred and the belief that forgiveness or merit can be gained by sufferings, whether self-inflicted or imposed by a religious superior—all of which are now universally and rightly condemned. Reaction to such excesses in the monastic orders has made it very difficult for many to regard the spiritual disciplines as essential to their well-being, spiritual and otherwise.

THE ORIGIN OF MONASTICISM

How did the idea of monastic life develop? The answer lies in the early church's history. The impulse of the Spirit and the impact of persecution scattered the early Christians. Wherever they went, they banded together and groups of the "called out ones" (the *ecclesia*) were established. Some historians suggest that bloody opposition to the new faith was sufficient to sustain the disciples' sense of identity and separate them from the surrounding world for the first three centuries. They were never allowed to forget that their citizenship was in heaven (Phil. 3:21), that they were in but not of the world (John 17:16), and that they had here no continuing city, being strangers and pilgrims upon the earth (Heb. 11:13–16).

However, with the conversion of the Roman emperor Constantine to Christianity and the promulgation of his Edicts of Toleration in A.D. 311, Christianity suddenly had legal standing and even enjoyed imperial patronage. Possessing status and security granted by the world, the church and most of its members began to think of the world as quite compatible with the profession of discipleship to Christ. Soon, though, a select group within the Christian fellowship found this situation unbearable, and individuals and small groups began to set themselves apart to engage in what they felt to be a more intensely spiritual mode of existence.[4]

At this same time a synthesis of Hellenistic, Jewish, and Christian thought in the teachings of the Alexandrian church father Origen (died 254) began to exercise widespread influence. He emphatically called disciples of Christ to a perfection and a mystical union with God far above and apart from ordinary worldly existence:

It was Origen's desire to express the Christian experience as an orderly, rational pattern of perfection based upon sound philosophical principles. Origen saw man as cooperating in the process of his own sanctification, the outcome of union with God. He further saw the process of attaining holiness/union as an ascent to be accomplished by steps or degrees. These steps had to be taken by a man. His only access to these stages of development was the unremitting practice of asceticism.[5]

Out of such conditions and as the magnificent social and political order of the Roman Empire stumbled toward its end, people hungry for God took to the Egyptian desert as a refuge in which to find holiness and union with God. Abhorrence of the world mingled with a hunger for God and purity, and with not a little romanticism about the lofty calling, to produce one of the most astonishing phenomena in world history.

Soon, from Syria in the north to middle Egypt in the south, a distinctive mode of existence, "eremetical monasticism"—the individual living completely alone in the wilderness—was recognized as a special mode of life that one might choose as a Christian disciple. Predators, human and animal, along with spiritual, psychological, and physical needs destroyed many of these Christian hermits who followed leaders such as Saint Antony (died 396) into the desert.

Pachomius, a contemporary and fellow countryman of Antony, dealt with these dangers by creating communities of hermits (as contradictory as that may sound) and thus instituting the "cenobitic" or *enclosed* communal life. Each hermit had his own dwelling place and was therefore a hermit. But all were enclosed by one protective wall. There were minimal contacts in their common labor, religious service, and teaching, but each disciple could safely pursue his union with God without the threats and dangers of complete desert solitude. Thus was born what we have come to know as monasteries.

CONSUMING ASCETICISM

Many invaluable contributions to individual lives, to the church, and to civilization were made by the monastic orders from the fourth century up to the present day.[6] We should concede that, for some people, appropriate forms of the monastic life can be a valid mode of discipleship to Christ in the present day as it has been in the past. But it is no less true that, as it was actually practiced, it easily and frequently departed in obvious ways from the kind of life lived by Jesus himself and by his immediate followers.

Jesus and his disciples were all clearly ascetic. Statements such as "Christianity is not a religion of asceticism, but rather one of faith and love"[7] (from the monumental study of asceticism by Otto Zockler), simply misunderstand the connection between ascetic practices and the ability to walk in faith and love in the manner of Christ and his friends. But just as clearly as they were ascetic in their mode of existence, Christ and his followers also were *not* monks, in any shape or form. In the power of the life of grace, fueled by their disciplines, they did not flee the world as some monastics did, but stood firmly in its midst—kept by God the Father as Jesus had prayed (John 17) and holding forth the word of life to others (Phil. 2:15–16).

No one who has looked squarely upon the life of Jesus and the apostles can imagine them engaging in the strange behavior of a Macarius of Alexandria, or a Serapion, or a Pachomius: eating no cooked food for seven years, exposing the naked body to poisonous flies while sleeping in a marsh for six months, not lying down to sleep for forty or fifty years, not speaking a word for many years, proudly keeping a record of the years since one had seen a woman, carrying heavy weights everywhere one went, or living in iron bracelets and chains, explicitly vying with one another for the championship in austerities.[8]

Simeon Stylites (A.D. 309–459), for instance, built a column six feet high in the Syrian desert and lived on it for some time. But he soon grew ashamed of its small height and found one sixty feet high, three feet across, with a railing to prevent him from falling off in his sleep.

On this perch Simeon lived uninterruptedly for thirty years, exposed to rain and sun and cold. A ladder enabled disciples to take him food and remove his waste. He bound himself to the pillar by a rope; the rope became embedded in his flesh, which putrefied around it, and stank, and teemed with worms. Simeon picked up the worms that fell from his sores, and replaced them there, saying to them, "Eat what God has given you."[9]

ADVANCE ACROSS EUROPE

The monastic form of asceticism spread from the Egyptian/Syrian crescent westward and northward across Europe during the fifth and sixth centuries to the furthermost reaches of the British Isles. And the unusual austerities of the Irish saints are as remarkable as any of the Eastern monks. St. Finnchua is said to have spent seven years suspended by his armpits from iron shackles, so that he might get a place in heaven in lieu of one he thought he had somehow given away. He as well as St. Ite are said to have caused their bodies to be eaten into by beetles. St. Ciaran mixed his bread with sand. St. Kevin is said to have remained in a standing posture for seven years. And so forth, each example more fantastic than the one before.

From the beginnings, in the rules of St. Pachomius and St. Benedict (who is often pictured holding a bundle of switches), those who offended the monastic codes were severely whipped, often until their blood flowed. But around the twelfth century flagellation came into a new usage as a means of personal mortification. St. Peter Damian (died 1072) urged the use of "the discipline" upon the monastics as a means of "imitating Christ." In some groups the flagellation was self-administered; in others the superior of the order administered it—often in the church during the recitation of the penitential Psalms.

But it must be said that the earlier monasticism was far less severe in this matter than the later—though perhaps nothing ever surpassed the early desert hermits for overall rigor of life. The Benedictine rule, the model for the entire monastic movement, contained nothing of the more violent methods of penance and "discipline," such as self-flagellation, wearing the hair shirt, or *inclusio* (lengthy confinement of monks to very narrow cells, caves, or huts). From the twelfth century on, however, ascetic practices increased in number and severity, and efforts were made to extend such excessive practices to the church as a whole, not just to those who might voluntarily seek them. There were epidemics of self-flagellation, involuntary dancing, and stigmatization—this latter especially falling upon the rival orders of St. Francis and St. Dominic.

ASCETICISM FOR ASCETICISM'S SAKE?

Observing someone practicing such intense activities, ostensibly on behalf of the spiritual life, one cannot help but think that the point is somehow being missed. Like being in the presence of a person obsessed with diet or bodybuilding, the point no longer seems to be health or strength, but self-admiration, self-righteousness, and self-obsession.

In such bodybuilding groups, we often see muscle for muscle's sake. Similarly, in the excesses of spiritual "asceticism" we see asceticism for asceticism's sake. These people are no longer truly ascetic, no longer are they truly concerned about taking pains for the end of a healthy, outgoing union with the healthy, outgoing, and sociable Christ who also loves himself and all of God's creation.

The older Christian asceticism and its monasticism also failed in that many of its practitioners obviously became addicted to it, enjoyed it for its own sake—like joggers who want the "high" and the pride of strenuous exertion for their own sake more than for the contribution exercise makes to their total life and health. So it is here that Hume's scorn of "monkish virtue" could have found justifiable foundation within an understanding of the Christian gospel itself. Here it is a matter of taking pains about taking pains. It is in fact a variety of self-obsession—narcissism—a thing farthest removed from the worship and service of God. It is actually losing one's life through trying to save it.

TRANSITION TO PROTESTANTISM

So as might be expected, monastic asceticism fell into decadence with monotonous regularity. Its model of the spiritual life, for all its devotion and passionate intensity, was on the whole false to the life that was in Christ Jesus. From the ninth century onward, a series of reform movements emerged, including some new monastic orders.[10] But the essential misunderstanding of ascetic practice—which tied it to forgiveness, punishment, and merit rather than to "exercise unto godliness"—always ended in abuse and then failure, sooner or later, depending upon local circumstances.

Here is where the Protestant reaction against asceticism comes in: it was a reaction against *any* essential role of spiritual disciplines in the process of redemption. Indeed, the Protestant Reformation may have done more than all the internal reform attempts to perpetuate monastic asceticism, by pressuring it from the outside. Nothing brings discipline and unity to a group or institution more than exterior attack or rejection, such as Luther's attack on the asceticism he was taught as a young man. As Roland Bainton writes in *Here I Stand*:

He fasted, sometimes three days on end without a crumb. The seasons of fasting were more consoling to him than those of feasting. Lent was more comforting than Easter. He laid upon himself vigils and prayers in excess of those stipulated by the rule. He cast off the blankets permitted him and well-nigh froze himself to death. At times he was proud of his sanctity and would say, "I have done nothing wrong today." Then misgivings would arise. "Have you fasted enough? Are you poor enough?" He would then strip himself of all save that which decency required. He believed in later life that his austerities had done permanent damage to his digestion.[11]

Luther later thought that had he kept such activities up any longer, he would have killed himself with vigils, prayers, reading, and other works.

PROTESTANTISM CONTINUES THE OBSESSION

So we've seen that this obsession with merit and forgiveness of sins as the only essential issue for the Christian's concern simply would not permit the monastic system of Christianity to develop a pattern of spiritual disciplines that was biblically as well as psychologically and spiritually sound. Strangely enough, though, Protestantism continued that obsession. It precluded "works" and Catholicism's ecclesiastical sacraments as essential for salvation, but it continued to lack any adequate account of what human beings *do* to become, by the grace of God, the kind of people Jesus obviously calls them to be.

In the Reformed branches of Protestantism, with John Calvin as the chief inspiration, discipline became identified with something that the church exerts over its members to keep them in line. In Methodism, developing about three centuries after Calvinism, "the discipline" came to refer to a book that contained the essentials of

Methodist faith and practice and in which much of what we earlier listed as "disciplines" are referred to as "means of grace." In the 1924 edition of *The Discipline,* for example, the means of grace are divided into the Instituted and the Prudential. The Instituted includes prayer, searching the Scriptures, the Lord's Supper, fasting, and "Christian conference." The Prudential includes "watching, denying ourselves, taking up our cross, and exercise of the presence of God."[12] Discerning any logical ordering principle in this arrangement is hard.

The Methodists were, of course, originally so called because they believed in methodical "godly exercise" as the sure route to spiritual maturity. John Wesley's writings and life spell out the "method" of the Methodists in detail. But almost nothing of it remains in current practice, and in this denomination we have one of the clearest illustrations of the tendency, noted at the end of the last chapter, to admire a great Christian leader in words, but never to think of simply *doing* what he or she did in order to do the work of the Kingdom of God.

Luther and his followers seem to have thought that the teaching and preaching of the gospel, along with the administration of the sacraments, was all that was really essential for the formation of the spiritual life. The Augsburg Confession informs us that:

The church is the assembly of saints, in which the gospel is taught purely and the sacraments administered rightly. For the unity of the church it is enough to agree concerning the teaching of the gospel and the administration of the sacraments.

The various Baptist and Pentecostal groups concur and go one step further, subtracting the sacraments from what is essential. The substance of Luther's views on this matter have become almost totally dominant in all branches of Western Protestantism. As one dictionary of religion rather quaintly puts it: "The official maintenance of correct doctrinal views and of approved religious habits on the part of church members, which was formerly seriously undertaken, has now generally given way to moral suasion and spiritual influence."[13] In other words with no significant exception, this mind-set has given way to no requirement except attendance upon church services for a few hours per month or year.

Even this may go too far. Elton Trueblood pointed out some years ago:

There is not one unique feature that can be predicated of the practical life of the average member of the Protestant church, and there is very little that can be predicated of the practical life of the average member of the Catholic church. It is not a foregone conclusion that they are scrupulously regular in attendance at anything, or that they tithe their monies. We have no idea what they believe on controversial social issues.[14]

THE CONTINUING ERROR

So the replacement of salvation (new life in Christ) for one of its effects or components (the forgiveness of sins) has dominated both the monastic system of Christianity and the reaction against it in which we still live today. To deal with sin the monastic system tried to avoid contact with it in the world. It also tried to merit forgiveness by strenuous efforts of various kinds. It desired to be *out* of the world to avoid being *of* the world.

Paul, long before, had explained to the Christians in Corinth that it was not necessary to avoid people outside of the family of God, for, he said, "Then it would be necessary to go out of the world" (1 Cor. 5:10), plainly implying that this was not to be done. Jesus prayed not that his friends would be taken out of the world (John 17:15), but that, not being of the world, they would be kept from evil *while yet in the world.*

Monasticism in fact proved that you could be "out of the world" and still be of it; and its ever-increasing excesses were but a witness to the futility of contesting this fact. Better, it demonstrated that you never really *could* get out of the world (short of death) and that the effort to do so only proved that you were fundamentally *of* it, operating still upon basically "worldly" principles and motivations. Impressed with this proof, Protestantism made the mistake of simply rejecting the disciplines as essential to the new life in Christ. As a result, then, it has never been able to develop a coherent view of our part in salvation that would do justice either to the obvious directives of the New Testament for the disciple of Christ or to the facts of human psychology.

A NEW LOOK AT ASCETICISM

To have a correct appreciation of the spiritual disciplines we must look more closely at the language and history of asceticism in the Western world. In Acts 24:16 the apostle Paul states: "And herein do I exercise (asko) myself, to have always a conscience void of offence toward God and toward men." This is the only New Testament use of the Greek term asko, from which our English word "asceticism" derives. The more common New Testament word for "exercise" is qumnazo, which occurs not only in 1 Timothy 4:7, but also in 2 Peter 2:14 and in Hebrews 5:14 and 12:11. It is from this latter Greek term that we derive our English word "gymnasium," with its familiar associations of sport and battle—images much loved and used by St. Paul in his descriptions of the spiritual life.

"Ascetic" is the English equivalent to the Greek adjective askateos, derived from the verb askein, meaning to practice, to exercise; to toil, work, or labor; or to provide, furnish, or adorn. The noun form of the word refers to practice, exercise, study, custom, regimen, diet, or training. Other forms of the word refer to the condition of being practiced or tried, to a school or place of study or exercise, to a teacher or master in a certain activity, and so forth.

Homer, author of The Iliad and The Odyssey, uses these terms only with reference to technical adornment and artistic effort; but from the time of Herodotus and Pindar onward they acquire their reference to the mental and spiritual endeavors of humankind.[15] The Greek philosophers from the Sophists through Philo and Epictetus included ascetic practices in their views of all proper human education or development. The term was never used in a negative sense, but rather, in a positive, affirming sense.

CLASSICAL ASCETICISM

In this classical linguistic background there is nothing whatso-ever of hatred of the body, of the indulgence in its punishment for punishment's sake, or of the earning of merit simply through pow-er of will and self-control—the very things we now believe to be the essence of asceticism and spiritual discipline. Asceticism is sim-ply a matter of adaptation of suitable means to obviously valuable ends. The ascetic is one who enters the training appropriate for his or her development into an accomplished athlete (*athlasis*) of body, mind, or spirit. If one wishes to speak or run or carve or fight or sing well, one must prepare the relevant parts of mind and body by exercising them. One must "take pains," must exert oneself, in the appropriate ways. This continues to be true when we move into the spiritual life and is an essential and enduring theme in the religion of the Old and New Testaments.

The use of the law, for example, is one of the major elements of asceticism in the Old Testament. In Joshua 1:8 we read: "This book of the law must ever be on your lips; you must keep it in mind day and night so that you may diligently observe all that is written in it. Then you will prosper and be successful in all that you do" (JB). One notices, once again, the bodily basis for a spiritual and mate-rial condition of life. The law is to be *on the lips*. People are to memorize the law and say it out loud to themselves as they go through the day.

Psalm 119 is a continuous song of praise to the life that results from "hiding the word in the heart" (v. 11). Psalm 1 describes the life of the one who turns his or her mind from the ways of the world and whose "delight is in the law of the Lord; and in his law doth he meditate day and night."

The hiding of the law in the heart and constant meditation upon it are—as anyone who has done it will know—not separable from a certain use of the body. The part our body plays in this experi-ence is definitely under our control. And the indirect effects of the direct experience with the law then make our meditative person "like a tree firmly planted by streams of water, which yields its fruit in its season, and its leaf does not wither; and in whatever he does, he prospers" (Ps. 1:3, NAS).

Here we have an activity of mind and body undertaken with all the strength we have to make our total being cooperate effectively with the divine order. As a pastor, teacher, and counselor I have repeatedly seen the transformation of inner and outer life that comes simply from memorization and meditation upon Scripture. Personally, I would never undertake to pastor a church or guide a program of Christian education that did not involve a continuous program of memorization of the choicest passages of Scripture for people of all ages.

The inspired writers of the words quoted above were simply recording certain observable facts of the spiritual life, facts we neglect at the grave peril of ourselves and of those under our spiritual care. Although these facts do involve much more than just "natural" abilities, they are no more mysterious than the fact that saying a telephone number out loud will enable you to remember it until you get it dialed or the fact that eating food will give you strength you will not otherwise have. Asceticism rightly understood is so far from the "mystical" as to be just good sense about life and, ultimately, about spiritual life.

O. Hardman's excellent study, *Ideals of Asceticism,* quite correctly summarizes the essence of religious asceticism as the voluntary practice of activities "for the deliverance and protection of the soul from defilement, for the increase of its powers by the discharge of its proper functions in accordance with its own conception of the moral and spiritual order, and for the consequent achievement and enjoyment of its full status."[16] Teachers who condemn asceticism correctly practiced in the contemporary context will almost certainly do more harm than good, unless they have some other method for their students that effectively lays hold on life in the Kingdom of God.

ONE FINAL CLARIFICATION—THE TRUE NATURE OF THE SPIRITUAL DISCIPLINE

Let's lay aside, then, ideas of spiritual discipline as the mere outward performance of certain actions or as the expression of self-hatred or the attainment of merit through suffering. And let's make a final clarification of the basic nature of spiritual disciplines, relating them to human existence and to the ideal of spiritual life in God.

Let's return to the biblical scene of Christ's last evening with his disciples in the Garden of Gethsemane. The disciples were full of good intentions, but Jesus understood their condition. In the light of this knowledge he advised a course of action that would enable them to do what he knew they sincerely wanted to do. "Watch and pray," he said, "that ye enter not into temptation; the spirit indeed is willing, but the flesh is weak" (Matt. 24:41).

The plain meaning of this advice to his sleepy and worried friends was that by engaging in a certain type of action—the keeping of vigil combined with prayer—they would be able to attain a level of spiritual responsiveness and power in their lives that would be impossible without it. In this simple but profound episode we find the whole nature and principle of the kind of activity that is a spiritual discipline. Such an activity implants in us, in the embodied personality that is the carrier of our abilities (and disabilities!) a readiness and an ability to interact with God and our surroundings in a way not directly under our control.

Peter and the other disciples would not in their moment of need have the ability to stand fast in the confrontation with Christ's enemies. But *had* they watched and prayed, as they were advised, the requisite ability would have been there when it was needed. They would have been in a condition of body and mind to secure the Father's assistance to stand as firmly as Jesus himself did. Here as always—whether in our natural life or in our spiritual life—the mark of disciplined persons is that they are able to do what needs to be done when it needs to be done.

THE ISSUE IN DISCIPLINE—THE BODY'S ESSENTIAL PART IN SPIRITUALITY

The entire question of discipline, therfore, is how to apply the acts of will at our disposal in such a way that the proper course of action, which cannot always be realized by direct and untrained effort, will nevertheless be carried out when needed.

The preparation for *all* of life's actions including the spiritual, essentially involve bodily behaviors. Watching or vigil, for example, is a bodily behavior. Of course it is not only a bodily behavior, but the point we are in greatest danger of missing in our contemporary culture is that it also is not purely "spiritual" or "mental," and that *whatever is purely mental cannot transform the self.*

One of the greatest deceptions in the practice of the Christian religion is the idea that all that really matters is our internal feelings, ideas, beliefs, and intentions. It is this mistake about the psychology of the human being that more than anything else divorces salvation from life, leaving us a headful of vital truths about God and a body unable to fend off sin.

Screwtape has a wonderful comment on the effects of failing to use the body in our religion. He advises Wormwood to have his man

remember, or to think he remembers, the parrotlike nature of his prayers in childhood. In reaction against that, he may be persuaded to aim at something entirely spontaneous, inward, informal, and unregularised; and what this will actually mean to a beginner will be an effort to produce in himself a vaguely devotional *mood* in which real concentration of will and intelligence have no part. One of their poets, Coleridge, has recorded that he did not pray "with moving lips and bended knees" but merely "composed his spirit to love" and indulged "a sense of supplication." That is exactly the sort of prayer we want; and since it bears a superficial resemblance to the prayer of silence as practised by those who are very far advanced in the Enemy's service, clever and lazy patients can be taken in by it for quite a long time. At the very least, they can be persuaded that the bodily position makes no difference to their prayers; for they constantly forget, what you must always remember, that they are animals and that whatever their bodies do affects their souls. [17]

Of course the condition of life in God that we seek is not to be thought of as a merely mechanical result. It is a widespread fallacy that careful and thorough preparation precludes freedom, spontaneity, and personal interaction. In fact the very person best prepared for any situation is the one who experiences the greatest freedom and spontaneity in it. The spiritual life is a life of interaction with a personal God, and it is pure delusion to suppose that it can be carried on sloppily. The will to do his will can only be carried into reality as we *take measures* to be ready and able to meet and draw upon him in our actions.

TAKING MEASURES—WHAT CAN WE DO?

In the simplest possible terms, the spiritual disciplines are a matter of taking appropriate measures. To reject them wholesale is to insist that growth in the spirit is something that just happens all by itself. It is hard to see how any serious disciple of Christ could possibly believe that. To reject the standard, classical disciplines we've discussed, to hold that practices such as solitude, fasting, service, and others aren't essential to spiritual growth, is at least conceivable. But when a believer does reject them, he or she must then assume the responsibility of putting other effective activities in their place.

Perhaps this can be done, and we at least are willing to leave the question open for now. But to be spiritual disciplines, any such activities substituted would have to be activities of mind and body, done to bring our whole selves into cooperation with the divine order, so we can experience more and more a vision and power beyond ourselves.

WORKING TOWARD ACTING NATURALLY

Dr. William C. De Vries, who installed the first artificial heart in a human being, told of the many times he had practiced such an installation in animals. And in his discussion was this simple yet profound explanation: "The reason you practice so much is so that you will do things automatically the same way every time."[18]

It is such "automatic" or unthinking readiness that Jesus points us to when he tells us that in our good deeds we are not to let our left hand know what our right hand is doing. Certainly this is not something that can be *consciously* enacted, for the effort to hide our right from our left hand would have precisely the effect of calling attention to what our right hand is doing. Only the right hand's habit of doing good can indirectly prepare it to act *unconsciously*.

The same law of indirect preparedness rules all human existence, from playing the flute to intercessory prayer. We shouldn't totally ignore conscious intent but we cannot rely on it alone. Why? Until we have taken the steps to achieve such unconscious readiness, we cannot honestly intend to carry out the good deed, any more than we can honestly intend to speak Japanese without engaging in the learning activities that prepare us to speak that language.

Perhaps it is at this point that we can appropriately speak of forgiveness of sins. Forgiveness comes to those with a new life in them: a life of loving confidence in God that is inseparable from the intention to please and be like him. God upholds the intention of such people, and within the psychological reality of their mutual love he enables them to do as they intend. As Jesus said: "He that has my commandments, and keeps them, he it is that loves me" (John 14:21). Obedience is the natural outflow of the experienced faith and love.

Love brings the firm intention to avoid what is wrong and assures us of God's forgiveness. William Law puts the matter well:

Although the goodness of God, and His rich mercies in Christ Jesus, are a sufficient assurance to us, that He will be merciful to our unavoidable weaknesses and infirmities, that is to such failings as are the effects of ignorance or surprise; yet we have no reason to expect the same mercy towards those sins which we have lived in, through a want of intention to avoid them.[19]

NOTES

Epigraph 1. Margaret R. Miles, "Toward a New Asceticism." *The Christian Century* (October 28, 1981): 1097

Epigraph 2. Elton Trueblood, *Alternative to Futility* (Waco, TX: Word, 1972), 97.

1. David Hume, *Enquiry into Morals,* ed. L. A. Selby-Bigge, (Oxford: Oxford University Press, 1957), 270.

2. John M'Clintock and James Strong, preparers, *Cyclopaedia of Biblical, Theological, and Ecclesiastical Literature* (New York: Harper, 1895), 1:454.
3. Quoted in Ira Goldwin Whitchurch, *The Philosophical Bases of Asceticism in the Platonic Writings and in Pre-Platonic Tradition* (New York: Longmans, Green, 1923), 108.
4. See Owen Chadwick, *Western Asceticism: Selected Translations with Introductions and Notes* (Philadelphia: Westminister, 1958), 16: see also Anthony C. Meisel and M. L. del Mastro, eds., *The Rule of St. Benedict* (Garden City, NY: Doubleday, 1975), Introduction, 12–13.
5. Meisel and del Mastro, eds., *The Rule of St. Benedict,* Introduction, 13.
6. Friedrich Heer, *The Medieval World* (New York: New American Library, 1963), 61ff.; also, O. Hardman. *The Ideals of Asceticism: An Essay in the Comparative Study of Religion* (New York: Macmillan, 1924), 191–200.
7. Otto Zockler, *Askese und Monchtum* (Frankfurt am Main: Heyder & Zimmer, 1897), 136.
8. Will Durant. *The Age of Faith,* vol. 4 of *The Story of Civilization* (New York: Simon and Schuster, 1950), 58ff.
9. *Ibid.,* 60.
10. Heer, *The Medieval World,* 63.
11. Roland H. Bainton, *Here I Stand: A Life of Martin Luther* (New York: New American Library, 1953), 34.
12. David G. Downey, ed., *Doctrines and Discipline of the Methodist Episcopal Church* (New York: Methodist Book Concern, 1924), 132f. But see also the remarks on the practice of Wilberforce and Fletcher in Hardman, *The Ideals of Asceticism,* 152n.
13. Shailer Mathews and G. B. Smith, eds., *A Dictionary of Religion and Ethics* (London: Waverly, 1921), 133.
14. Trueblood, *Alternative to Futility,* 85.
15. Gerhard Kittel, ed., *Theological Dictionary of the New Testament,* trans. G. W. Bromiley (Grand Rapids, MI: Eerdmans, 1968), 494–96.
16. Hardman, *The Ideals of Asceticism,* 16.
17. C. S. Lewis, *The Screwtape Letters and Screwtape Proposes a Toast* (New York: Macmillan, 1962), 20.
18. "NBC News," December 3, 1983.
19. William Law, *The Power of the Spirit* (Ft. Washington, PA: Christian Literature Crusade, 1971), 27.

9. Some Main Disciplines for the Spiritual Life

But to obtain these gifts, you need more than faith; you must also work hard to be good, and even that is not enough. For then you must learn to know God better and discover what he wants you to do. Next, learn to put aside your own desires so that you will become patient and godly, gladly letting God have his way with you. This will make possible the next step, which is for you to enjoy other people and to like them, and finally you will grow to love them deeply. The more you go on in this way, the more you will grow strong spiritually and become faithful and useful to our Lord Jesus Christ.

2 PETER 1:5–8, LB

A discipline for the spiritual life is, when the dust of history is blown away, nothing but an activity undertaken to bring us into more effective cooperation with Christ and his Kingdom. When we understand that grace (*charis*) is gift (*charisma*), we then see that to grow in grace is to grow in what is given to us of God and by God. The disciplines are then, in the clearest sense, a means to that grace and also to those gifts. Spiritual disciplines, "exercises unto godliness," are only activities undertaken to make us capable of receiving more of his life and power without harm to ourselves or others.

Though we may not be aware of it, we experience "disciplines" everyday. In these daily or "natural" disciplines we perform acts that result in a direct command of further abilities that we would not otherwise have. If I repeat the telephone number aloud after looking it up, I can remember it until I get it dialed. Otherwise, I probably couldn't. If I train rigorously I can bench press 300 pounds; otherwise not. Such ordinary activities are actually disciplines that aid our physical or "natural" life.

The same thing happens with disciplines for our spiritual life. When through spiritual disciplines I become able heartily to bless those who curse me, pray without ceasing, to be at peace when not given credit for good deeds I've done, or to master the evil that comes my way, it is because my disciplinary activities have inwardly poised me for more and more interaction with the powers of the living God and his Kingdom. Such is the potential we tap into when we use the disciplines.

THE DISCIPLINES

What then are the particular activities that can serve as disciplines for the spiritual life? And which should we choose for our individual strategy for spiritual growth?

In answering these practical questions, we need not try to come up with a complete list of disciplines. Nor should we assume that *our* particular list will be right for others. Quite a few well-known practices will have a strong claim to be on every list. On the other hand, there are a number of good activities that may not usually be thought of as disciplines, and yet others that have served through the ages as spiritual disciplines but are now largely forgotten. For example, there is the *peregrinatio,* or voluntary exile, introduced by the Irish St. Brenden (born 484) and widely practiced for some centuries thereafter.[1] We have mentioned several times the vigil or "watch," where one rejects sleep to concentrate on spiritual matters. The keeping of a journal or spiritual diary continues to be an activity that serves some individuals as a vital discipline, though it probably would not show up on any "standard" list. Sabbath keeping as instituted in the Old Testament can be a most productive discipline. Physical labor has proven to be a spiritual discipline, especially for those who are also deeply involved in solitude, fasting, study, and prayer. (1 Thess. 4:11–12)

One unusual activity that can be an effective spiritual discipline for those who are used to "the better things in life" is to do grocery shopping, banking, and other business in the poorer areas of the city. This has an immense effect on our understanding of and behavior toward our neighbors—both rich and poor—and upon our understanding of what it is to love and care for our fellow human beings.

In shaping our own list of spiritual disciplines, we should keep in mind that very few disciplines can be regarded as absolutely indispensable for a healthy spiritual life and work, though some are obviously more important than others. Practicing a *range* of activities that have proven track records across the centuries will keep us from erring. And if, later, other activities are really more what we need, our progress won't be seriously hindered, and we'll probably be led into them.

So, to help us make our all-important choices, let's list those activities that have had a wide and profitable use among disciples of Christ and approach them in a prayerful, experimental way. The following list is divided into the disciplines of "abstinence" and the disciplines of "engagement." We'll discuss what each of these activities is and how each can make an especially important contribution to spiritual growth.

Disciplines of Abstinence

solitude
silence
fasting
frugality
chastity
secrecy
sacrifice

Disciplines of Engagement

study
worship
celebration
service
prayer
fellowship
confession
submission

THE DISCIPLINES OF ABSTINENCE

"Abstain from fleshly lusts which war against the soul" (1 Peter 2:11).

Reminding us that the word "asceticism" is the correlate of a Greek word for *training,* as in athletes training for a race, W. R. Inge notes that disciplines of abstinence should be practiced by everyone, leading to a sober and moderate use of all God's gifts.

If we feel that any habit or pursuit, harmless in itself, is keeping us from God and sinking us deeper in the things of earth; if we find that things which others can do with impunity are for us the occasion of falling, then abstinence is our only course. Abstinence alone can recover for us the real value of what should have been for our help but which has been an occasion of falling. . . . It is necessary that we should steadily resolve to give up anything that comes between ourselves and God.[2]

He concludes his discussion of abstinence by quoting from Bishop Wilson of the Isle of Man: "Those who deny themselves will be sure to find their strength increased, their affections raised, and their inward peace continually augmented."[3]

In the disciplines of abstinence, we abstain to some degree and for some time from the satisfaction of what we generally regard as normal and legitimate desires. "Normal" desires include our basic drives or motivations, such as those for food, sleep, bodily activity, companionship, curiosity, and sex. But our desires for convenience, comfort, material security, reputation or fame, and variety are also considered under this heading. Psychologists have no generally accepted classification of these "normal" drives or of their precise interrelationships, though obviously most of the ones just mentioned must be satisfied to some degree for the sake of human life and health.

Keep in mind that the practice of abstention does not imply that there is anything essentially wrong with these desires as such. But in today's distorted condition of humanity, it is these basic desires that have been allowed to run a rebellious and harmful course, ultimately serving as the primary hosts of sin in our personalities.

We can clearly see this by considering the nature of the major types of sin. The seven "deadly" sins recognized throughout church history are pride, envy, anger, sloth, avarice, gluttony, and lasciviousness. Gregory the Great (A.D. 540–604) described these as "a classification of the normal perils of the soul in the ordinary conditions of life."[4] Each is a case of one or more legitimate desires gone wrong. An adequate course of spiritual discipline will single out those tendencies that may harm our walk with God. By the carefully adapted arrangement of our circumstances and behavior, the spiritual disciplines will bring these basic desires into their proper coordination and subordination within the economy of life in his Kingdom.

SOLITUDE

We have already seen what a large role solitude played in the life our Lord and the great ones in His Way. In solitude, we purposefully abstain from interaction with other human beings, denying ourselves companionship and all that comes from our conscious interaction with others. We close ourselves away; we go to the ocean, to the desert, the wilderness, or to the anonymity of the urban crowd. This is not just rest or refreshment from nature, though that too can contribute to our spiritual well-being. Solitude is choosing to be *alone* and to dwell on our experience of isolation from other human beings.

Solitude frees us, actually. This above all explains its primacy and priority among the disciplines. The normal course of day-to-day human interactions locks us into patterns of feeling, thought, and action that are geared to a world set against God. Nothing but solitude can allow the development of a freedom from the ingrained behaviors that hinder our integration into God's order.

It takes twenty times more the amount of amphetamine to kill individual mice than it takes to kill them in groups. Experimenters also find that a mouse given no amphetamine at all will be dead within ten minutes of being placed in the midst of a group on the drug. In groups they go off like popcorn or firecrackers. Western men and women, especially, *talk* a great deal about being individuals. But our conformity to social pattern is hardly less remarkable than that of the mice—and just as deadly!

In solitude we find the psychic distance, the perspective from which we can see, in the light of eternity, the created things that trap, worry, and oppress us. Thomas Merton writes:

That is the only reason why I desire solitude—to be lost to all created things, to die to them and to the knowledge of them, for they remind me of my distance from You: that You are far from them, even though You are in them. You have made them and Your presence sustains their being and they hide You from me. And I would live alone, and out of them. *O beata solitudo!*[5]

But solitude, like all of the disciplines of the spirit, carries its risks. In solitude, we confront our own soul with its obscure forces and conflicts that escape our attention when we are interacting with others. Thus, "Solitude is a terrible trial, for it serves to crack open and burst apart the shell of our superficial securities. It opens out to us the unknown abyss that we all carry within us . . . [and] discloses the fact that these abysses are haunted."[6] We can only survive solitude if we cling to Christ there. And yet what we find of him in that solitude enables us to return to society as free persons.

Solitude will also pain and threaten our family and friends. The author Jessamyn West comments: "It is not easy to be solitary unless you are born ruthless. Every solitary repudiates someone."[7] Others need us to keep *their* lives in place; and when we retreat, they then have to deal with their souls. True, they need God more than they need us, but they may not understand this. We must carefully respect their pain and with much loving prayer make wise arrangements on their behalf; and we must do all possible to help them understand what we are doing and why.

Of all the disciplines of abstinence, solitude is generally the most fundamental in the beginning of the spiritual life, and it must be returned to again and again as that life develops. This factual priority of solitude is, I believe, a sound element in monastic asceticism.

Locked into interaction with the human beings that make up our fallen world, it is all but impossible to grow in grace as one should. Just try fasting, prayer, service, giving, or even celebration without the preparation accomplished in withdrawal, and you will soon be thrown into despair by your efforts, very likely abandoning your attempt altogether.

On the other hand, we must reemphasize, the "desert" or "closet" is the primary place of *strength* for the beginner, as it was for Christ and for Paul. They show us by their example what we must do. In stark aloneness it is possible to have silence, to be still, and to *know* that Jehovah indeed is God (Ps. 46:10), to set the Lord before our minds with sufficient intensity and duration that we stay centered upon him—our hearts fixed, established in trust (Ps. 112:7–8)—even when back in the office, shop, or home.

Thomas à Kempis distilled more of what was right in the monastic calling than any other, and he had this to say:

The great holy men, where they might, fled men's fellowship and chose to live to God in secret places. One said: As ofttimes as I was among men I came back a less man, that is to say less holy. . . . If in the beginning of thy conversion thou keep thy cell and dwell well therein it shall be to thee afterwards as a dear and well beloved friend and most pleasant solace. In silence and quiet the devout soul profiteth and learneth the secrets of the scriptures. . . . Leave vain things to the vain. . . . Shut thy door upon thee and call to thee Jesu thy love: dwell with him in thy cell for thou shalt not find elsewhere so great peace.[8]

Henry David Thoreau saw how even our secular existence withers from lack of a hidden life. Conversation degenerates into mere gossip and those we meet can only talk of what they heard from someone else. The only difference between us and our neighbor is that he has seen the news and we have not. Thoreau put it well. As our inward quiet life fails, "we go more constantly and desperately to the post office," but "the poor fellow who walks away with the greatest number of letters, proud of his extensive correspondence, has not heard from himself this long while. . . . Read not The Times," he concludes, "read The Eternities!"[9]

SILENCE

In silence we close off our souls from "sounds," whether those sounds be noise, music, or words. Total silence is rare, and what we today call "quiet" usually only amounts to a little less noise. Many people have *never* experienced silence and do not even know that they do *not* know what it is. Our households and offices are filled with the whirring, buzzing, murmuring, chattering, and whining of the multiple contraptions that are supposed to make life easier. Their noise comforts us in some curious way. In fact, we find complete silence shocking because it leaves the impression that nothing is happening. In a go-go world such as ours, what could be worse than that!

Silence goes beyond solitude, and without it solitude has little effect. Henri Nouwen observes that "silence is the way to make solitude a reality."[10] But silence is frightening because it strips us as nothing else does, throwing us upon the stark realities of our life. It reminds us of death, which will cut us off from this world and leave only us and God. And in that quiet, what if there turns out to be very little to "just us and God"? Think what it says about the inward emptiness of our lives if we must *always* turn on the tape player or radio to make sure something is happening around us.

Hearing is said to be the last of our senses to go at death. Sound always strikes deeply and disturbingly into our souls. So, for the sake of our souls, we must seek times to leave our television, radio, tape players, and telephones turned off. We should close off street noises as much as possible. We should try to find *how* quiet we can make our world by making whatever arrangements are necessary.

Silence and solitude do go hand in hand, usually. Just as silence is vital to make solitude real, so is solitude needed to make the discipline of silence complete. Very few of us can be silent in the presence of others.

Yet most of us *live* with others, so how can we practice such a discipline? There are ways. For instance, many have learned to rise for a time in the middle of the night—to break the night's sleep in half in order to experience such silence. In doing so, they find a rich silence that aids their prayer and study without imposing on others. And though it sounds impossible, meaningful progress into silence can be made without solitude, even within family life. And sharing this discipline with those you love may be exactly what is needed.

As with all disciplines, we should approach the practice of silence in a prayerful, experimental attitude, confident that we shall be led into its right use for us. It is a powerful and essential discipline. Only silence will allow us life-transforming concentration upon God. It allows us to hear the gentle God whose only Son "shall not strive, nor cry; neither shall any man hear his voice above the street noise" (Matt. 12:19). It is this God who tells us that "in quietness and trust is your strength" (Isa. 30:15, NAS).

But we must also practice the silence of *not speaking*. James, in his Epistle, tells us that those who seem religious but are unable to bridle their tongues are self-deceived and have a religion that amounts to little (James 1:26). He states that those who do no harm by what they say are perfect and able to direct their whole bodies to do what is right (James 3:2).

Practice in not speaking can at least give us enough control over what we say that our tongues do not "go off" automatically. This discipline provides us with a certain inner distance that gives us time to consider our words fully and the presence of mind to control what we say and when we say it.

Such practice also helps us to listen and to observe, to pay attention to people. How rarely are we ever truly listened to, and how deep is our need to be heard. I wonder how much wrath in human life is a result of not being heard. James says, "Let every man be swift to hear, slow to speak, slow to wrath" (1:19). Yet when the tongue is moving rapidly, it seems wrath will usually be found following it. God gave us two ears and one mouth, it's been said, so that we might listen twice as much as we talk, but even that proportion is far too high on the side of talking.

In witnessing, the role of talking is frequently overemphasized. Does that sound strange? It's true. Silence and especially true listening are often the strongest testimony of our faith. A major problem for Christian evangelism is not getting people to talk, but to silence those who through their continuous chatter reveal a loveless heart devoid of confidence in God. As Miguel de Unamuno says, "We need to pay less attention to what people are trying to tell us, and more to what they tell us without trying."[11]

Why do we insist on talking as much as we do? We run off at the mouth because we are inwardly uneasy about what others think of us. Eberhard Arnold observes: "People who love one another can be silent together."[12] But when we're with those we feel less than secure with, we use words to "adjust" our appearance and elicit their approval. Otherwise, we fear our virtues might not receive adequate appreciation and our shortcomings might not be properly "understood." In not speaking, we resign how we appear (dare we say, how we *are?*) to God. And that is hard. Why should we worry about others' opinions of us when God is for us and Jesus Christ is on his right hand pleading our interests (Rom. 8:31–34)? But we do.

How few of us live with quiet, inner confidence, and yet how many of us desire it. But such inward quiet is a great grace we *can* receive as we practice not talking. And when we have it, we may be able to help others who need it. After we know that confidence, we may, when others come fishing for reassurance and approval, send them to fish in deeper waters for their own inner quiet.

Here is the testimony of a young person entering into the practice of solitude and silence:

The more I practice this discipline, the more I appreciate the strength of silence. The less I become skeptical and judgmental, the more I learn to accept the things I didn't like about others, the more I accept them as uniquely created in the image of God. The less I talk, the fuller are words spoken at an appropriate time. The more I value others, the more I serve them in small ways, the more I enjoy and celebrate my life. The more I celebrate, the more I realize that God has been giving me wonderful things in my life, the less I worry about my future. I will accept and enjoy what God is continuously giving to me. I think I am beginning to really enjoy God.[13]

FASTING

In fasting, we abstain in some significant way from food and possibly from drink as well. This discipline teaches us a lot about ourselves very quickly. It will certainly prove humiliating to us, as it reveals to us how much our peace depends upon the pleasures of eating. It may also bring to mind how we are using food pleasure to assuage the discomforts caused in our bodies by faithless and unwise living and attitudes—lack of self-worth, meaningless work, purposeless existence, or lack of rest or exercise. If nothing else, though, it will certainly demonstrate how powerful and clever our body is in getting its own way against our strongest resolves.

There are many ways and degrees of fasting. The desert fathers such as St. Antony often subsisted for long periods of time on bread and water—though we must understand that their "bread" was much more substantial than what we have today. Daniel and his friends would not eat the king's meat or drink his wine; they had vegetables and water only (Dan. 1:12). At another time, Daniel "ate no pleasant bread, neither came flesh nor wine in my mouth, neither did I anoint myself at all, till three whole weeks were fulfilled" (10:3). Jesus in the time of his preparation for temptation and ministry seems to have forgone all food for more than a month (Matt. 4).

Fasting confirms our utter dependence upon God by finding in him a source of sustenance beyond food. Through it, we learn by experience that God's word to us is a life substance, that it is not food ("bread") alone that gives life, but also the words that proceed from the mouth of God (Matt. 4:4). We learn that we too have meat to eat that the world does not know about (John 4:32, 34). Fasting unto our Lord is therefore feasting—feasting on him and on doing his will.

The Christian poet Edna St. Vincent Millay expresses the discovery of the "other" food in her poem entitled "Feast":

> I drank at every vine.
> The last was like the first

> I came upon no wine
>   So wonderful as thirst.
> I gnawed at every root.
>   I ate of every plant.
> I came upon no fruit
>   So wonderful as want.
> Feed the grape and the bean
>   To the vintner and the monger;
> I will lie down lean
>   With my thirst and my hunger.[14]

Hence, when Jesus directs us not to appear distressed and sad when we fast (Matt. 6:16–18), he is not telling us to mislead those around us. He is instead explaining how we will feel—we really will not be sad. We are discovering that life is so much more than meat (Luke 12:33). Our belly is not our god, as it is for others (Phil. 3:19; Rom. 16:18); rather, it is his joyful servant and ours (1 Cor. 6:13).

Actually fasting is one of the more important ways of practicing that self-denial required of *everyone* who would follow Christ (Matt. 16:24). In fasting, we learn how to suffer happily as we feast on God. And it is a good lesson, because in our lives we *will* suffer, no matter what else happens to us. Thomas à Kempis remarks: "Whosoever knows best how to suffer will keep the greatest peace. That man is conqueror of himself, and lord of the world, the friend of Christ, and heir of Heaven."[16]

Persons well used to fasting as a systematic practice will have a clear and constant sense of their resources in God. And that will help them endure deprivations of *all* kinds, even to the point of coping with them easily and cheerfully. Kempis again says: "Refrain from gluttony and thou shalt the more easily restrain all the inclinations of the flesh."[17] Fasting teaches temperance or self-control and therefore teaches moderation and restraint with regard to *all* our fundamental drives. Since food has the pervasive place it does in our lives, the effects of fasting will be diffused throughout our personality. In the midst of all our needs and wants, we experience the contentment of the child that has been weaned from its mother's breast (Ps. 131:2). And "Godliness with contentment is great gain" (1 Tim. 6:6).

Fasting, though, is a hard discipline to practice without its consuming all our attention. Yet when we use it as a part of prayer or service, we cannot allow it to do so. When a person chooses fasting as a spiritual discipline, he or she must, then, practice it well enough and often enough to become experienced in it, because only the person who is well habituated to systematic fasting as a discipline can use it effectively as a part of direct service to God, as in special times of prayer or other service.

FRUGALITY

We turn now to some disciplines of abstinence that may for some not be as basic to the process of full redemption as solitude, silence, and fasting are. But they are still of very great importance, since they allow us to come to grips with behavioral tendencies that can destroy us or at least render us ineffective in the service of Christ.

In frugality we abstain from using money or goods at our disposal in ways that merely gratify our desires or our hunger for status, glamour, or luxury. Practicing frugality means we stay within the bounds of what general good judgment would designate as necessary for the kind of life to which God has led us.

That there is a general sense of what is "necessary" is indicated by the "sumptuary laws" enacted by secular authorities in both the ancient world and in more recent times. The ancient Spartan, for example, was prohibited from possessing a house or furniture that required more elaborate tools than the axe or saw. The Romans frequently wrote laws limiting expenses on entertainments. English law contained many enactments governing the food and clothing of various social ranks.

Such laws are hardly imaginable in the Western world of today, where no extravagance is thought to be shameful, but only a more or less astonishing exercise of one's presumably sacred right to "pursue happiness." The prophetic word from Old and New Testament alike is clear, however. James (5:1) says: "Go to now, ye rich men, weep and howl for the miseries that shall come upon you." For the sake of subsequent discussions we must note that James's warning to the rich is not simply because they are rich, but because they "have lived in pleasure on the earth, and been wanton" (5:5).

The spiritually wise person has always known that frivolous consumption corrupts the soul away from trust in, worship of, and service to God and injures our neighbors as well. O. Hardman forcefully puts the point:

It is an injury to society as well as an offence against God when men pamper their bodies with rich and dainty foods and seriously diminish their physical and mental powers by excessive use of intoxicants. . . . Luxury in every form is economically bad, it is provocative to the poor who see it flaunted before them, and it is morally degrading to those who indulge in it. The Christian who has the ability to live luxuriously, but fasts from all extravagance, and practices simplicity in his dress, his home, and his whole manner of life, is, therefore, rendering good service to society.[18]

While frugality *is* a service to God and humankind, our concern here is with it as a discipline. As such, it frees us from concern and involvement with a multitude of desires that would make it impossible for us "to do justice, to love mercy, and to walk humbly with thy God" (Mic. 6:8). It makes it possible for us to concentrate upon that "one thing needful," the "good part" Mary chose (Luke 10:42).

In our current world, a large part of the freedom that comes from frugality is freedom from the spiritual bondage caused by financial debt. This kind of debt is often incurred by buying things that are far from necessary, and its effect, when the amount is substantial, is to diminish our sense of worth, dim our hope for the future, and eliminate our sensitivity to the needs of others. Paul's admonition, "Let no debt remain outstanding, except the continuing debt to love one another" (Rom. 13:8) is therefore good spiritual advice as well as wise financial counsel.

John Joseph Surin was once asked why, when so many people seem to wish to be great in God's eyes, there are so few who are truly saintly. "The chief reason," he replied, "is that they give too big a place in life to indifferent things."[19] Frugality as a settled style of life frees us from indifferent things. Insofar as *simplicity* (the arrangement of life around a few consistent purposes, explicitly excluding what is not necessary to human well-being) and *poverty* (the rejection of all possessions) are spiritual disciplines at all, they are such largely as expressions of frugality. We shall discuss these points further in the next chapter.

CHASTITY

In naming a discipline that deals specifically with the sexual drive we lack appropriate terminology. I shall use the term "chastity," although it, like "simplicity," properly refers to the *result* of a discipline under grace rather than to disciplinary activities themselves. In exercising the spiritual discipline of chastity, we purposefully turn away from dwelling upon or engaging in the sexual dimension of our relationships to others—even our husbands or wives.

Sexuality is one of the most powerful and subtle forces in human nature, and the percentage of human suffering tied directly to it is horrifying. The human abuse stemming from sex, both outside of and within marriage, makes it imperative that we learn "how to possess our vessel in sanctification and in honor" (1 Thess. 4:4). And an essential part of this learning consists in the practice of abstaining from sex and from indulging in sexual feelings and thoughts, and thus learning how to not be governed by them.

Abstention within marriage by mutual agreement was also counseled by St. Paul as an aid to fasting and prayer (1 Cor. 7:5). Contrary to much modern thought, it is absolutely vital to the health of any marriage that sexual gratification not be placed at the center. Voluntary abstention helps us appreciate and love our mates as whole persons, of which their sexuality is but one part. And it confirms us in the practice of being very close to people without sexual entanglements. Chastity thus has an important part to play within marriage, but the main effect we seek through it is the proper disposal of sexual acts, feelings, thoughts, and attitudes within our life as a whole, inside of marriage and out. Sexuality cannot be allowed to permeate our lives if we are to live as children of God and brothers and sisters of Jesus Christ.

Is this to say our sexuality is something to shun? That would be impossible. We are sexual beings: "male and female created he them" (Gen. 1:27). This crucial passage ties sexuality to our creation in the image of God. It is a part of our power with which to serve him. In sexuality the intermingling of persons, the knowing and being known that is characteristic of God's basic nature, is provided in a special form for embodied personality. In the full sexual union, the person is known in his or her whole body and knows the other by means of his or her whole body. The depth of involvement is so deep that there can be no such thing as "casual sex." It is a contradiction of terms—something very well understood by the apostle Paul, who, accordingly, taught that fornication is a sin against one's own body (1 Cor. 6:18).

So, our sexuality reaches into the essence of our being. Therefore chastity does not mean nonsexuality, and any *pose* to that effect will certainly do great harm. And this is a *very* important point. The suffering that comes from sexuality does come in large part from improper indulgence in sexual thoughts, feelings, attitudes, and relations. But much also comes from *improper abstinence*.

In no domain of human life is it more true that "hope deferred maketh the heart sick" (Prov. 13:12), and it makes many minds sick as well. Jesus clearly saw that abstinence from sexual relations still allowed for gross sexual impropriety and disturbance—some of which he called "adultery in the heart" (Matt. 5:28)—and that a right abstinence was something that called for very special qualifications (Matt. 19:11–12). This realism about sex is carried on by Paul, who taught about a wrong kind of abstention when he wrote it is "better to marry than to burn" (1 Cor. 7:9).

Of course, we must understand that the "burning" here in question is something very serious in its implications, not just a trivial "inward" matter. It spills out into human life in many ways: severe distortion of thought and emotion, inability to engage in normal and appropriate sexual relations, disgust and hatred between frustrated men and women, even abuse of children, sexual perversion, and sex murders. Chastity rightly practiced as a part of an overall rich walk with God can draw the poison from sexual abstinence and prevent the sickness of heart and mind that now runs amok in the sexual dimension of life in today's world.

Dietrich Bonhoeffer observes that "the essence of chastity is not the suppression of lust but the total orientation of one's life toward a goal."[20] Healthy abstention in chastity can only be supported by loving, positive involvement with members of the opposite sex. Alienation from them makes room for harmful lusts, and so this discipline must be underscored with compassion, association, and helpfulness. If our family situations were as they should be, a close and compassionate relationship between the sexes would be the natural outflow of the relationships between mother and son, father and daughter, sister and brother, and so forth. A recent study indicates that fathers who care for their children, cleaning, feeding, holding them from their earliest days on, rarely abuse them sexually. That is because they effectively love them, and such effective love prevents our harming one another. To practice chastity, then, we must first practice love, practice seeking the good of those of the opposite sex we come in contact with at home, work, school, church, or next door. Then we will be free to practice the discipline of chastity as appropriate and gain only positive results from it.

SECRECY

In the discipline of secrecy—and here again, the word is not perfectly suited to our purposes—we abstain from causing our good deeds and qualities to be known. We may even take steps to prevent them from being known, if it doesn't involve deceit. To help us lose or tame the hunger for fame, justification, or just the mere attention of others, we will often need the help of grace. But as we practice this discipline, we learn to love to be unknown and even to accept misunderstanding without the loss of our peace, joy, or purpose.

Few things are more important in stabilizing our walk of faith than this discipline. In the practice of secrecy, we experience a continuing relationship with God independent of the opinions of others. "Thou shalt hide them in the secret of thy presence from the pride of men: thou shalt keep them secretly in a pavilion from the strife of tongues," Psalms 31 states.

Thomas à Kempis comments on the "great tranquility of heart" that comes to those who rise above "praisings and blamings":

Thou are not the holier though thou be praised nor the more vile though thou be blamed or dispraised. What thou art, that thou art; that God knoweth thee to be and thou canst be said to be no greater. . . . For a man ever to do well and to think little of himself is token of a meek soul. For a man not to wish to be comforted by any creature is a token of great purity and inward trust. He that seeketh no outward witness for himself, it appeareth openly that he hath committed himself all wholly to God.[21]

One of the greatest fallacies of our faith, and actually one of greatest acts of unbelief, is the thought that our spiritual acts and virtues need to be advertised to be known. The frantic efforts of religious personages and groups to advertise and certify themselves is a stunning revelation of their lack of substance and faith. Jesus, surely with some humor, remarked that a city set on a hill cannot be hid (Matt. 5:14). I would not like to have the task of *hiding* Jerusalem, or Paris, or even Baltimore. The Gospel stories tell us how hard Jesus and his friends tried to *avoid* crowds and how badly they failed. Quite candidly, if it is possible for our faith and works to be hidden, perhaps that only shows they are of a kind that *should* be hidden. We might, in that case, think about directing our efforts toward the cultivation of a faith that is impossible to hide (Mark 7:24).

Secrecy rightly practiced enables us to place our public relations department entirely in the hands of God, who lit our candles so we could be the light of the world, not so we could hide under a bushel (Matt. 5:14–16). We allow *him* to decide when our deeds will be known and when our light will be noticed.

Secrecy at its best teaches love and humility before God and others. And that love and humility encourages us to see our associates in the best possible light, even to the point of our hoping they will do better and appear better than us. It actually becomes possible for us to "do nothing out of selfish ambition or vain conceit, but in humility consider others better than ourselves," as Philippians 2:3 advises. And what a relief that can be! If you want to experience the flow of love as never before, the next time you are in a competitive situation, pray that the others around you will be more outstanding, more praised, and more used of God than yourself. Really pull for them and rejoice for their successes. If Christians were universally to do this for each other, the earth would soon be filled with the knowledge of God's glory. The discipline of secrecy can lead us into this sort of wonderful experience.

Secrecy has yet another important dimension as a spiritual discipline. The needs that arise in our efforts to serve God can often be handled by looking to God only, not telling others that there is a need, but counting on God to tell them. Over a century ago, George Mueller of Bristol, England, supported a vast ministry, including a number of houses for orphans, without advertising his needs or those of his work. He was inspired to do this in part by the similar work of A. H. Franke in Halle, Germany, during the early 1700s. But his aim was to establish before the world and the church a testimony that God provides faithfully for those who trust in him. He reasoned:

Now if I a poor man, simply by prayer and faith, obtained without asking any individual, the means for establishing and carrying on an orphan house: there would be something which, with the Lord's blessing, might be instrumental in strengthening the faith of the children of God, besides being a testimony to the consciences of the unconverted, of the reality of the things of God.[22]

If we see needs met because we have ask God alone, our faith in God's presence and care will be greatly increased. But if we always tell others of the need, we will have little faith in God, and our entire spiritual life will suffer because of it.

SACRIFICE

In the discipline of sacrifice, we abstain from the possession or enjoyment of what is necessary for our living—not, as in frugality, from what is really to some degree superfluous anyway. The discipline of sacrifice is one in which we forsake the security of meeting our needs with what is in our hands. It is total abandonment to God, a stepping into the darkened abyss in the faith and hope that God will bear us up. Abraham knew about such abandonment when he was prepared to sacrifice Isaac. He was actually counting upon his Lord to raise Isaac from the dead to fulfill the promise of lineage, as Hebrews 11:19 explains. The poor widow of Luke 21:2–4 abandoned herself to God's care as she gave sacrificially. She gave more to God with her two pennies than all the rich gentlemen writing out their large, tax deductible checks around her.

Strangely enough, even though sacrifice may seem more of a service, it is always more of a discipline. Our need to give is greater than God's need to receive, because he is always well supplied. But how nourishing to our faith are the tokens of God's care in response to our sacrifice. The cautious faith that *never* saws off the limb on which it is sitting never learns that unattached limbs may find strange, unaccountable ways of not falling.

Once while in graduate school at the University of Wisconsin, my wife and I decided to give away what we had left after paying the bills at the first of the month. It was not much to give away, but we did it. And we told no one. How odd then that a twenty-dollar bill was found pinned to the steering wheel of our car a week or so later! With hamburger at thirty-nine cents a pound, we lived like royalty until the next month, convinced we were enjoying the provisions of the King. With the discipline of sacrifice, we practice a different dimension of faith, and often we are surprised at its results.

THE DISCIPLINES OF ENGAGEMENT

"Arise, take up thy bed, and go thy way" (Mark 2:11).

The disciplines of abstinence must be counterbalanced and supplemented by disciplines of engagement. Abstinence and engagement are the outbreathing and inbreathing of our spiritual lives, and we require disciplines for both movements. Roughly speaking, the disciplines of abstinence counteract tendencies to sins of commission, and the disciplines of engagement counteract tendencies to sins of omission. Life, as we have seen in an earlier chapter, does not derive its power of growth and development from withdrawal but from action—from engagement.

Abstinence, then, makes way for engagement. If the places in our blood cells designed to carry oxygen are occupied by carbon monoxide, we die for lack of oxygen. If the places in our souls that are to be indwelt by God and his service are occupied by food, sex, and society, we die or languish for lack of God and right relation to his creatures. A proper abstinence actually breaks the hold of improper engagements so that the soul can be properly engaged in and by God.

STUDY

In the spiritual discipline of study we engage ourselves, above all, with the written and spoken Word of God. Here is the chief positive counterpart of solitude. As solitude is the primary discipline of abstinence for the early part of our spiritual life, so study is the primary discipline of engagement.

Our early experience may be so full that we neglect study. But relationship with God, as with any person, soon requires a contribution from us, which will largely consist of study. Calvin Miller well remarks: "Mystics without study are only spiritual romantics who want relationship without effort."[23]

We have already commented a number of times upon the use of Bible study as a discipline, but it would be difficult to overstate the point. Here is David Watson's comment on the days before his operation for the cancer that ultimately took his life:

As I spent time chewing over the endless assurances and promises to be found in the Bible, so my faith in the living God grew stronger and held me safe in his hands. God's word to us, especially his word spoken by his Spirit through the Bible, is the very ingredient that feeds our faith. If we feed our souls regularly on God's word, several times each day, we should become robust spiritually just as we feed on ordinary food several times each day, and become robust physically. Nothing is more important than hearing and obeying the word of God.[24]

In study we also strive to see the Word of God at work in the lives of others, in the church, in history, and in nature. We not only read and hear and inquire, but we *meditate* on what comes before us; that is, we withdraw into silence where we prayerfully and steadily focus upon it. In this way its meaning for us can emerge and form us as God works in the depths of our heart, mind, and soul. We devote long periods of time to this. Our prayer as we study meditatively is always that God would meet with us and speak specifically to us, for ultimately the Word of God is God speaking.

Does this sound like a scholarly pursuit? Actually, study isn't necessarily that at all. It does, however, involve giving much time on a regular basis to meditation upon those parts of the Bible that are most meaningful for our spiritual life, together with constant reading of the Bible as a whole. We should also make every effort to sit regularly under the ministry of gifted teachers who can lead us deeply into the Word and make us increasingly capable of fruitful study on our own. Beyond this, we should read well the lives of disciples from all ages and cultures of the church, building a small library as we make them our friends and associates in The Way.

WORSHIP

The study of God in his Word and works opens the way for the disciplines of worship and celebration. In worship we engage ourselves with, dwell upon, and express the greatness, beauty, and goodness of God through thought and the use of words, rituals, and symbols. We do this alone as well as in union with God's people. To worship is to see God as *worthy,* to ascribe great worth to him.

Here, for example, is worship: "Thou art worthy, O Lord, to receive glory and honour and power: for thou hast created all things, and for thy pleasure they are and were created" (Rev. 4:11). And again: "Worthy is the Lamb that was slain to receive power, and riches, and wisdom, and strength, and honour, and glory, and blessing. . . . Blessing, and honour, and glory, and power, be unto him that sitteth upon the throne, and unto the Lamb for ever and ever" (Rev. 5:12–13). As we worship in this manner, giving careful attention to the details of God's actions and to his "worthiness," the good we adore enters our minds and hearts to increase our faith and strengthen us to be as he is.

If in worship we are met by God himself, our thoughts and words turn to perception and experience of God, who is then really *present to us* in some degree of his greatness, beauty, and goodness. This will make for an immediate, dramatic change in our lives. Such a thing happened with Isaiah, who once at worship *saw* the Lord, "sitting upon a throne, high and lifted up, and his train filled the temple," surrounded by the seraphim crying to one another: "Holy, Holy, Holy, is the Lord of Host; the whole earth is full of his glory" (6:1-3). It has happened to many others.

Nevertheless, the direct divine encounter is not essential to true worship, and it may also occur outside of the context of purposeful worship, as it did with Elijah, Ezekiel, and Paul. *Worship is our part,* even though divinely assisted, and therefore it can be a discipline for the spiritual life.

Practically speaking, the Christian's worship is most profitable when it is centered upon Jesus Christ and goes through him to God. When we worship, we fill our minds and hearts with wonder at him—the detailed actions and words of his earthly life, his trial and death on the cross, his resurrection reality, and his work as ascended intercessor. Here, in the words of Albertus Magnus (died 1280), we "find God through God Himself; that is, we pass by the Manhood into the Godhood, by the wounds of humanity into the depths of His divinity."[25] There is so much to *do* in this worship that we will never finish. And as we worship in this way our lives are filled with his goodness, which is also God's.

The converted slave trader John Newton penned this hymn of worship:

> Content with beholding His face,
> My all to His pleasure resigned;
> No changes of season or place

> Would make any change in my mind;
> While blessed with a sense of his love,
> A palace a toy would appear;
> And prisons would palaces prove,
> If Jesus would dwell with me there.[26]

CELEBRATION

Here is one of the most important disciplines of engagement, yet most overlooked and misunderstood. It is the completion of worship, for it dwells on the greatness of God as shown in his goodness *to us*. We engage in celebration when we enjoy ourselves, our life, our world, *in conjunction with* our faith and confidence in God's greatness, beauty, and goodness. We concentrate on *our* life and world as God's work and as God's gift to us.

Typically this means that we come together with others who know God to eat and drink, to sing and dance, and to relate stories of God's action for our lives and our people. Miriam (Exod. 15:20), Deborah (Judg. 5), and David (2 Sam. 6:12–16) provide us with vivid biblical examples of celebration, as does Jesus' first public miracle at the wedding in Cana (John 2), or the appointed feasting periods of the nation of Israel. Celebration was also maintained by the church in its established feast days up to the Protestant era and is continued to today by the Roman Catholic and the Orthodox communions.

Holy delight and joy is the great antidote to despair and is a wellspring of genuine gratitude—the kind that starts at our toes and blasts off from our loins and diaphram through the top of our head, flinging our arms and our eyes and our voice upward toward our good God.

The unabashedly sensual and earthy character of celebration or jubilee is nowhere more clearly portrayed than in the instructions contained in Deuteronomy 14. Here a tithe of goods produced was to be used in a feast before the Lord on a vacation trip to the big city of Jerusalem. If the city was too far for individuals to carry their own produce as provision, the tithe was to be sold "for money," and the money taken to Jerusalem where—are you ready for this?—"Thou shalt bestow that money for whatsoever thy soul lusteth after, for oxen, or for sheep, or for wine, or for strong drink, or whatsoever thy soul desireth: and thou shalt eat there before the Lord thy God, and thou shalt rejoice, thou, and thine household, and the Levite that is within thy gates" (14:26–27). The "strong drink" mentioned here was, shall we say, not exactly sassafras tea! But the point of this exercise, nonetheless, was precisely "that thou mayest learn to fear the Lord thy God always" (14:23).

The book of Ecclesiastes contains similar admonitions. For example: "Then I realized that it is good and proper for a man to eat and drink, and to find satisfaction in his toilsome labor under the sun during the few days of life God has given him—for this is his lot. Moreover, when God gives any man wealth and possessions, and enables him to enjoy them, to accept his lot and be happy in his work—this is a gift of God. He seldom reflects on the days of his life, because God keeps him occupied with gladness of heart" (5:18–20, NIV; see also 2:24 and 3:12–23).

Be assured that I'm not in favor of drunkenness as a spiritual discipline, or even so much as a good thing. Abuse of alcohol is currently a curse upon the earth. Celebration is not the whole life or discipline of the faithful, and it requires supplementation and correction by the rest of a balanced practice. But this world is radically unsuited to the heart of the human person, and the suffering and terror of life will not be removed no matter *how* "spiritual" we become. It is because of this that a healthy faith before God cannot be built and maintained, without heartfelt celebration of his greatness and goodness *to us* in the midst of our suffering and terror. "There is a time to weep, and a time to laugh; a time to mourn, and a time to dance" (Eccles. 3:4) It is the act and discipline of faith to seize the season and embrace it for what it is, including the season of enjoyment.

Certainly this will seem far too hedonistic to many of us. But we dishonor God as much by fearing and avoiding pleasure as we do by dependence upon it or living for it. Listen once more to Uncle Screwtape. He is chiding his demon protégé, Wormwood, for allowing his "patient" to read a book he really enjoyed and take a walk in the country that filled him with joy.

"In other words," says Screwtape, "you allowed him two real positive pleasures. Were you so ignorant as not to see the danger of this?" Then he elaborates:

The man who truly and disinterestedly enjoys any one thing in the world, for its own sake, and without caring twopence what other people say about it, is by that very fact forearmed against some of our subtlest modes of attack. You should always try to make the patient abandon the people or food or books he really likes in favor of the "best" people, the "right" food, the "important" books. I have known a human defended from strong temptations to social ambition by a still stronger taste for tripe and onions.[27]

Elsewhere Screwtape remarks that when demons are dealing with any pleasure in its healthy and normal and satisfying form, they are on the enemy's ground. We've won many a soul through pleasure, he says, "All the same, it is His invention, not ours. He made the pleasures: all our research so far has not enabled us to produce one."[28]

Faith in its celebration sometimes becomes a delirious joy coursing through our bodily being, when we really begin to see how great and lovely God is and how good he has been *to us*. Even those commonly thought to be ruined (Luke 6:20–23; Matt. 5:3–12)—the poor, the depressed, the persecuted—have a godlike well-being in his company and Kingdom. Feasting, dancing, singing, oration become insuppressible. "For by thee," we shout, "I have run through a troop: and by my God I have leaped over a wall" (Ps. 18:29). "Thou hast turned for me my mourning into dancing: thou hast put off my sackcloth, and girded me with gladness; to the end that my glory may sing praise to thee, and not be silent. O Lord my God, I will give thanks unto thee forever!" (Ps. 30:11–12). But that is not yet enough. The hills must sing and the trees break out in applause for God (Isa. 55:12). Every created thing must praise the Lord (Ps. 148–150).

Celebration heartily done makes our deprivations and sorrows seem small, and we find in it great strength to do the will of our God because his goodness becomes so real to us.

SERVICE

In service we engage our goods and strength in the active promotion of the good of others and the causes of God in our world. Here we recall an important distinction. Not every act that *may* be done as a discipline *need* be done as a discipline. I will often be able to serve another simply as an act of love and righteousness, without regard to how it may enhance my abilities to follow Christ. There certainly is nothing wrong with that, and it may, incidentally, strengthen me spiritually as well. But I may also serve another to train myself away from arrogance, possessiveness, envy, resentment, or covetousness. In that case, my service is undertaken as a discipline for the spiritual life.

Such discipline is very useful for those Christians who find themselves—as most of us by necessity must—in the "lower" positions in society, at work, and in the church. It alone can train us in habits of loving service to others and free us from resentment, enabling us in faith to enjoy our position and work because of its exhalted meaning before God.

Paradoxically perhaps, service is the high road to freedom from bondage to other people. In it, as Paul realized, we cease to be "menpleasers" and "eyeservants," for we are acting unto God in our lowliest deeds: "Slaves, obey in everything those who are your earthly masters, not with eyeservice, as menpleasers, but in singleness of heart, fearing the Lord. Whatever your task, work heartily, as serving the Lord and not men, knowing that from the Lord you will receive the inheritance as your reward; you are serving the Lord Christ" (Col. 3:22–24, RSV).

Can this be applied by the mother of six who must leave her little children uncared for in a derelict neighborhood to support them by scrubbing office floors at night? Can it be applied by the refugee from Central America who pushes his ice cream cart around the neighborhood, ringing his bell as he goes? Yes it can be, if they have heard and received from the heart the gospel of the Kingdom of God—though this provides not the least shadow of an excuse for others failing to do all they reasonably can to help them.

And, truly, it *must* be so applied by them. For they are where they are, and God has yet to bless anyone except where they are. Needless to say, only clear teaching and example, with much practice in the discipline of service, can make us strong here.

But I believe the discipline of service is even more important for Christians who find themselves in positions of influence, power, and leadership. To live as a servant while fulfilling socially important roles is one of the greatest challenges any disciple ever faces. It is made all the harder because the church does not give special training to persons engaged in these roles and foolishly follows the world by regarding such people as "having it made," possibly even considering them qualified to speak as authorities in the spiritual life because of their success in the world.

Some of the most important things Jesus had to say concerned the manner in which leaders were to live:

Ye know that the princes of the Gentiles exercise dominion over them, and they that are great exercise authority upon them. But it shall not be so among you: but whosoever will be great among you, let him be your minister; and whosoever will be chief among you, let him be your servant. Even as the Son of man came not to be ministered unto, but to minister, and to give his life a ransom for many (Matt. 20:25–28).

We misunderstand this passage if we read it merely as instructions on how to become great. It is, rather, a statement on how those who *are* great are to behave. To be "great" and to live as a servant is one of the most difficult of *spiritual* attainments. But it is also the pattern of life for which this bruised and aching world waits and without which it will never manage a decent existence. Those who would live this pattern must attain it through the discipline of service in the power of God, for that alone will train them to exercise great power without corrupting their souls. It is for this reason that Jesus told his disciples to wash one another's feet and set them an example (John 13:14). But where are our seminary courses that would teach leaders in all areas of life—even the church—how to do this and accustom them to it as the fine and easy thing to do?

Service to others in the spirit of Jesus allows us the freedom of a humility that carries no burdens of "appearance." It lets us be what we are—simply a particularly lively piece of clay who, as servant of God, happens to be here now with the ability to do this good and needful thing for that other bit of clay there. The experience of active love freed up and flowing by faith through us on such occasions will safeguard us from innumerable pitfalls of the spiritual life.

We must, then, strive to meet all persons who cross our path with openness to service for them—not, of course, in any anxious, obsequious, overly solicitous manner, but with ease and confidence born of our vision of our lives together in the hands of God.

PRAYER

Prayer is conversing, communicating with God. When we pray we talk to God, aloud or within our thoughts. In the nature of the case, prayer almost always involves other disciplines and spiritual activities if it is to go well, especially study, meditation, and worship, and often solitude and fasting as well.

It would of course be a rather low-voltage spiritual life in which prayer was chiefly undertaken as a discipline, rather than as a way of co-laboring with God to accomplish good things and advance his Kingdom purposes. Yet prayer *can* be a discipline, and a highly effective one, as we see from our Lord's advice to those with him in the Garden of Gethsemane: "Watch and pray, that ye enter not into temptation."

Indeed, the indirect effects of prayer upon the conduct of our lives is so obvious and striking that they have been mistakenly treated at times as the only point of prayer. Even when we are praying for or about things other than our own spiritual needs and growth, the effect of conversing with God cannot fail to have a pervasive and spiritually strengthening effect on *all* aspects of our personality. That conversation, when it is truly a conversation, makes an indelible impression on our minds, and our consciousness of him remains vivid as we go our way.

O. Hardman has an excellent description of how the one immersed in prayer then meets the world with its stupid policies, its grasping for privilege and security, its suspicion, ingratitude, and resistance to good:

Continuing instant in prayer after the conclusion of each period of definite communion with God, he will set himself to undertake every legitimate risk, to do the right without fear of consequences, and to embrace in loving purpose those who are opposed to him no less than those who are in agreement with him, in the attempt to realise the vision and to exercise the sympathy with which prayer has endowed him. The many groups into which his fellows are divided will be seen by him in the light of the whole, and he will ever strive to bridge gulfs and so assist in the realisation of that living unity which is experienced by him in anticipation when, in his moments of intensest prayer, he is caught up to God and filled with the joy of union. Economic, social, political, national, and racial antagonisms are waiting for this sole solution of the deadlock which they present. There is no other way.[29]

How misguided are those who regard prayer as irrelevant to social conditions! No doubt many things called "prayer" are quite useless in every respect, but nothing is more relevant to social conditions than the transformation of persons that comes from prayer at its best in the life of the disciple of Christ.

Praying with frequency gives us the readiness to pray again as needed from moment to moment. The more we pray, the more we think to pray, and as we see the results of prayer—the responses of our Father to our requests—our confidence in God's power spills over into other areas of our life. Out of her vast experiences with prayer in the harrowing life of a missionary wife and mother, Rosalind Goforth explains: "Perhaps the most blessed element in this asking and getting from God lies in the strengthening of faith which comes when a definite request has been granted. What is more helpful and inspiring than a ringing testimony of *what God has done?*"[30]

However, prayer as a discipline has its greatest force in strengthening the spiritual life only as we learn to *pray without ceasing* (1 Thess. 5:17; Phil. 4:6). We can train ourselves to invoke God's presence in every action we perform. This is an experiential fact that has been proven in the lives of many disciples of Jesus, ancient and modern. God will meet us in love, and love will keep our minds directed toward him as the magnet pulls the needle of the compass. Habit will be confirmed in gracious interaction, and our whole lives will be bathed in the presence of God. Constant prayer will only "burden" us as wings burden the bird in flight.

But prayer will not be established in our lives as it must be for us to florish, unless we are practicing other disciplines such as solitude and fasting. In many Protestant churches prayer and Bible study are held up as *the* activities that will make us spiritually rich. But very few people actually succeed in attaining spiritual richness through them and indeed often find them to be intolerably burdensome. The "open secret" of many "Bible believing" churches is that a vanishingly small percentage of those talking about prayer and Bible reading are actually doing what they are talking about. They have not been shown how to change their life as a whole, permeating it with appropriate disciplines, so that prayer and Bible reading will be spiritually successful. Examples of those who are especially effective at prayer and study, such as David Brainerd, or John Fletcher, or Charles Finney, are presented in such a way that hearers do not discover the totality of spiritual disciplines which they carefully practiced to pray as they did. The emphasis upon the character of overall discipline throughout the life must not be missed if prayer is to be the powerful work and effectual discipline God intended it to be, one of his most precious gifts to us.

FELLOWSHIP

In fellowship we engage in common activities of worship, study, prayer, celebration, and service with other disciples. This may involve assembling ourselves together in a large group or meeting with only a few. Personalities united can contain more of God and sustain the force of his greater presence much better than scattered individuals. The fire of God kindles higher as the brands are heaped together and each is warned by the other's flame. The members of the body must be in *contact* if they are to sustain and be sustained by each other. Christian redemption is not devised to be a solitary thing, though each individual of course has a unique and direct relationship with God, and God alone is his or her Lord and Judge. But The Life is one that requires some regular and profound conjunction with others who share it. It is greatly diminished when that is lacking.

The diverse gifts or graces of the Spirit—all of which are needed in some measure by each person from time to time—are distributed among the separate members of the body of Christ, the church. The unity of the body rightly functioning is thus guaranteed by the people reciprocating in needs and ministries. There are no "oughts" or "shoulds" or "won't-you-pleases" about this. It is just a matter of how things actually work in the new life:

Each man is given his gift by the Spirit that he may use it for the common good. One man's gift by the Spirit is to speak with wisdom, another's to speak with knowledge. The same Spirit gives to another man faith, to another the ability to heal, to another the power to do great deeds. The same Spirit gives to another man the gift of preaching the word of God, to another the ability to discriminate in spiritual matters, to another speech in different tongues and to yet another the power to interpret the tongues. Behind all these gifts is the operation of the same Spirit, who distributes to each individual as he wills (1 Cor. 12:7–11, Phillips).

Because of this reciprocal nature within the corporate body of Christ, fellowship is required to allow realization of a joyous and sustained level of life in Christ that is normally impossible to attain by all our individual effort, no matter how vigorous and sustained. In it we receive the ministry of all the graces of the Spirit to the church.

CONFESSION

Confession is a discipline that functions within fellowship. In it we let trusted others know our deepest weaknesses and failures. This will nourish our faith in God's provision for our needs through his people, our sense of being loved, and our humility before our brothers and sisters. Thus we let some friends in Christ know who we really are, not holding back anything important, but, ideally, allowing complete transparency. We lay down the burden of hiding and pretending, which normally takes up such a dreadful amount of human energy. We engage and are engaged by others in the most profound depths of the soul.

The New Testament church seems to have assumed that if a brother or sister had some sickness or other affliction, it might have been due to a sin that was separating that person from the full flow of redeeming life. So in the Letter of James we are told: "Confess your faults one to another, and pray one for another, that ye may be healed. The effectual fervent prayer of a righteous man availeth much" (5:16). We must accept the fact that unconfessed sin is a special kind of burden or obstruction in the psychological as well as the physical realities of the believer's life. The discipline of confession and absolution removes that burden.

But confession also helps us to *avoid* sin. The proverb tells us that "He that covereth his sins shall not prosper: but whoso confesseth and forsaketh them shall have mercy" (Prov. 28:13). The "confesseth" obviously is an aid to the "forsaketh," for persisting in sin within a close community—not to mention the fellowship of a transparent body of Christ—is unsupportable unless it is hidden. It is said confession is good for the soul but bad for the reputation, and a bad reputation makes life more difficult in relation to those close to us, we all know. But closeness and confession force out evildoing. Nothing is more supportive of right behavior than open truth.

And the baring of the soul to a mature friend in Christ or to a qualified minister enables such friends to pray for specific problems and to do those things that may be most helpful and redemptive to the one confessing. Confession alone makes *deep* fellowship possible, and the lack of it explains much of the superficial quality so commonly found in our church associations. What, though, makes confession bearable? Fellowship. There is an essential reciprocity between these two disciplines.

Where there is confession within a close community, *restitution* cannot be omitted and it too serves as a powerful discipline. It is difficult not to rectify wrong done once it is confessed and known widely. Of course not all sin calls for restitution. But it is unthinkable that I should sincerely confess to my brother or sister that I have stolen a purse or harmed a reputation and then blithely go my way without trying to make some restoration for the loss.

In general, our own innate integrity, a force within our personality, *requires* such restitution. This often is not a pleasant experience, but it actually strengthens us in our will to do the right thing. Confession then is one of the most powerful of the disciplines for the spiritual life. But it may be easily abused, and for its effective use it requires considerable experience and maturity, both in the individual concerned and in the leadership of the group—which leads us to our final discipline.

SUBMISSION

The highest level of fellowship—involving humility, complete honesty, transparency, and at times confession and restitution—is sustained by the discipline of submission.

In the letter to the Hebrews we read: "Obey them that have the rule over you, and submit yourselves: for they watch for your souls, as they that must give account, that they may do it with joy and not with grief" (13:7). In 1 Peter those older in The Way are told to take the oversight of the flock of God, not by being forced to do so and not as lords over God's heritage, but *as examples to the flock* (5:2–3). The younger are then told to submit themselves to this gentle oversight by the elders, and all are caught up together as a community of mutual servants in mutual submission: "Yea, all of you be subject one to another, and be clothed with humility: for God resisteth the proud and giveth grace to the humble" (5:5; see also Eph. 5:21).

The order in the redemptive community here implied obviously is not a matter of an iron hierarchy in which unwilling souls are crushed and driven. Instead, it functions in the power of truth and mercy inhabiting mature personalities, being the expression of a kingdom not of this world (John 18:36)—but truly a kingdom nonetheless. Otherwise the church would revert to the model of purely human government. Unfortunately, we see this actually happening in certain misguided attempts at Christian community. The Way of Jesus knows no submission outside the context of *mutual* submission of all to all. (Eph. 5:21, Phil. 2:3)

Submission, though, is a call for help to those recognized as able to give it because of their depth of experience and Christlikeness—because they truly are "elder" in The Way. In submission we engage the experience of those in our fellowship who are qualified to direct our efforts in growth and who then add the weight of their wise authority on the side of our willing spirit to help us do the things we would like to do and refrain from the things we don't want to do. They oversee the godly order in our souls as well as in our fellowship and in the surrounding body of Christ.

But these "wise" people will not be looking at themselves as "leaders" actually. Their being examples we submit to is but one aspect of *their* submission to *servanthood*. It is a case of true leadership, not of the *drivership* that so often prevails in secular society and in some church groups where those "in control" do not know of an alternative. How *truly* blessed is this free "order that is in beatitude."[31] Here are the beginnings of that kingdom "cut out without hands" (Dan. 2:34), which will in time fill the earth and make the kingdoms of this world into the kingdom of our God and of his Christ!

ARE THESE DISCIPLINES ADEQUATE?

Here then are some main disciplines for the spiritual life. As we have indicated, there are many other activities that could, for the right person and upon the right occasion, be counted as spiritual disciplines in the strict sense stated of our previous chapter. The walk with Christ certainly is one that leaves room for and even *calls for* individual creativity and an experimental attitude in such matters. Yet the range or extension of the disciplines is largely determined by our own established tendencies to sin that must be resisted, as well as by the possible avenues of loving service to God and humankind that offer themselves to such creatures as we are.

Which disciplines must be central to our lives will be determined by the chief sins of commission and omission that entice or threaten us from day to day. Arrogance, envy, wrath, sloth, avarice, gluttony, and lasciviousness—the seven "deadly" sins of theological and literary history—along with many others are not phantoms or jokes, but hard-bitten realities whose dreadful effects can be viewed hour by hour. They call for a comparably hard-nosed, tough response on our part, supported by infinite grace.

The above list of disciplines provides just such a response. The activities mentioned—when we engage in them conscientiously and creatively and adapt them to our individual needs, time, and place—will be more than adequate to help us receive the full Christ-life and become the kind of person that should emerge in the following of him. Other disciplines can be added, but these are the foundational ones. If practiced faithfully, they will guide us right no matter what other disciplines we may add.

NOTES

1. *Lives of the Saints,* translated with an introduction by J. F. Webb (Baltimore, MD: Penguin, 1973), 18ff.
2. W. R. Inge, *Goodness and Truth,* (London: Mowbray, 1958), 76–77.
3. *Ibid.,* 77.
4. Quoted in Henry Fairlie, *The Seven Deadly Sins Today* (Washington, DC: New Republic Books, 1978), 5.
5. Thomas Merton, *The Seven Storey Mountain* (New York: Harcourt Brace Jovanovich, 1978), 421.
6. Louis Bouyer, *The Spirituality of the New Testament and the Fathers,* vol. 1 of *A History of Christian Spirituality* (New York: Seabury, 1982), 313.
7. Quoted in the *Los Angeles Times,* July 24, 1983, part 4, p. 3.
8. Thomas à Kempis, Irwin Edman, ed., *The Imitation of Christ,* in *The Consolations of Philosophy* (New York: Random House, Modern Library, 1943), 153–55.
9. Henry David Thoreau, *Thoreau: Walden and Other Writings,* ed. Joseph Wood Krutch, (New York: Bantam, 1962), 366.
10. Henri Nouwen, "Silence, The Portable Cell," *Sojourners* (July 1980): 22.
11. Miguel de Unamuno, "Saint Emmanuel the Good, Martyr," *The Existential Imagination,* F.R. Karl and Leo Hamalian, eds. (Greenwich, CT.: Fawcett Publications, 1963), p. 103.
12. Eberhard Arnold, "Why We Choose Silence Over Dialogue," *The Plough,* a publication of the Bruderhof communities, no. 11, (July/August 1985): 12.

13. Communicated to me by Dr. Dirk Nelson.
14. Edna St. Vincent Millay, *Collected Poems of Edna St. Vincent Millay,* ed. Norma Millay (New York: Harper & Row, 1956), 158.
16. Thomas à Kempis, *The Imitation of Christ,* 174.
17. Ibid., 152.
18. O. Hardman, *The Ideals of Asceticism: An Essay in the Comparative Study of Religion* (New York: Macmillan, 1924), 211–12.
19. Quoted in William R. Parker and Elaine St. Johns, *Prayer Can Change Your Life* (Carmel, NY: Guideposts Associates, 1957), 40.
20. Dietrich Bonhoeffer, *Letters and Papers from Prison* (London: Fontana, 1953), 163.
21. Thomas à Kempis, *The Imitation of Christ,* 177.
22. Roger Steer, *Admiring God: The Best of George Mueller* (London: Hodder and Stoughton, 1987), 54.
23. Calvin Miller, *The Table of Inwardness* (Downers Grove, IL: Inter-Varsity Press. 1984), 83.
24. David Watson, *Fear No Evil: A Personal Struggle with Cancer,* (London: Hodder and Stoughton, 1984), 39.
25. Albertus Magnus, *Of Cleaving unto God,* trans. Elisabeth Stopp (London: Mowbray, 1954), 13.
26. John Newton, "How Tedious and Tasteless the Hours," in *The Broadman Hymnal* (Nashville, TN: Broadman Press, 1940), no. 24.
27. C. S. Lewis, *The Screwtape Letters and Screwtape Proposes a Toast* (New York: Macmillan, 1962), 60, 41.
28. *Ibid.,* 41.
29. Hardman, *The Ideals of Asceticism,* 218–19.
30. Rosalind Goforth, *How I Know God Answers Prayer* (Grand Rapids, MI: Zondervan, 1921), 2.
31. This marvelous phrase is from St. Thomas Aquinas, *Summa Theologica,* Part One of the Second Part, Question 90, Article 2, Objection 3.

10. Is Poverty Spiritual?

The brother in humble circumstances ought to take pride in his higher position. But the one who is rich should take pride in his low position, because he will pass away like a wild flower.

JAMES 1:9–10, NIV

As for the rich in this world, charge them not to be haughty, nor to set their hopes on uncertain riches but only in God who richly furnishes us with everything to enjoy. They are to do good, to be rich in good deeds: liberal and generous, thus laying up for themselves a good foundation for the future, so that they may take hold of the life which is life indeed.

1 TIMOTHY 6:17–19, RSV

SHOULD WE BE POOR?

Possessions and money cause uneasiness today in the minds of many sincere Christians. It is not just that they fear failing in their clear responsibilities to help others with the goods at their disposal. Rather, they are haunted by the more radical thought that their service to God would be better if they were poor—or at least if they owned nothing beyond what is required to meet their day-to-day needs. They are troubled by the idea that the very possession of surplus goods or money is evil.

How, they wonder, can it be right for them to have more than they need when so many do not have the necessities? And would they not be able to trust God far better and have greater faith, if they had less material goods to rely on? Again, would they not be freer to serve God if they did not have to take care of their possessions? Even Adam Smith, that recognized dean of capitalists, commented that "the beggar, who suns himself by the side of the highway, possesses that security which kings are fighting for."[1] Should we not be like the birds of the air, which "sow not, neither do they reap, nor gather into barns" (Matt. 6:26)? *That* seems to be the true life of faith.

If that's true, though, how could we fail to include poverty in our list of the central disciplines for the spiritual life? There is a very good reason why not. The idealization of poverty is *one of the most dangerous illusions of Christians in the contemporary world*. Stewardship—which requires possessions and includes giving—is the true spiritual discipline in relation to wealth.

POSSESSING, USING, AND TRUSTING IN RICHES

There can be no doubt that we often fail to give of our goods when we should. There is no justification for that, just as there is none for living wastefully or in frivolous consumption and luxury. Frugality is both a discipline and a primary Christian virtue. But it must be noted that such failures concern the *use* of goods, not their possession. Poverty and wealth, on the other hand, have to do with the *possession* of things. Condemnation and guilt over mere possession has no part in scriptural faith and is, in the end, only a barrier to the right use of the riches of the earth.

Yet too often a burning sense of outrage at social injustice and an elevated sense of 'spirituality' keep us from thinking accurately. When dealing with wealth and poverty it is not only necessary to understand this distinction between the possession and the use of riches but also to understand the difference between these and *trust in* riches.

To *possess* riches is to have a right to say how they will or will not be used. To *use* riches, on the other hand, is to cause them to be consumed or to be transferred to others in exchange for something we desire. The difference between possession and use immediately becomes clear when we think about how we sometimes use and control the use of riches we do not own, as when we influence the decisions of those who do own them. It's possible to use or consume goods we do not own, and it is possible to own what we do not and perhaps cannot use.

To *trust* in riches, on the other hand, is to count upon them to obtain or secure what we treasure most. It is to think that they will bring us happiness and well-being. When we also possess the riches we trust in, we may suppose that we are secure, like the rich fool of the Gospel account (Luke 12:19), or even suppose that we are *better* than those who are poor. If we trust in riches we will also love them and come to serve them. In our actions we will place them above the truly ultimate values of human life, even above God and his service.

In the light of these distinctions it becomes clear that we *can* possess without using or trusting. Possession only gives us a substantial say over how goods may be used. And we *can* use without possessing or trusting. And we are painfully aware how we can trust (and serve) wealth without either possessing or using it. Those poor people whose faith is in riches they neither own nor can use are among the most unhappy people on earth.

POVERTY AND INJUSTICE

At present we find ourselves in a world where, as a matter of fact, few people are rich and powerful, while many are poor and weak. Some who are well-off often have actively wronged their neighbors to get or keep their wealth; others wrong their neighbors by allowing them to suffer rather than share with them. There is an obvious inequality in the distribution of the goods needed for life, and much of the inequality is a reflection of injustice. This we know all too well.

The wealthy also obviously and persistently misuse their wealth in many ways. For example, they live in decadent luxury and use their riches to coerce those who are poorer. Or they invest in such a way that harmful practices and evil people are supported. And many of them seek and trust and serve their wealth to the harm of body, soul, and loved ones.

The problems posed for human life by wealth and poverty are not just concerns for theology and social or personal ethics. They go to the very foundations of the social order. We talk in clinically detached terms of "the economy," but it is economic issues that open the door to the most repressive and bloody regimes, of the political Right as well as Left.

These regimes offer "solutions" that require the murder of millions—ten or more million under the Nazis, ten million in the Ukraine, three million in Cambodia. In our modern world the primary arguments upon which such regimes come to power are mainly economic—economic justice or equality is the professed goal. But at some point, "economic" considerations are translated into the ruin or termination of human lives. Sometimes this is due to "the establishment;" other times "the requirements of the revolution" are served.

In such circumstances it is easy to see why many concerned people might brand wealth itself as evil and the possession of wealth as essentially bad. They will then naturally pit God against riches and against the wealthy as a class. A scholar of the stature of Alastair MacIntyre flatly states: "The New Testament quite clearly sees the rich as destined for the pains of Hell."[2] Father Ernesto Cardenal, a Catholic priest and the minister of culture for the Sandinista government of Nicaragua, interprets Christ as saying "that the rich can never enter the kingdom of God."[3] I believe that these well-known figures are only saying out loud what the majority of socially concerned people now take the Christian religion to teach.

JOHN WESLEY'S LAMENT OVER PROSPEROUS CHRISTIANS

But this attitude is not really new. John Wesley (1703–1791), like many today, was deeply troubled about the relationship of riches to Christian life. His own followers were mostly from the lower economic classes. He observed, however, that the form of life resulting from his preaching made his converts prosperous, which then resulted in their becoming selfish, indulgent, and lacking in self-denial. In his touching sermon on "The Inefficacy of Christianity" he cries out: "I am distressed! I know not what to do!" He even suggests that "true, scriptural Christianity has a tendency, in the process of time, to undermine and destroy itself." It begets diligence and frugality, which make one rich. Riches, in turn, "naturally beget pride, love of the world, and every temper that is destructive of Christianity."[4]

For all of Wesley's religious genius—and it was great—he could not understand the possibility of a Christian teaching and discipline that would produce people capable of holding possessions and power without being corrupted by them (1 Tim. 6:17–19). He could not believe—perhaps could not conceive of the idea—that those who have money *need not* love it and so carry in themselves the root of all evil. (1 Tim. 6:9–10).

But surely he must have known that no one loves and trusts money more than those who have none. And certainly he knew that "If I give all I possess to the poor and surrender my body to the flames, but have not love, I gain nothing" (1 Cor. 13:3, NIV). Giving alone cannot secure a proper relationship to God. Yet he came up with a deeply flawed solution: "I can see only one possible way: find out another who can. Do you gain all you can, and save all you can? Then you must in the nature of things grow rich. Then if you have any desire to escape the damnation of hell, *give* all you can; otherwise I can have no more hope of your salvation than that of Judas Iscariot."[5]

A TEST FOR PREJUDICE AGAINST WEALTH

A simple test reveals an individual's attitude toward the religious and moral significance of wealth. Suppose that by owning a great deal of property and money you are able, in the long run, to give much more away and do much more good for others or the promotion of God's purposes than if you simply gave your surplus away to the poor as it came to hand or if you followed some other course of service that dissolved your financial base. Plus, *as* a prosperous industrialist, businessperson, merchant, government official, publisher, farmer, or university administrator, suppose that you have a wide range of influence over your employees or associates and others in the community and you use that influence to set an example in living and to testify to the reality of Christ's Kingdom.

Suppose that to possess and use your property, money, and influence effectively you must live a life that involves an above average standard of living. The question then is: would you necessarily be holier and a better steward of God's grace and goods if you were merely to *rid* yourself as quickly as possible of your property and money?

Let's take that test again. One sincere, devout Christian is poor; he as just enough money to get by on. Another equally sincere, devout Christian is a successful businessperson who exercises his natural business abilities in an honest and faithful way; he maintains significant financial resources and uses them wisely for godly purposes. Is the poor person a better person and servant of God *merely* for having only enough money to get by on?

My experience in presenting people with this test indicates that the more devout or socially concerned they are, the more likely they are to think that you are the better person for being poor—all else being equal. They believe that if the good achieved by holding possessions is *very* great and cannot be achieved in another way available to you, then you may be "forgiven," as it were, for not being poor.

Looking once again at Wesley we find that his attitude ran along these lines. In his *Journal* for September 6, 1750, he notes a published account of the passing of "one of our preachers." The deceased had hardly enough possessions to pay for his funeral, and Wesley observes with gratification: "Enough for any unmarried preacher of the Gospel to leave to his executors!"

He clearly thought it a good thing that the man should have so little possessions at his death. But would it not have been equally well, or even better, had he been found to have had great possessions carefully managed for the good of others and the glory of God? Especially if it turned out that he did more good in that way than he could have done by giving it all away? Surely it would have.

POVERTY NO ADVANTAGE

While certain individuals may be given a specific call to poverty, in general, being poor is one of the poorest of ways to help the poor. Further, I have yet to find anyone who was the better person simply for being poor. In some instances, people might do fewer bad things than they would if they had had more means. Poverty may in some cases be said to have secured the *lack* of opportunity to do evil, but that will not recommend it to those who are not looking for such an opportunity in the first place.

Also, the giving away of ones goods—and possibly giving *all,* thus becoming poor—may be a praiseworthy act under certain circumstances. But the virtue or discipline here is in the giving, not in the resultant state of poverty. And once all has been given away, further giving is precluded. No one can give what they do not possess. If giving is good, having is also good—providing one's spiritual balance is retained. If giving much is good, having much is also good. If giving more is good, having more is also good.

THE DECEITFULNESS OF RICHES

Of course riches *are* deceitful (Matt. 13:22). In the absence of a vividly superior life in God's Kingdom, wealth creates in most of us an illusion of security and well-being that causes us to trust it rather than "the living God, who giveth us richly all things to enjoy" (1 Tim. 6:7). Those in the grip of this illusion will then certainly be the servants of money—of mammon—not of God (Matt. 6:24). And that will seem *to them* just plain good sense.

It may also be said with assurance that *most* rich people do trust and serve mammon. Thus Jesus rightly said: "How hardly shall they that have riches enter into the kingdom of God" (Mark 10:23). But this is not due just to the power of wealth to mislead. It is also caused by the failure of the church to reach the wealthy with news of their opportunities for life under God's rule.

In any case, the delusions caused by possessions cannot be prevented by having none. We do not have to own things to love them, trust them, even serve them. The percentage of those in bondage to wealth is no greater among the rich than among the poor. It is not money or gain, but *the love of it,* that is said by Paul to be the root of all evil (1 Tim. 6:10), and none love it more desperately and unrealistically than those without it. This must be kept firmly in mind when we come to the gospel story of the "rich young ruler," which has so often been taken to support poverty (or at least the giving away of all we have) as a requirement for the "really serious" Christian.

THE CASE OF THE "RICH YOUNG RULER"

In this story we see a young nobleman coming to Jesus, calling him "good master," and asking him what he should do to receive eternal life (Luke 18:18). After pointing out that God alone is good, Jesus told him that he should keep the commandments. The young man professed, in his blindness, to have fulfilled that condition entirely. This meant, that he always worshiped, served, and trusted God above all else (Exod. 20:3–6).

To help him understand the falsity of his smug declaration, Jesus gave him not an *additional* commandment, but an instruction that could reveal to him the real object of his trust and worship: "You still lack one thing. Sell everything you have and give to the poor, and you will have treasure in heaven. Then come, follow me" (Luke 18:22, NIV). Because the young man's heart was indeed in the wrong place, he turned away. Jesus' word revealed his true god. For even though he sincerely professed to keep the commandments and had recognized divinity in Jesus, he was unwilling to forsake his riches and keep the first commandment by following him.

In the discussion with his disciples following this event, Jesus reflected out loud on how hard it is for the rich to enter the Kingdom. This was a shock to his hearers because in those days the rich were, of all people, thought most certainly to be under the blessing of God—just as now the prejudice runs in favor of the poor. Hence, those who heard Jesus say this asked in surprise: "Who then can be saved?" (Luke 18:26). He replied that things impossible within the range of human power are nevertheless possible with God.

It is almost universally held today that in this passage Jesus says it is easier for the poor to be saved than the rich, but he says no such thing. You only have to look at his words to see this. The point of the passage has nothing to do with the *relative* positions of poor and rich. What he teaches here is simply that it is no easy thing for the rich to enter under the rule of God.

Let's be clear about one thing. Whoever cannot have riches without worshiping them above God should get rid of them, *if* that will enable him or her to trust and serve God rightly. If it does not enable them to do that, then there well may be no point at all in getting rid of the riches. And whether or not there is a point to it will depend upon the effect on those who receive the given-away money. There is no guarantee the recepients will actually benefit from it. The wealth may actually do harm.

We can be sure that Jesus was not ignorant of these facts. An avaricious, covetous poor man is no better than an avaricious, covetous rich man. Poverty in itself is no recommendation to God and no means of grace.

GIVING ALL AWAY AS A WITNESS

Both St. Antony and St. Francis of Assisi were greatly impressed with this Gospel story of the rich ruler and believed that through it God told them personally to have no possessions. They should know whether or not this is so, and I would never argue against it. By adopting a form of poverty, moreover, they made a powerful statement to their times and to ours about the way we can be independent of possessions and dependent upon God and his people.

What the two did was a beautiful thing, an enduring treasure of the church and of Christ. But we are talking about something very different from this sort of poverty. We are discussing poverty as either (1) a condition intrinsically holy in itself, (2) as a generally useful discipline for the spiritual life, or (3) as God's best plan for utilizing the wealth of this world.

THE DISCIPLINE AND SERVICE OF POSSESSIONS

Say we decided to give away all the money we had, where would the money go? It would go somewhere—someone will continue to be affected by it. We must never forget that the riches of this world, whether they are to be regarded as good or evil, are realities that do not just disappear if we abandon them. They will continue to exert their effects. Possessions and use of them *will* occur. Someone will control them, and the fact that *we* do not possess them does not mean that they will be better distributed. So to assume the responsibility for the right use and guidance of possessions through ownership is far more of a discipline of the spirit than poverty itself. Our possessions vastly extend the range over which God rules through *our* faith. Thus they make possible activities in God's power that are impossible without them. We must not allow our quite justifiable revulsion at the debauchery of those who happen to be rich to blind us to this crucial fact.

Poverty as a general practice cannot solve humankind's bondage to wealth. Freedom from possessions is not an outward thing as much as an inward one. It is something that can come from the inward vision of faith alone. This is the point of Bonhoeffer's remark that "to be without desire is a mark of poverty."[6] But to abandon the goods of this world to the enemies of God is to fail the responsibilities we are given at creation to have dominion, to rule over all life forms above the plants (Gen. 1:26).

Likewise, charity and social welfare programs, while good and clearly our duty, cannot even *begin* to fulfill our responsibilities as children of light to a needy world. It is pure delusion to imagine that they can. They simply concern too small a portion of the goods of life. Specifically, they cannot take the place of adequately prepared, godly men and women who will assume the responsibility, under God and by his power, of owning and directing the world's wealth and goods. Such people must rise up and, in union with Christ and his people everywhere, guide social, economic, and political processes so that the conditions that cause the need for charity are lessened to a point where that need can be met. Such men and women are the only ones who can effectively lead humankind to fulfill its ancient charge of supervision over the earth.

It is precisely these facts about God's purpose in our creation and the nature of our life that explain the almost universal failure of people to actually carry through with poverty as a *life*-style. St. Francis's cult of poverty did not even survive to the end of his own life. Some of his disciples, the "Fraticelli," were denounced as heretics and burned for continuing to exhalt poverty.[7]

This, of course, does not prove that he was wrong. But the implicit Manicheanism—the placing of material goods outside of holiness—inherent in St. Francis's idealization of nonpossession had the effect of abandoning wealth to Satan and excluding those who control it from the service of God. This terrible mistake—which did not originate with St. Francis—can only be reversed by understanding that possession and right rule over material wealth is a spiritual service of the highest order. And our response must be to develop a ministry that prepares people for that service.

POVERTY: VOWED AND REAL

The failure of poverty as a life unto God is also clear from the way it is generally practiced by those who vow it explicitly. In fact, the destitution of real poverty would make most of the activities associated with the work of the Christian life and ministry impossible. So most of the so-called poverty voluntarily accepted in the church's history is, naturally enough, not poverty at all. As St. Francis de Sales sharply observed: "That poverty which is praised, caressed, esteemed, succored, and assisted is closely allied to riches."[8]

The truly poor of the earth know poverty for what it is: it is crushing deprivation and helplessness. The vow of poverty, on the other hand, allows a person to continue to enjoy the security, provision, and care of a religious order—made available through the wealth of others. I am not criticizing this arrangement. Far from it. In fact, it makes excellent sense for freeing individuals for ministry of various kinds. But none of that support is available to the *truly* poor of the earth. Poverty as vowed only amounts to foregoing formal ownership of things, not foregoing *access to* and *use of* them—which, in fact, the vow usually guarantees.

This removal of the idea of poverty from the reality of poverty is what allows it to be romanticized among all groups of Christians—and even permits a certain "poverty chic" to flourish in some quarters of secular society. Wesley, though no advocate of vows of poverty, listed his deceased preacher's possessions as one shilling and fourpence, in addition to his clothes, linen and woolen, stockings, hat, and wig. All of these together were not sufficient to meet the funeral expenses, which amounted to one pound seventeen shillings and threepence. Certainly this minister often knew want, and his self-sacrificing manner of life is not to be despised as a virtue or as a discipline. But he did not lack for status within his society or for reliably regular provisions of food and shelter that he did not own.

POVERTY IS NOT SIMPLICITY

Another aspect of the romanticization of poverty is its identification with simplicity. But the life for the poverty stricken is simple only in the sense that the motions of a person in a straight jacket tied to a tree are simple: there's not much to them. No one is more torn and fragmented by the manifold demands of life than the poor; they just can't do much about them. If Adam Smith had been stuck for life in the position of "the beggar who suns himself by the side of the highway," he would have been able to appreciate just how little the beggar possessed "that security which kings are fighting for." And anyone who has had to deal with the needs of food, housing, health, transportation, and education from the position of *real* poverty knows how bafflingly complex it is. Merely getting a sick baby to a doctor, for example, or obtaining a few days supply of food can easily occupy most of a day or more. One of the few luxuries enjoyed by people of all ranks in life is speculating how much better life is for those in *other* positions.

Simplicity as a spiritual attainment, on the other hand, is—like poverty under Bonhoeffer's description given above—a matter of an inward order. The person who has grown to the place where he or she can truly say with Paul, "This one thing I do" (Phil. 3:13), or who truly "seeks first the kingdom of God and His righteousness" (Matt. 6:33), is a person who has entered into simplicity. They easily put all demands that come to them in "their place" and deal harmoniously, peacefully, and confidently with complexities of life that seem incomprehensible to others, for they know what they are doing.

In the spiritual life, simplicity is not opposed to complexity, and poverty is not opposed to possessions. In fact, as simplicity makes great complexity bearable, so poverty as Bonhoeffer explains it— freedom from desire—makes possessions safe and fruitful for the glory of God.

JESUS' TEACHING

But did not Jesus himself say that the rich are cursed or "woeful" while the poor are blessed? Certainly he did, and in so doing he gave one of the most important applications of his often repeated principle that the first (in human judgment) shall be last (in God's view) and the last (in human judgment) shall be first (in God's).

But what this means can be understood only if we understand the *manner* in which he taught, which is the same for all teachers who have any real power to guide life. Jesus' teaching does not lay out safe generalizations by which we can engineer a happy life. Instead, it is designed to startle us out of our prejudices and direct us into a new way of thinking and acting. It's designed to open us up to experience the reign of God right where we are, initiating an unpredictable process of personal growth in vivid fellowship with him.

In Luke 14 we find him present at a Sabbath dinner. There are the guests jockeying for the "best seats" at the table, ones where their honor would be appropriately secured. So Jesus takes the occasion to advise them on how to succeed with their little project. He tells them to take the *worst* seat they can find, the one near the doorpost, way out in the kitchen, or at the card table set up in the farthest corner of the house. Then when the host arrives he will see you there and exclaim: "What in the world are *you* doing down there! Here. You come right up here and sit by me. Everybody move over and make room so that my dear friend can sit close to me while we talk."

Surely Jesus must have smiled a bit as he concluded: "Then you will be honored in the presence of your fellow guests. For everyone who exalts himself will be humbled, and he who humbles himself will be exalted" (Luke 14:10–11 NIV).

And then he turned on his host—no longer smiling perhaps, or only very slightly—and told him never to invite his friends or brothers or relatives or rich neighbors to dinner. (This of course was what he had just done for this dinner.) Rather, he should ask the poor, the maimed, the lame and the blind to eat with him.

Think about this situation. If you read this scripture without understanding the *manner* of Christ's teaching you would take his words as *Laws*. It *says* you are never to invite your mother to a dinner at your house, doesn't it? If you take any but the worst seat at the table where you are invited you would be disobedient to him. And you would abase yourself every chance you got so that you would ultimately be exalted.

And yet we know that none of this will do. The words of Jesus in this passage typify his manner of teaching. In all cases where he touches upon specific actions and conditions of life, his purpose is not to give generalizations or laws on how *always* to behave. Instead, he refutes false generalizations that are observed as law in the practice of those to whom he speaks. Once we understand this we see that he is not forbidding us to have mother to dinner, nor is he providing us with a sure-fire way to succeed in self-exhaltation.

The false generalizations Jesus is pointing out are embarrassingly obvious in the circumstances of Luke 14. The first is: always take the place at table that makes you appear most favorably in the prevailing pecking order. The second is: only invite those to dinner who can in some way recompense you. Make commerce of hospitality. Jesus here challenges us to step beyond these "futile ways inherited from your fathers" (1 Pet. 1:18) to see how we might be met by God, who certainly is not running *his* affairs by such silly rules.

BLESSED POOR: CURSED RICH?

The same manner of teaching is employed by Jesus throughout the Gospels and in his "blesseds" and "curseds" of Luke 6 and Matthew 5.

"Blessed are the poor." Can you *really* imagine that poverty is enough to secure blessedness? Think of all the kinds of people who are poor. Think of the person in extreme poverty who hates and fears the idol to whom he sacrifices his children. He lives in the most brutal and degrading of relations to his family and neighbors. And is he yet blessed? Because he is poor, does *he* have the Kingdom of God? Jesus taught *that*? Again, we certainly know he did not!

And "Woe unto you that are rich." A woman with some wealth worships and devotes herself to Jesus Christ in the most thorough and enlightened way and through him loves God with all her being. She is conscious of her wealth as a gift from God for which she must exercise stewardship, and makes every effort to bless her neighbors with it. Is she really cursed?

Such a one was Mrs. Katharina Bovey, memorialized on the wall of Westminister Abbey in these words:

It pleased God to bless her with a considerable estate, which, with a liberal hand guided by wisdom and piety, she employed to His glory and the good of her neighbors. Her domestic expenses were managed with a decency and dignity suitable to her fortune; but with a frugality that made her income abound to all proper objects of charity, to the relief of the necessitous, the encouragement of the industrious and the instruction of the ignorant. She distributed not only with cheerfulness but with joy, which upon some occasions of raising or refreshing the spirit of the afflicted, she could not refrain from breaking forth into tears flowing from a heart thoroughly affected with compassion and benevolence.

But this lady has only woe, and not blessing, for she is rich. Right? As Professor MacIntyre and Father Cardenal see it, the New Testament teaching sends her to hell. But had she happened to be poor, on the other hand, no matter what her faith and character, her blessing would have been secured.

If one had purposely set out to make the teachings of Jesus appear foolish, it would be hard to find a better means than this interpretation of his teachings. Though advanced by those who claim the highest intellectual qualifications and moral concerns, what we have here is actually the same legalism as is found in those who believe Jesus sends you to hell for wearing lipstick and bright clothing, for "social" drinking, or for not speaking (or *for* speaking) in tongues. It is crucial to see this, and not allow it to disappear into elevated discussions about socioeconomic conditions, class struggles, and imperialism—which in their own right are, of course, separate matters of utmost seriousness and spiritual consequence.

In the Beatitudes and the "woefuls," then, Jesus refutes, from the vantage point of the Kingdom, human generalizations about who is *certainly* unblessable and who *certainly* "has it made."[9] The Beatitudes are not a list one must be on in order to be blessed, nor is the blessing they announce caused by the condition specified in those said to be blessed. Poverty, for example, whether in spirit or in pocketbook, is not the cause or reason for blessedness—entry into the Kingdom of God is the reason, as The Teacher explicitly stated. In these teachings Jesus lays his axe to the root of the off-center human value system and proclaims *irrelevant* those factors the world uses in deciding who is or is not well off.

KINGDOM VIEW OF WELL-BEING

To see riches and poverty for what they are we must stand firmly within the Kingdom view of well-being. The essential point can be put into one shocking statement: *under the rule of God, the rich and the poor have no necessary advantage over each other with regard to well-being or well-doing in this life or the next.*

St. Antony left us these beautiful words:

Some of those who stop in inns are given beds, while others having no beds stretch themselves on the floor and sleep as soundly as those in beds. In the morning, when night is over, all alike get up and leave the inn, carrying away with them only their own belongings. It is the same with those who tread the path of this life: both those who have lived in modest circumstances, and those who had wealth and fame, leave this life like an inn, taking with them no worldly comforts or riches, but only what they have done in this life, whether it be good or bad.[10]

RESPECT AND HONOR TO THE POOR

Only if we believe with our whole being in the equality of rich and poor before God can we walk in their midst as Jesus did, unaffected in our personal relations by the distinction. If we don't, our inability to treat our rich and our poor neighbors alike leaves us guilty and confused about our responsibilities to them. The New Testament teaching is that we are to honor *all* people (1 Pet. 2:17). Hence we are to honor the poor. We are to respect them and to show our respect in all the natural ways. We are to do no less and no more to the rich.

The distinction between rich and poor is permanently affixed to human life. However much our modern ideologies may deny it, that distinction is the natural and inevitable consequence of differentiations within people's histories and family contexts and in genetic endowment. That is an arrangement instituted by God, which explains why Scripture never suggests that poverty is to be abolished. It is not even clear what it would mean for every individual to have the same economic power, as it *is* clear what it would mean for everyone to be decently fed, clothed, and housed. One can at least *imagine* the later, but not the former. No political devices can change the simple reality of this distinction. But much can and must be done in all dimensions of life to eliminate the harmful *effects* of the rich/poor distinction in a fallen world, such as freeing those with ethnic and cultural differences from socially enforced economic deprivation.

While the biblical teachings do not speak of eliminating poverty; they *always* insist that the needy are to be cared for, that the poor are not to be taken advantage of but defended and given opportunity, and that they are to be taken into consideration in all aspects of life. In the Old Testament manifold provisions for the poor are made and repeatedly emphasized. The New Testament goes so far as to state that pure and undefiled religion essentially involves our "looking after orphans and widows in their distress" (James 1:27), they being the poorest of the poor under usual circumstances.

The overarching biblical command is to love, and the first act of love is always the giving of attention. Therefore the poor are not to be avoided, forgotten, or allowed to become invisible. We are to *see* them as God's creatures, of equal significance with anyone else in the divine purpose. "The rich and poor have this in common: The Lord is the Maker of them all" (Prov. 22:2).

The apostle Paul tells us: "Do not be proud, but be willing to associate with people of low position. Do not be conceited" (Rom. 12:16). Jesus Christ "did not consider equality with God something to cling to, but made Himself nothing, taking the very nature of a servant" (Phil. 2:6–7). The vision of Kingdom blessedness and righteousness both directs and enables Christians to imitate Jesus' actions in every phase of their lives. Such a vision permits Jesus' mind to be in them (Phil. 2:5) through their association with people of all conditions.

When our attitude is saturated with that vision and with Christ's model, any advantages we may have within the world's set of values do not mislead us or affect the quality of our human associations. Because of our vision of faith we are comfortable with the poor and the other "unblessables" and are able to be with them in a spirit and manner that does not set them off from us. The same is true for the rich. We share the human condition gladly and without affectation, as did our Savior, whose spirit has pervaded us.

By contrast, those without the mind of Christ make a use of distinctions between people the mature disciple would never make. They cannot respect the poor within their value system. Even their special efforts, no matter how "charitable," emphasize their lack of solidarity with the poor. They are of course trying "to be big about it." But disciples, whose very life is a gift of incarnation, really see nothing special in their actions toward the unblessables. They are not "being big about it" *because they truly see nothing to be big about* in the situation. The left hand simply does not know what the right hand is doing (Matt. 6:3).

NEW EYES THROUGH THE CROSS

Our problem is not primarily with how we see the poor, but with how we see ourselves. If we still think and convey by our behavior that in some way we are fundamentally different and better as persons from the man sleeping in the discarded boxes in the alley, we have not been brought with clear eyes to the foot of the cross, seeing our own neediness in the light of it. We have not looked closely at the lengths to which God had to go to reach *us*. We have not learned to live always and thankfully in the cross's shadow. From that vantage point alone is our solidarity with the destitute to be realized.

How do we respond to that man sleeping in those discarded boxes? Does it take great and awkward effort even to acknowledge his presence, or to speak to him if need be, or to take his hand or help him with his few possessions? Are we frightened of him though the circumstances are perfectly safe? Do we shrink from being seen near him or dealing with him? Is his smell and dirtiness alone enough to repel us from him? Or, how about others not in such extreme condition? Does the fact that a person is without work or an apartment or an automobile make us treat him or her as if he or she were "different"? If so, then we have not truly beheld our own ruined condition, and because of this we *cannot* heartily love that person.

RICH OVER POOR IN THE CHURCH?

James addresses a case all too familiar to us today. "A man comes into your meeting wearing a gold ring and fine clothes, and a poor man in shabby clothes also comes in" (2:2, RSV). The rich man receives much attention and is given a good seat, while the poor man is hustled off to stand in a corner or to sit on the floor. In such cases, James says, we insult the poor, whom God has chosen to be rich in faith (2:5), and fail to care for our neighbor *as we would be cared for*. We fail to keep the "royal law" of neighbor love and therefore are lawbreakers on a level with murderers or adulterers (2:8–11).

What an indictment! And yet one hardly ever finds a church or a Christian free from knee-jerk favoritism toward those who are impressive in the world's scale of values. And it is heartbreaking to behold. The most biblical of churches are permeated with favoritism toward the rich and comfortable, the beautiful and famous—or at least toward "our kind of people."

Yet, many will insist, this is necessary for the advancement of the cause of Christ. We cannot sustain our programs, we are told, unless we can attract and hold the right kinds of people. These people seem to have forgotten that the church's business is to *make* the right kind of people out of the wrong kind. More often than not the wrong kind in God's eyes are precisely the "right" kind by the world's standards—or are even "our kind."

ASSOCIATING WITH THE POOR AND NEEDY

So, the main cause of uneasiness in the hearts of many well-provided Christians today is that inadequate vision of the Kingdom of God that prevails in Christian circles and that produces an anemic faith. But once, through adequate preaching and teaching, we vividly understand our relationship with the poor we will find there is much to be done and our anemic faith gets a healthy transfusion. Opportunities to serve people of impoverished and weakened conditions will come to us every day. The cup of cold water we'll have always ready, for our vision of Kingdom realities will make us much more sensitive to occasions to help and give. It may also lead us to make a point of discovering need, rather than always waiting for it to be thrust upon us.

And all of this activity will be natural, never gaudy. When we remember that we are, overall, as needy as those we serve and that to receive is not as blessed as to give, our deeds of giving will naturally be low-keyed and unassuming. Perhaps we will find ways in which we can meet needs without anyone knowing the source, as Matthew 6:4 says, "so that our giving may be in secret."

One way to gain such understanding is to experience the life of the poor in some further measure—though we must never give in to the temptation to act as if we are poor when we are not. No adequate elaboration of practical strategies can be undertaken here. But, depending upon our family and other circumstances, we might, as suggested earlier, do some of our ordinary business in the poorer districts of our community. It may even be as simple as getting out of our cars and onto public transportation. One of the great social and economic divisions in many parts of the world is between those who must ride public transportation and those who can transport themselves.

We must take care not to *force* such things upon our dependents, but shopping, banking, even living in the poorer districts of our area will do much to lend substance to our grasp of how the economically deprived experience their world—and ours. This will add a great substance to our understanding, prayers, and caring that can never be gained by an occasional "charity run" or by sending money to organizations that work with the poor.

Remember, Jesus did not *send* help. He came among us. He was victorious under *our* conditions of existence. That makes all the difference. We continue on his incarnational model when we follow the apostle's command "to associate with people of low position" by unassumingly walking with them in the path of their daily affairs, not just on special occasions created because of their need.

NO DIVISION BETWEEN SACRED AND SECULAR

From within this Kingdom perspective on human worth and well-being emerges a solution to the major social problems of wealth and poverty. That solution consists in a new type of human being, people who have assimilated the character of Christ into all areas of life and society. These people clearly see that giving is only a part and by no means the largest part of stewardship before our Lord. These people understand it is part of their responsibility to control the world's possessions in a way that ministers to all. The poor are much more to be benefited by the godly controlling the goods of this world than by their performing a pious handwashing that only abandons those goods to the servants of "mammon." We are not speaking of political power as normally understood, but of personal vocation fulfilled in the power of God. Possession and direction of the forces of wealth are as legitimate an expression of the redemptive rule of God in human life as is Bible teaching or a prayer meeting. For example, it is as great and as difficult a *spiritual* calling to run the factories and the mines, the banks and the department stores, the schools and government agencies for the Kingdom of God as it is to pastor a church or serve as an evangelist.

There truly is no division between sacred and secular except what we have created. And that is why the division of the legitimate roles and functions of human life into the sacred and the secular does incalculable damage to our individual lives and to the cause of Christ. Holy people must stop going into "church work" as their natural course of action and take up holy orders in farming, industry, law, education, banking, and journalism with the same zeal previously given to evangelism or to pastoral and missionary work.

Long ago William Law, accordingly, characterized the devout person in this way:

He, therefore, is the devout man, who lives no longer to his own will, or the way and spirit of the world, but to the sole will of God; who considers God in everything, who serves God in everything, who makes all the parts of his common life parts of piety, by doing everything in the Name of God, and under such rules as are conformable to His glory. [11]

The organized churches must become schools of spiritual discipline where Christians are taught how to own without treasuring (Matt. 6:21); how to possess without, like the "rich young ruler", being possessed (Mark 10:22); how to live simply, even frugally, though controlling great wealth and power.

We continue to be misled by the world's view of well-being, which holds riches to *be* well-being, and that is why we react by thinking of possessions as inherently and essentially evil, instead of as a domain of spiritual work of the purest sort. So, obviously, we fail to develop adequate teaching and examples for those who do prosper. We can only lamely suggest that maybe they ought *not* to prosper when we should be showing those who do, those to whom much has been given, how to serve God and humankind through their prospering.

POSSESSIONS AS EXTENSIONS OF THE BODY

Actually, the attempt to associate material goods with evil is an extension of the spirit of *Antichrist,* which denies that Christ has come *in the flesh* (1 John 4:3). But the *"redemption"* of material goods is absolutely necessary, for they are active realities in the created world. And their redemption is to be carried out by our possessing them in submission to God, as the redemption of the body is to be carried out by submitting the bodily members to righteousness.

Possessions, then, are an extension of the body and of the self, for through them our will and character extend their range, just as they do through our tongue, our arms, and our legs. Our possessions increase the range within which we can reign in life by Christ Jesus and see spiritual power defeat the deadly reign of sin. To write them off from redemption is but another aspect of that Docetism, earlier noted, that wrote the body itself off.

As the tendency to sin in the body is not its natural or necessary condition, so it is with wealth. Wealth is but a part of created reality, pronounced by God as good. But like the body before redemption the wealth of this fallen world usually tends toward evil. This "normal" tendency can and must be removed through possession and purification by us, its owners, who live to see it submitted to God. We must recognize nothing but radical faithlessness and irresponsibility in the pious-sounding talk about the holiness of poverty and the evil—or holiness—of riches as such. Riches are not holy, riches are not evil. They are creations we are to use for God.

PROSPERITY'S NEED FOR GRACE

But attitude is all. When we prosper, we need guidance and grace more than ever. The apostle Paul understood the necessity of disciplined grace for prosperity. The usual Christian quotes his words, "I can do everything through him who gives me strength" (Phil. 4:13, NIV), only when facing deprivation and hard times. But that was not Paul's meaning. In the previous verses he said: "I have learned to be content whatever the circumstances. I know what it is to be in need, and I know what it is to have plenty. I have learned the secret of being content in any and every situation." Thus, when he adds that Christ gives him strength for everything, he is also saying that Christ enables him also to prosper.

He succeeds in abundance because of his relation to Christ just as much as he succeeded by grace in his times of need. Few people understand that they need help to prosper, for they have not yet cleared their hearts and minds of the world's perspective on well-being. Once again, our teaching and pastoral ministry are tragically defective on this point. I have never heard anyone exclaim, upon coming into great wealth, "I can do all things through Christ who strengtheneth me!"

But this is one of the most serious omissions that can be made in the spiritual life and shows how unwise we are. Once we understand this, we see why "the prosperity of fools destroys them" (Prov. 1:32). We see why the gospel is for the up-and-in as well as the down-and-out, equally so and equally essential. How do we keep from making this prevalent mistake? We can be protected from error on this point only by an unprejudiced, full, and constant presentation of the nature of Christ's Kingdom and a full use of the disciplines for the spiritual life as we described earlier. We need disciplined grace.

WESLEY'S FORMULA REVISED

Ironically, for all of his method-ism, John Wesley remained a child of the Reformation, like his contemporary David Hume. The possibilities of disciplined grace remained hidden to him, and he was unable to understand a Christian asceticism that could produce a people able to hold possessions and power without being corrupted by them.

Of course *giving* must have a great place in the life of Christ's disciple, no matter what else. But it cannot take the place of keeping, using, and controlling possessions as responsible stewards of God's creation for our individual time in his world. Here is where Wesley erred, failing to appreciate the aspects of stewardship other than charity. His famous formula, "Get all you can; save all you can; give all you can," must be supplemented. It should read: *get* all you can; *save* all you can; freely *use* all you can within a properly disciplined spiritual life; and *control* all you can for the good of humankind and God's glory. *Giving* all you can would then naturally be a part of an overall wise stewardship.

"ALL NATIONS SHALL COME TO YOUR LIGHT"

Because the issues surrounding poverty and wealth in the spiritual life are so complex and confusing, so easily misunderstood, and yet of such overwhelming importance, we conclude this chapter with a restatement of some main points.

Poverty as utter destitution is not, in general, a discipline for the spiritual life or a condition of spiritual superiority in any respect. It may be a condition of life into which we are placed, as many are. If so, we will be neither disadvantaged nor advantaged in knowing God's care for us or in our standing before him, *so long as* we steadfastly seek first his rule over us and the kind of righteousness characteristic of him (Matt. 6:33). When we step outside his rule, of course, the worldly perspective takes over. The poor and the powerless are indeed beyond blessing if the world's vision and its scale of values is correct. No doubt destitution has upon occasion had the good side-effect of driving people to God as a refuge, but that doesn't prove that it's an especially desirable or necessary way of coming to God.

Sometimes poverty is idealized within various cultural traditions, but that poverty is not destitution; it is nonpossession coupled with security of provision for basic needs. This type of poverty may be useful as a discipline for the spiritual life, if undertaken in a right faith. It is not, however, a condition especially virtuous in itself, because possession is not an evil in itself. Nor does it automatically guarantee freedom from inner servitude to wealth. It is also not a superior spiritual condition in general. There is nothing especially holy about not possessing material goods, even though that life-style may be appropriate for given individuals.

Finally, and very importantly for the life of disciplined grace, such nonpossession is not a condition well suited to making provision for others who are destitute. In fact, to make it *the* especially holy calling is to destroy all possibility of Christ's people guiding the world for the best of all people, which requires that the godly substantially own and otherwise control the wealth of the earth.

The role of Christian ministry or the special "religious" vocations is to embody and communicate the gospel of God's government to all and to prepare those who can stand in the crucial "secular" areas of the world to be religious caretakers of the world's goods. If taught well, such Christians within important secular environments will then be on the job *to see to it* that what needs to be done with the goods of this world is done as it needs to be done.

The church certainly is to lead the way in charitable works, and after that is to exhort and advise all public agencies concerning policies of general welfare. But this is not to be the fundamental aspect of its service to the world. Its fundamental work is to show those who gather in its meetings how to enter into full participation in the rule of God where they are. In this way the church will ultimately bring all nations to itself to find out how humanity can realize the universal ethical vision of righteousness and well-being. Through vision and discipline taught and practiced, our Christian ministers and teachers should shape a people who can form the foundation and framework of a world that is the unique dwelling place of The Immortal God.

NOTES

1. Adam Smith, in D. D. Raphael, ed., *British Moralists 1650–1800*, vol. 2, (Oxford: Clarendon, 1969), 245.
2. Alastair MacIntyre, *After Virtue: A Study In Moral Theory*, 2d ed. (Notre Dame, IN: University of Notre Dame Press, 1984), 182.
3. Ernesto Cardenal, interview in the *Los Angeles Times*, December 11, 1983, part 4, p. 2.
4. John Wesley, *Sermons on Several Occasions*, 2 vol. (New York: Waugh and Mason, 1836), II: 441. The problem of what to do with the abundance generated by Protestant piety did not first arise with the Methodists, but in the Genevan church of John Calvin. See O. Hardman, *The Ideals of Asceticism: An Essay in the Comparative Study of Religion* (New York: Macmillan, 1924), 209ff.
5. Wesley, *Sermons on Several Occasions, II: 441*.
6. Dietrich Bonhoeffer, *Letters and Papers from Prison* (London: Fontana, 1953), 81. This is, essentially, Eckhart's teaching on poverty as a spiritual attainment. See his sermon, "Blessed Are The Poor," in *Meister Eckhart*, trans. Raymond B. Blakney (New York: Harper, 1941), especially 227–28.
7. Kenneth Clark, *Civilization: A Personal View* (New York: Harper & Row, 1969), 78f.
8. Francis de Sales, *Introduction to the Devout Life*, trans. John K. Ryan (Garden City, NY: Double day, Image Books, 1957), 163.
9. See the interesting formulation of the *world's* "beatitudes" in J. B. Phillips, *When God Was Man* (New York: Abingdon, 1955), 26–27.
10. St. Antony, in E. Kadloubovsky and G. E. H. Palmer, eds., *Early Fathers from the Philokalia* (London: Faber and Faber, 1963), 30.
11. William Law, *A Serious Call to a Devout and Holy Life*, many editions, opening words.

11. The Disciplines and the Power Structures of This World

Men are so accustomed to establish and defend their existence by violence, by bayonets, bullets, prisons, and gallows, that it seems to them as if such an arrangement of life were not only normal, but were the only one possible. Yet it is just this arrangement and maintenance of the commonwealth by violence, that does most to hinder people from comprehending the causes of their sufferings, and consequently from being able to establish a true order.

LEO TOLSTOY

The barbarians are not waiting beyond the frontiers; they have already been governing us for quite some time. And it is our lack of consciousness of this that constitutes part of our predicament. We are waiting not for a Godot, but for another—doubtless very different—St. Benedict.

ALASTAIR MACINTYRE

For to us a child is born, to us a son is given, and the government will be on his shoulders. And he will be called Wonderful Counselor, Mighty God, Everlasting Father, Prince of Peace. Of the increase of his government and peace there will be no end.

ISAIAH 9:6-7, NIV

Today we represent ourselves through our public media, our arts, our education, and our political life as a people of great practicality. This tendency extends to our church life also, where the laying out of clear organizational objectives and the efficient marshalling of means is frequently regarded as the key to successful ministry. While the exaltation of the practical is especially characteristic of American culture, it has now spread around the world, as the idealization of political revolution and of technological development sweeps everything before it. This modern outlook sharply criticizes The Way of Christ as impractical in relation to the ideals of justice, peace, and prosperity.

That criticism is largely justified when applied to the form usually taken by Christian faith throughout our history. More often than not, faith has failed, sadly enough, to transform the human character of the masses, because it is usually unaccompanied by discipleship and by an overall discipline of life such as Christ himself practiced. As a result, when faced with the real issues of justice, peace, and prosperity, what is called faith in Christ has often proved of little help other than the comfort of a personal hope for what lies beyond this life.

Surely Jesus did not have only this scant comfort in mind when he promised all necessary provision would be supplied to those who above all seek God's rule and righteousness in their lives, as he says in Matthew 6:33. He understood instead that in this quest alone lay the true practicality, the only effective path to justice, peace, and prosperity.

What is "practicality"? An action or a practice can be appraised as "practical" or "impractical" only in the light of the goals and purposes to be realized. The secular world thinks of justice, peace, and prosperity in negative terms. Justice means that no one's rights are infringed. Peace means no war or turmoil. Prosperity means no one is in material need. The strategy in relation to these negative goals is naturally one of *avoidance.* Steps are taken to prevent injury, war, and want, steps that often have some good effect. But they are ultimately and disasterously ineffective, as the record of history shows.

The worldy system of understanding tries to produce justice, peace, and prosperity directly in people's lives by placing restraints upon what would harm them. But the effort, besides being ineffective, also proves impractical. The gospel of Christ, by contrast, comes to create a new person pervaded by the positive realities of faith, hope, and love—toward God primarily and therefore toward all men and women and creatures. From this positive transformation of the self, justice, peace, and prosperity can result as God's rule is fulfilled in human life.

We shouldn't disparage practicality. It is of the essence of spirituality as well as of intelligence, faith, and love. But nothing is really practical in relation to human aspirations for the world if it does not proceed from deep insight into the realities of the human heart and does not call into question the fundamental forces that move human life and history. And that lack of insight is starkly and constantly revealed by our tendency to ask "Why?" when faced by the evils people do.

"THE EVIL THAT MEN DO"

In the southern California community of Wilmington there is an area described in news reports as a "1950s prototype of the close-knit all-American neighborhood." Some families have lived there for twenty or thirty years, and now overlap through children who have grown up together and intermarried. On the evening of January 14, 1983, the community gathered to celebrate a baptism. Shortly after midnight the party was attacked with guns and knives by members of a street gang from south Los Angeles, a few miles away. Within seconds dead and dying young men were scattered across the streets, sidewalks, and lawns. Wounded men, women, and children writhed in agony, their bodies and lives irreparably damaged. Some time later a young woman from the community looked back on this horror-filled scene in bewilderment: "Why? That's what everybody wants to know. Why did something like this happen?"[1]

A widely known teacher and author in the field of education, Herbert Kohl, describes the response of his children to the massacre of Palestinian refugees in Bierut. They were unable to understand how *Jewish* soldiers could let this happen, how it was possible that the people who had experienced the horrors of the ghettos and the concentration camps could have *anything* to do with the slaughter of helpless Palestinians. He found it impossible to answer their questions to his own satisfaction and commented: "I don't understand how people who are probably loving parents and loyal friends turn themselves into murderers. . . . Christians and Jews and Arabs were involved in the negation of love and the debasement of justice in Lebanon. The best I can say is that some kinds of ideological obsessions drive people to treat others as not human."[2]

BUT WHY SHOULD WE ASK "WHY"?

It may be the mere *immensity* of human evil that makes us ask "Why?" when we are forced to look at some part of it. The destruction and brutalization of the weaker by the stronger goes on at so many levels of social structure and has so many dimensions that its magnitude and complexity alone are enough to stun the mind.

Six hundred thousand people starve to death in the Nazi siege of Leningrad during World War II. Untold millions die as Estonia, China, or Cambodia undergo forced collectivization. A bomb falls on Hiroshima and multitudes of people are melted outright or turned into slowly dying monstrosities. In the United States of America fifty thousand little children disappear every year, most never to be heard from again, perhaps to be sexually abused and killed or enslaved. We now have six hundred thousand young men and women under the age of sixteen who earn their living as prostitutes. In the United States a black market for children is reported to exist where a white male child has a going price of $30,000, with other types going for less. Battering and abuse within families passes itself on from generation to generation, seeming to grow more widespread as the social structure grows more and more fragmented and inhumane and as the victims of victims of abuse find less and less in their surroundings to sustain and redirect them.

These facts were gathered without special research, merely by attending to generally reliable sources of public information for a few weeks. The evils done by people to people are constantly before us. We not only know about them, but they are an object of constant personal concern. We know that *we* are never wholly secure from them. And yet we ask "Why?"

But *why* do we ask "Why?" What is it about our lives that always leaves us astonished and wondering at the evils people do? Indeed, at the evils *we* do? What makes us expect any better, given a track record like the one just cited? There is something very deep here to be explored, for it is closely tied to our cowlike confidence in banal decency and to our corresponding failure to take appropriately strong measures against evil as it rests in our own personalities and in our world.

DENIAL OF THE DEPTHS OF EVIL

No doubt a good deal of our surprise at evil comes from the well-known psychological mechanism of denial. The mind preserves its own ability to stay on balance and carry on by denying, refusing to look at or be conscious of, things awful enough to paralyze us. The full horror of actual human behavior is like the face of the Medusa in Greek mythology. We sense that if we look squarely at it we will be turned to stone.

And then we are aided in our denial by the fact that on most occasions most people do treat others well. They are considerate and helpful or at least not destructive in the fashion of the situations mentioned above. For this we must give thanks, since otherwise life would not be possible. Whatever the condition of their hearts, the overt behavior of our companions and neighbors is characteristically mild and inoffensive, and often compassionate and loving.

Moreover we recognize that, when coolly considered, the evils that emerge in the heat of human events are not things that any normal person thinks to be inherently good or would wish on others. At most, they will only be admitted as "necessary" evils or as something to be explained by extenuating circumstances of some kind. We ask "Why?" in the face of the undeniably monstrous cases of evil because we cannot imagine any necessity or extenuating circumstance in these cases.

But such explanations do not go to the heart of the matter. The persistence of evil rests upon the general drift of human life in which we all share. It rides upon a motion so vast, so pervasive and ponderous that, like the motion of the planet earth, it is almost impossible to detect. We delude ourselves about the sustaining conditions of people's evil deeds *because we wish to continue living as we now live and continue being the kinds of people we are.* We do not want to change. We do not want our world to be really different. We just want to escape the *consequences* of its being what it truly is and of our being who we truly are.

We certainly think it would be wonderful if we and all others would try to make a difference—to do what we should—and we often say so. But we do not want to bother with becoming the sort of people who actually, naturally do that. In fact, to look at our media—our novels, our movies, our television—sometimes it seems we may think being such a person might be rather dull and unexciting. Imagine a television series called "Miami Virtue" instead of "Miami Vice." We are drawn to evil, excited by it. Yet, interestingly enough, we seem surprised when it becomes reality.

READINESS TO DO EVIL

Our "Why?" in the face of evil, then, signals a lack of insight—willing or unwilling—into the forces that inhabit the normal human personality and thereby move or condition the usual course of human events. Above all, it shows a failure to understand that the immediate support of the evils universally deplored lies in the simple *readiness* of "decent" individuals to harm others or allow harm to come to others when the conditions are "right." That readiness comes into play whenever it will help us realize our goals of security, ego gratification, or satisfaction of bodily desires. This systematic readiness that pervades the personality of normal, decent human beings is fallen human nature. To understand this is the first level of understanding the "why" of the evil people do.

This ever-present *readiness* fills common humanity and lies about us like a highly flammable material ready to explode at the slightest provocation. Here is a main part of that deeper level of reality into which the prophetic vision reaches as it reads the times. Isaiah's exquisitely penetrating analysis of his society was: "The man of high estate will be tinder, his handiwork a spark. Both will burn together and no one put them out" (1:31, JB). Paul sees the unregenerate as a "vessel of wrath" (Rom. 9:22) and as "children of wrath" (Eph. 2:8). Human wrath is an explosive, unrestrained impulse to hurt or harm. And it is a fact of life, especially associated with that very wantonness and chaos that so impresses us in the more shocking monstrosities that occur. It is a brother of revenge and almost always supports itself upon the self-righteousness of having been wronged. Thus it can "justifiably" cast off all restraint.

REAPING THE WHIRLWIND

Much of the wisdom and analysis in the book of Proverbs is directed toward wrath, a fundamental and very complex form of evil. "A fool's wrath is quickly known" (12:16), but "He that is slow to wrath is of great understanding" (14:29). Fear and wrath mingle to form the automatic, overt response of the "normal, decent human being" to any person or event that threatens his or her security, status, or satisfaction. Once this response floods in, all of the other tendencies to evil in the human organism begin ticking away, sure to take their course if not somehow deactivated or repressed. That, however, normally does not happen until damage is done, setting off new cyles of wrath and reaction. As we so correctly say, "All hell breaks loose." It is to forestall this that we are advised to be swift to hear, *slow* to speak, and *slow* to wrath (James 1:19–20). Once the word with its load of wrath is unleashed, the larger processes of evil are set in motion. The little detonator sets off the bullet or the bomb. We have then sown the wind and will reap the whirlwind (Hos. 8:7).

The level of this deadly "readiness" to do evil in all of its forms is variable from individual to individual, but it is very high in almost everyone. It is no mere abstract possibility but a genuine *tendency*, constantly at work. It does not take much to get most people to lie, for example, or to take what does not belong to them, and shamefully little to get them to think of how nice it would be if certain others were dead. Thus, if in our lives we are not protected by a hearty confidence in God's never failing and effective care for us, these "readinesses" for various kinds of wrongdoing will be constantly provoked into action by threatening circumstances. And when we act, others around us will, of course, react. And then we will react to them, and so forth, until we and others are stunned into quiescence by the spiraling disasters.

We can daily observe these downward spirals at all levels of life from international relations to the individual locked into his or her little personalized cell of wrongdoing and suffering. Only the common grace of God toward us and the presence in the world of the Holy Spirit and the institutionalized church prevents our daily lives, resting upon the edge of the volcano of readiness, from being unbearably worse.

Once we see what people are prepared to do, the wonder ceases to be that they occasionally do gross evils and becomes that they do not do them more often. We become deeply thankful that something is restraining us, keeping us from fully doing what lies in our hearts.

THE LONGING TO CHANGE: *METANOIA*

We, then, must change from within. And that is what most of us truly want. The repentance in which we pine for our life and world to *really* be different, the authentic *metanoia* which Christ opens us to in his gospel (Mark 1:15, 6:12), comes upon us as we are given a vision of the majesty, holiness, and goodness of God. It's a vision sufficient to impart a vivid realization of our terrible readiness to mistrust God and hurt others and ourselves as we take things into our own hands. This sharp, heartbreaking realization of *our condition* silences all argument and hair-splitting rationalization. It makes us simultaneously recoil from God, because we realize that he also sees us for what we are, and yet we reach out for help and refuge in him.

Simon Peter was an experienced fisherman, and he knew his business well. After using Peter's ship as a pulpit one morning, Jesus wished to pay a little rent and so advised him to "launch out into the deep, and let down your nets for a catch" (Luke 5:4). Peter replied that the fish weren't running, that they had been out all night, thank you just the same, and had caught nothing. But, with a weary "If you say so," he piled the nets back into the boat and shoved off. The nets fanned out and sank down, enclosing such a mass of fishes that here and there the nets ripped apart. The men frantically signaled their partners in another ship to come and help, and soon *both* ships were so full with fish that they were about to sink.

At some point a certain realization began to grip Peter's mind. *Whose* suggestion was this that he had treated so casually? He was literally "floored," falling to his knees at Jesus' feet, saying: "Oh, sir, please leave us—I'm too much of a sinner for you to have around" (5:8, LB). Peter was overwhelmed by the "otherness" of Jesus. Holiness is, fundamentally, *otherness* or separateness from the ordinary realm of human existence in which we believe we know what we are doing and what is going on. It is the idea of "something else," in current terminology. Peter was saying, "Lord you are something else altogether from me! How can you stand to be around me?" This "something else" presented in Jesus and his gospel makes it starkly clear that we are something dreadfully less. It is the burning sense of this that both breaks our pride and confidence and makes us long to be a disciple.

When Isaiah "saw also the Lord" filling the temple with majesty, and attendant seraphim crying out the holiness and glory of God (6:1–3), he saw himself at the same time as utterly *undone* and *cut off*: "I am a man of unclean lips and I dwell in the midst of a people of unclean lips: for mine eyes have seen the King, the Lord of Hosts." The prophet was brought by his vision into touch with "the exceeding sinfulness of sin" (Rom. 7:13) and with the deplorable condition of his *lips,* the main thoroughfare of evil in human life. He was even prepared for his lips to be burned with fire from the altar because of their sickening condition (6:7). That God is also gracious and that we are saved by grace was irrelevant to this point. Isaiah fully grasped why human life is as it is, for over against what God is he saw himself as he was. And he burned to be "other." People who have undergone such repentance can readily understand the readiness of evil in us all.

THE TROUBLED SEA

What individuals are ready to do, what sits in them ready to burst forth, goes far to explain why people do the gastly things they do. They are *set* to do them. There is a "real presence" of evil scarcely beneath the surface of every human action and transaction. But this still does not go far enough. The magnitude of evil in human deeds is also a result of the institutional structures or common practices that emerge at the social level in politics, art, business, journalism, education, the intellectual life, government service, sexual and family relations, and sports and entertainment.

This is our "sytem." A woman who earns half a million dollars per year on Wall Street is "more acceptable" to her colleagues if she uses cocaine, so she surrenders to this force, this practice in the world around her, as it plays upon her desires (James 1:14). Another woman is able to get parts in dramatic productions and advance in her career as an actress by being appropriately "available" to men who make decisions. A contractor can meet his budget by skimping on materials and bribing an "understanding" inspector. A worker in a plant is excluded from training in advanced techniques because he is an American Indian. A professor is influenced in his grading by the need to have many students, or he manufactures data in order to get grants, produce publications, and gain advancement over his colleagues. A young black woman cannot train well enough to get a scholarship to a university because her high school is not supported financially. A minister shades his example and teaching to the inclinations of his "more important" hearers to gain their support and advance his career.

The social structures exhibited in such cases are, strictly speaking, not *in* any individual, but in the world where we live, though they totally depend for their existence and power upon the *readinesses* that are in us individually. Structural evils are practices that—whether they are stated or not explicitly formulated—are accepted and enforced by others in the context of our actions.

But none of these evils would continue to function if the Ten Commandments (Exod. 20) and the two great principles of love of

God and neighbor (Matt. 19:37–40) were generally observed. In that case, malnutrition, war, oppression, class and tribal conflict, overpopulation, crime and violence, and family strife would eventually cease to be possible as mass conditions, because individuals would not cooperate in their development and would take measures to stop it.

TRUTH ALONE CRUSHES EVIL

Such non-cooperation would transform the social and political as well as the personal areas of our life almost beyond recognition. I admit, it is difficult to imagine what such a world would be like. Try picturing a world where lying doesn't exist. Imagine that human beings became constitutionally incapable of telling a lie in word or behavior. Almost all evil deeds and intents are begun with the thought that they can be hidden by deceit. When we realize that "success" with lying almost always depends upon collusion with others, we understand that if only a large percentage of the population were unstintingly truthful, lying would be forced out of life. Suddenly we can see how the kingdom of evil rests on lies, and why Satan is called a liar and the father of lies (John 8:44). The kingdom of evil is structurally very weak, for all its fearsome appearance. Pull one string and the whole unravels.

But individuals cannot be counted on to do what is right. Hence they are easily moved in the wrong direction, and these movements reverberate and build throughout their communities. They are like a droplet of water, which has little structural rigor. Because of its mobile nature, a droplet responds to every quiver of the droplets about it, and they begin to move in sympathy with each other. Soon a huge wave is generated, large enough possibly to crush a ship or roll over the coastline and destroy a city.

The prophet Isaiah also had the insight that the wicked resemble a tossing sea, whose natural motions cast dirt and filth about (57:20). The vast forces in the sea of humanity that make possible large-scale evil are generated as individuals pool their wickedness in joint action or joint inaction that very soon is far beyond their own control, beyond anyone's control. Fear, wrath, arrogance, revenge, and lust take on extrahuman proportions. At this point the righteous are powerless to halt the process (Ps. 11:3). As with the more individualized destructive spirals mentioned earlier, the madness must—like a wave—run its course until it collapses back into fragmented individuals and gutted communities.

THE EFFECT OF RIGHTEOUS INDIVIDUALS

But the righteous can stop the wave before it starts, *if* they are stable in their righteousness, empowered by God, and distributed through society appropriately. The impersonal power structures in the world are, though independent of any one person's will and experience, nevertheless dependent for their force upon *the general readiness of normal people to do evil.*

A slogan of the sixties asked: suppose they gave a war and nobody came? Obviously there would be no war. But in the case of a complex phenomenon such as war, the righteous must reach much deeper than resistance or noninvolvement. They must reach into the dispositions that make war seem a plausible course of action and make people come when the battle cry is sounded. War is not an isolated phenomenon but rides upon the coattails of cultural, economic, racial, and even religious practices, ideas, and attitudes that have their life in the social context. These are sparks that kindle the raging holocaust of war.

Also *within* nations, relations between the various social groups are carried on in such a way as to provide fertile ground for suffering, injustice, and violence. All of the big words, such as "labor," "management," "black," "white," "Jew," "Wasp," "Hispanic," "redneck," "rich," "poor," "feminist," "police," "government," "professional," "blue collar," "law," "health care," "welfare," "Right," "Left," and so forth, gain their concrete substance by attachment to the habitual responses, good and bad, of the normal, "decent" human being.

ARE MASS EVILS BASED ON IDEOLOGY?

This association of the big words and slogans with identifiable social blocks and pressures leads some to try to explain the inhumanity of people to other people as the result of "ideological obsession." No doubt ideas and ideological constructions have a certain fascination about them, but I think that this diagnosis—one offered mainly by those who devote their life to working with ideas—does not really touch on the *operative* factors in mass evil.

Ideology *alone* would never prove capable of energizing the machines of evil. It is a fact that by far the largest part of evil done under ideological banners draws upon long-cultivated resentments or hatreds that, in the moment of the deed, take the form of the wrath, frenzy, loathing, lust, greed, or revenge of a specific individual. Then in the case of many persons involved, they veil themselves as a feeling of blind duty or obligation to the good of *my* people.

This very same set of factors operates *within* the smaller societal groupings, especially within families, neighborhoods, and work groups to keep the pot of hurt and evil constantly boiling with wrongs of commission and omission. If these concrete factors were eliminated or appropriately restrained or redirected within the individuals involved, ideology would be rendered largely innocuous; while, if they are not, ideology will make little difference in what is bound to happen. Only the rationalization will be different.

THE PRACTICAL PROBLEM

From the practical point of view, then, the radical problem concerning the power structures of this world is how to transform *normal* human character away from its usual high level of readiness to disregard God and harm others for the sake of our own fear, pride, lust, greed, envy, and indifference. How can individual human beings be brought to a place where the social structures on many levels, from family or friends to the nation-state and beyond, no longer expect them to do things that are wrong? Individual change *is* the answer, even though many believe strongly the answer lies in social change.

I'm not suggesting that all forms of social institution are equally good or bad, or denying that we should strive for the very best cultural, educational, economic, legal, political, social, and religious arrangements in human affairs. Nor do I deny that the readiness for evil in the given individual has as its proximate cause the social context into which a person is born and upon which he or she is nurtured. The *obvious* truth of this is what tempts some, such as J. J. Rousseau, to suppose that evil's hold upon humankind can be broken merely by changing the social and economic arrangements under which we live.

Good certainly can be accomplished by some changes of this kind, as history shows. But the failure of such change as a total strategy for dealing with the evil of the human heart in both its individual and social dimensions is powerfully demonstrated by the many "revolutions" that have occurred in the nineteenth and twentieth centuries where one oppressor is exchanged for another, while humankind has barely managed to stay afloat in rivers of blood. How totally appropriate—not only in the face of these social or political "revolutions," but also in the light of the innumerable illusive "solutions" to lesser problems—is the world-weary saying: "The more things change, the more they are the same!"

O. Hardman points out that the times of most earnest discipline for the Kingdom of God by Christians have usually been times when social conditions were vastly modified for the better. But, he adds:

True social progress can never be effected solely by programmes of reform, organised demand, and legislative action. High wages and abundant leisure, good housing and improved sanitation, are not able of themselves to guarantee progress or even to check deterioration. It is of far greater importance that people should be clean and sober in their habits, and thrifty in their use of time and money, and that all the relationships of the members of a community should be inspired by love rather than controlled by principles of legal justice and economic equality: and these things are most surely promoted by the presence of earnest Christians living ascetically in the midst of society under various types of organization.[3]

Of course those who feel that legislative and social reform are the answer to humankind's problems may yet insist that the hinderance to our progress is lack of knowledge and of adequately trained personnel. With the right knowledge and proper personnel, they think, we can eliminate the harm people do to one another and to themselves. This response is quite correct, just as is that of those who insist that the solution lies in the regeneration of the individual. For when understood in a way that would actually meet the need concerned, they amount to the same thing. But *neither* is correct unless we are talking about knowledge or social arrangements or experiences that *radically* transform human character and relationships.

THE ILLUSION OF OUR AGE—STAYING THE SAME

We must at some point stop looking for new information or social arrangements or religious experiences that will draw off the evil in the world at large, abolish war, hunger, oppression, and so forth, *while letting us continue to be and to live as we have since Adam.* This is the illusion of our age, the Holy Grail of modernity, a pleasant dream in the sleep of secularism. The monstrous evils we deplore are in fact the strict causal consequences of the spirit and behavior of "normal" human beings following generally acceptable patterns of life. They are not the result of strange flukes, accidental circumstances, or certain especially mad or bad individuals. The tyrants, satanic forces, and oppressive practices of this world play upon our "merely decent" lives as a master organist dominates his or her instrument but is wholly powerless without it.

The debate about whether "the answer" lies in social or in individual change goes on and on only because *both* sides are thinking at a very superficial level. Establishing the rights of labor and of the various ethnic groups, shifting ownership of the means of production from private to public hands, outlawing various types of discrimination, governmental outlays for welfare and education, and so on, will certainly make a difference—good or bad—but they will not eliminate greed, loneliness, resentment, sexual misery and harm, disappointment with one's lot in life, hunger for meaning and recognition, fear of sickness, pain, old age and death, or hatred of those of other cultures. They will not bring us to love and accept ourselves and our neighbors or enable us to enjoy our lives with peace of mind. But then neither will the vapid, mass produced experiences of repentance and faith—if we may indeed call them that—that now commonly are announced as entrance into a new and supernatural life.

This is not a theory, but an observable fact. The highest education, as well as the strictest doctrinal views and religious practice, often leave untouched the heart of darkness from which the demons come to perch upon the lacerated back of humankind. Fine laws of the highest social intent and widespread confession of the new birth or of firsthand contact with God still leave an awesome lack in national and international affairs or in the quality of community and family life.

IS THE CHURCH NOW MEETING THE NEED?

Generally speaking, the church does not seem to be doing very well in meeting the need at present. We have spoken earlier about its great expansion in numbers in recent decades. A great body of disciples is emerging in South America and Africa. It may be for them to show the way for humankind as they walk fully in the yoke with Jesus. But they will never do this or even solve the problems of their own peoples, if they take the spiritual attainments of the Western church as the height of Christian possibility. In the "first world" countries, Christians simply do not advance very far into the health and strength of Christ. Psychological counselors frequently find little difference between the basic attitudes, actions, and afflictions of their unbelieving clients and those of the believers with which they deal. Some recent studies suggest that depression, anxiety, personal and marital maladjustment are epidemic in church members across all denominational lines.[4] Of all professional groups, the clergy was second highest in divorce rate during 1987.

The more conservative wing of both Catholic and Protestant religion has come into a strong social position in this country in recent years and has been the object of an immense amount of good will and support. The greatest question it now faces is whether it can really present the world with a new humanity or whether it is only attractive for the moment because it seems to support certain traditional values that comfort a people bewildered and frightened about the future.

RADICAL DISEASE REQUIRES RADICAL TREATMENT

The single most striking thing about the Kingdom of God Jesus invites us to enter is that in it there can be utter confidence in God's care and provision. Faced by a mass of the bleeding, needy dregs of humanity (Matt. 4:24–25), he pronounced a blessing open to individuals of every category. The Beatitudes, as we have earlier noted, are categories of the unblessables according to common human appraisal: the spiritual paupers (5:3), the depressed and grief-wracked (5:4), the "wimps" and pushovers (5:5), those consumed by the injustices done to them (5:6), and so forth. Blessedness is available in each case because of relationship to God in his Kingdom.

But in our distorted judgment about the nature of life, we have tried to turn the Beatitudes into mere poetry, rather than treating them as realistic announcements about *how things are*. We try to make them fit in with that banal decency that supports the power structures in a world set against God. This strategy seems to have succeeded pretty well with the version in Matthew. But the starkness of Luke's version does not allow Jesus' intent to be subverted: Blessed are you poor, hungry, weeping, persecuted ones, for the Kingdom of God is yours for the taking! (Luke 6:20–23; 16:16) Jesus knew and practiced in his own life the sufficiency of God himself and God alone for every need that comes. He preached what he knew by experience. What he expressed in his gospel was his vision and his faith.

It is in his faith alone that we can find a basis from which the evil in human character and life can be dislodged. We have one realistic hope for dealing with the world's problems. And that is the *person and gospel of Jesus Christ, living here and now, in people who are his by total identification found through the spiritual disciplines.*

Why? This faith and discipline yields a new humanity, one for which "The Lord is my shepherd, I shall not want" or "Our Father who art in heaven" does not express a resolve, a hope, or a commitment, but a vision in whose firm grip Jesus' people live with abandon. Their vision is one that regards worry about what we will eat or drink or wear as completely pointless. The natural thing for them is to "be careful for nothing," as Philippians 4:6–7 says, "but in everything by prayer and supplication with thanksgiving let your requests be made known unto God. And the peace of God, which passeth all understanding, shall keep your hearts and minds through Christ Jesus." People of this new humanity are not afraid "even if the world blows up, and the mountains crumble into the sea" (Ps. 46:2, LB). Living is Christ, dying is gain (Phil. 1:21). Living and dying are the only options and both are transcendentally wonderful, because liberation from fear of death is an inevitable result of living in the faith of Jesus (see Matt. 10:28; Heb. 2:15). That is the faith I am speaking of.

FROM RADICAL FAITH TO RADICAL DISCIPLINE

Starting from this radical faith, such individuals are capable of undertaking a course of life that will transform their character and make them capable of bearing the wisdom and power of God *throughout* human society. They will then prove capable of assuming positions of leadership or "pastoring" in all levels of society so that the whole of humankind can, at the appropriate moment in history, receive the risen and ascended Christ as its effectively reigning Lord. The government shall be upon his shoulders in reality.

This is the future event we should keep in mind when learned people tell us that personal virtue is not an answer to social ills. The effect of this saying is to keep people working at changing society without attempting the radical transformation of character. It pleads for a continuation of "life as usual," which is precisely the source of the problem. Often, those who work in this way like to think of themselves as "radicals." They fail to go to the root of social order and disorder, though. The only true "radical" is the one who proposes a different character and life for human beings.

RESTRUCTURING FOR CHRIST'S REIGN

But how can the transition to Christ's reign through his people come to pass? Often, we are told that the rule of God upon the earth will be fulfilled in a great act of violence, in which multitudes of people are slain by God, followed by a totalitarian government of literally infinite proportions, headquartered in Jerusalem.

While it may be true that humankind deserves no better than this, the *kind* of government it associates with God does not seem compatible with the news that Jesus brought about God. Further, if this is what is to happen, why would the action be delayed so long? Simple force of the kind envisioned would have been effective whenever it might applied. I believe, to the contrary, that the coming rule of God is to be a government by grace and truth mediated through personalities mature in Christ. It will not be by force, but by the power of truth presented in overwhelming love. Our inability to conceive of it other than by force merely testifies to our obsession with *human* means for controlling other people.

But both human nature and the biblical record suggest to me that the coming government of God, which will displace the power structures of the present world, will not come by any mere progressive advancement of humankind in general. A distinct reentry of the person of Christ into world history is required to complete the work. Apart from a radically new principle of life, humanity simply cannot advance *that* far. It is only the real presence of Christ in his mature people interspersed throughout the "secular" life of humanity that will cause the necessary "withering away of the state." The state is emblematic of all those worldly power structures based on oppression and the power of pain and death. The real presence of Christ as a world-governing force will come solely as his called out people occupy their stations in the holiness and power characteristic of him, as they demonstrate to the world the way to live that is best in every respect.

THE SYSTEM OF JUDGES

There is a model for this social organization. The pattern of social organization adequate to human nature and society under God has been foreshadowed by the system of "judges" introduced into the nation of Israel by Moses at its inception. Moses had at first tried to counsel, guide, and aid all of the people in matters where they had need. This is a role often assumed by government. However there was then, and is now, a limit, in the very nature of human relationships, on what *one* person can do for social order and individual need—even when that one person is closely linked to God.

Thus Moses was advised by his wise father-in-law to "select out of all the people able men who fear God, men of truth, those who hate dishonest gain" (Exod. 18:21, NAS). Of these some were placed over groups of a thousand, some over hundreds, some over fifties, and some over tens, to "judge" the people as need required, bringing only extremely important matters to Moses himself. Moses took "wise, understanding and respected men," chosen by the various tribes of the nation and set them in the various levels of "judging."

Here is his description of what he told them to do: "You must give your brothers a fair hearing and see justice done between a man and his brother or the stranger who lives with him. You must be impartial in judgment and give an equal hearing to small and great alike. Do not be afraid of any man, for the judgment is God's.

Should a case be too difficult, bring it to me and I will hear it. And I gave you directions at that time for everything you were to do" (Deut. 1:16–18, JB).

The genius of this system is very great, maximizing the possibilities of individuals responding and being responsible to other individuals within a community under God. The first level of leadership was responsible for oversight of ten individuals. No doubt this meant ten men with their families. The second level (judges over fifties) dealt directly with only five individuals (judges of first level), and the third level dealt directly with only two (judges of the second level). The possibilities of advice, counsel, concrete understanding and guidance, as well as care for any needs, would be adequate to human nature—as they are so desperately inadequate in our modern society.

There is every reason to believe, when we penetrate into the life context of Old Testament events, that the attitude in which this system was to be carried out was that of thoughtful, compassionate neighbors who were living entirely within the letter and the spirit of the Ten Commandments and with the help of other counsels of God to the Jewish people. Those who were out of line would be brought into line, if at all possible, by the persuasion and example of the judge of ten, who was a neighbor in the most literal of senses, or in cooperation with those over him if that was required. Legitimate needs of the individual would be known and would be cared for from the resources of the community, wherein all lived with a consciousness of provision by God. To "judge" was to have the responsibility for making sure that justice was being done in the community, that things were going as they should.

Certainly this system never worked with anything like perfection—as was true of the entire system of Mosaic legislation—due to the failure of the individuals who occupied the places of authority and leadership. The leaders of Israel, as of all nations thus far, constitute an almost uninterrupted series of illustrations of how power unleashes the corruption of the human heart. But it was not as said in Lord Acton's well-known statement, that "Power corrupts, and absolute power corrupts absolutely." Rather, *power makes corruption apparent, and absolute power makes corruption absolutely apparent.* Thomas à Kempis was correct: "Occasions make not a man fail, but they show what the man is."[5] History awaits Christ and those disciplined to his character before the system of judges can become a functional social reality whereby the kingdoms of this world become the Kingdom of our God and of his Christ, as the stone cut out without hands fills the whole earth (Dan. 2).

For our world today we need not think in terms of the exact numbers and the exact hierarchical arrangement laid down by Moses. The essential point, however, must not be missed. Things will go right in human life and society only to the extent that a sufficient number of qualified people are adequately distributed and positioned to see to it that they go right. Justice cannot prevail until there are enough people properly equipped with Christ's character and power, in something like the Mosaic distribution throughout society, who cooperatively and under God constantly see to it that the good is secured and that the right is done. Such people are the vessels in the household of God, "meet for the master's use and prepared unto every good work," as 2 Timothy 2:21 puts it. Only then will brotherhood, justice, well-being, and, consequently, peace prevail upon the earth.

Is this possible? I don't believe it's a mere dream or a desperate delusion, once we understand how the disciplines mesh with grace, on the one hand, and embodied human personality, on the other. There *is* a way of life that, if generally adopted, would eliminate all of the social and political problems from which we suffer. This way of life comes to whole-hearted disciples of Christ who live in the disciplines of the spiritual life and allow grace to bring their *bodies* into alignment with their redeemed *spirits*.

FROM MOSES TO JESUS

The order instituted by Moses was given an experimental run from his own time up to the institution of the monarchy in Israel, seen in 1 Samuel 8. This period of "the judges" is one in which Israel was without a government as the word is commonly understood, and "every man did that which was right in his own eyes," as Judges 17:6 and 21:25 describe. The hierarchy of judges was in force in some fashion, commonly most visible in the form of "the elders," who sat regularly in some public place such as the city gate to care for any matter that required attention (Ruth 4:1–12). In time of need a "judge" became a national leader. These natural leaders are the judges of the book of Judges in our Old Testament.

It is a curious fact that many today who read that in the period of the judges all did "what was right in their own eyes" think that something terrible was covered by that phrase. Indeed, the people of this time went wrong in many ways. But to do as one pleases is the ideal condition of humanity, what is often called "freedom," and does not imply wrongdoing at all. In the book of Judges, doing what was right in one's own eyes was not opposed to doing what is right in God's eyes, but opposed to doing what some governmental official saw as right. God has all along intended that we walk with him on a personal basis, be pleased by the right things, and then do what is right in our own eyes. This is why we were made and what constitutes our individuality.

When Israel demanded a king and an established government to replace this condition of freedom under God, the Lord told Samuel—the last of the judges in the full, original sense—that "they have not rejected you, but they have rejected me, that I should not reign over them" (1 Sam. 8:7). When he gave them Saul as king, Samuel accordingly said: "And you have this day rejected your God, who himself saved you out of all your adversities and your tribulations; and you have said unto him, Nay, but set a king over us" (10:19).

As they earlier refused to speak directly with God and insisted that Moses do it for them (Deut. 5:24–27), so now they refused to let God directly govern them by his law and by empowering individuals for tasks as occasion demanded, without a standing government running on its own power. Theocracy was in some measure restored through the *destruction* of the monarchy and the time of exile. Then the language of God's "heavenly" rule, as a "God of heaven" (e.g., Ezra 6:10; 7:12, 23; Neh. 1:5; 2:4; Dan. 2:28, 44), emerges within the Old Testament writings, preparing the way for the dramatic announcement of John the Baptist and Jesus: "The kingdom *of heaven* is now available, turn in to it!" (Matt. 3:2, 4:17). Now all humankind is invited to live in a *family,* made possible by Our Father in heaven, whom we address in prayer. When the gospel of this family kingdom has been adequately presented in The *lives* of Christ's people, the end of *human* history as we are familiar with it will occur (Matt. 24:14), for humankind will fall under the effectual leadership of those who stand in the Kingdom and upon the earth as judges (1 Cor. 6:2).

CHRIST'S WAY NOT YET TRIED

Holman Hunt's famous painting "The Light of the World" presents Christ with a lamp in one hand knocking at a door. The door has no handle on the outside, and it is overgrown with weeds and vines. The interpretation posted below the painting in St. Paul's Cathedral in London remarks: "On the lefthand side of the picture is seen this door of the human soul. It is fast barred; its bars and nails are rusty; it is knitted and bound to its stanchions by creeping tendrils of ivy, showing that it has never been opened."

There is something profoundly right about this statement. On any fair interpretation of history, the way of Christ in God's Kingdom has, at least, not been tried *as a general way of managing human affairs.* The personnel for such an undertaking has been lacking. Here again we must give Chesterton his due. Christianity has not only been "found difficult and left untried," it has rarely been closely enough approached by people even to be found difficult.

There was a "fulness of time" at which Christ could come in the flesh (Gal. 4:4), and there is likewise a fullness of time for his people to stand forth with the concrete style of existence for which the world has hungered in its thoughtful moments and praised through its poets and prophets. As a response to this world's problems, the gospel of the Kingdom will never make sense except as it is incarnated—we say "fleshed out"—in ordinary human beings in all ordinary conditions of human life. But it will make sense when janitors and storekeepers, carpenters and secretaries, businessmen and university professors, bankers and government officials brim with the degree of holiness and power formerly thought appropriate only to apostles and martyrs. Its truth will illumine the earth when disciplined discipleship to Jesus is recognized as a condition of professional competence in all the areas of life, since from that alone comes strength to live and work as *we ought*.

KNOCKING ON THE DOOR OF THE CHURCH

The end of World War II is still observed in England. I recently happened to be at Westminister Abbey on May 8, VE day, while services of commemoration were being conducted. All of the beautiful biblical words about there being no more war and about justice and peace ruling the earth were movingly read. As we do on such occasions, we suspended all questions as to how this would come about and lost ourselves in wonder at the beauty of the end hoped for.

But, as I listened, the question of means reasserted itself in my mind. How, I wondered, do we expect all of this to come about? We know that we have some part in bringing the vision to realization. Although it is God's power and presence that will bring health and peace to the earth, that does not mean that we are mere spectators. That power and presence will not fall upon us like a stone. There *is* a human instrumentality involved, which is why God waits for a fullness of time determined by our capacities to receive what he would give. He calls us to be a part of his efforts. Our part is to understand the way God works *with* humanity to extend his Kingdom in the affairs of humankind, and to act on the basis of that understanding.

The key to understanding our part is the realization that God only moves forward with his redemptive plan through people who are *prepared* to receive freely and cooperate with him in the next step. This is as true in our day as it was for Abraham, Moses, Jeremiah, and John the Baptist. To suggest what this means for us, we return to Holman Hunt's marvelous painting.

The painter depicted Revelations 3:20: "Behold, I stand at the door and knock; if any man hear my voice, and open the door, I will come in to him, and I will sup with him, and he with me." But the door at which Christ is knocking, according to this passage, is *not* the door of the generic human heart, as is so often suggested. Rather, it is—as the passage clearly indicates—the door of a *church*. We shall get nowhere in our attempts to understand the gospel, the church, and our own lives today unless we understand that *Christ is outside the church* as we commonly identify it.

Every group tries to tell us: "We have Christ in here with us." This may be true, but he also is always on the outside. It is to people *in* the church that Christ calls, and what he is offering is a special fellowship they do not now have. Christ is really out in the world, where we have not yet had the courage to follow him fully. Only "outside" is great enough for him. But still he knocks at our little door and invites us to invite him in. If we do open the door he will come in and share with us, even though he will, in his greatness, find our little church—so very necessary to us—too small and confining. He especially wants to do this because those in the church are, generally speaking, the very ones who are best prepared to freely receive him and cooperate with him in his vast purposes for humanity and this world.

CHRISTIAN LEADERS RESPONSIBLE FOR THE FUTURE OF THE WORLD

This is why the responsibility for the condition of the world in years or centuries to come rests upon the leaders and teachers of the Christian church. They alone have at their disposal the *means* to bring the world effectively under the rule of God. On the one hand, they have the "all power" that is in the hands of the One who bid them go and teach all human groupings to do as he commanded, and promised to be with them always (Matt. 28:18–20). On the other hand, the teachers of the gospel have Christ's Kingdom fellowship to live in and to offer to all. They have millions of people who regularly come to them, submitting to their leadership in the spiritual life even when unclear about what that means. And, further, they have concrete practices of submission to righteousness within which, given adequate teaching and example, their hearers can make regular and remarkable progress into the character and power of Christ himself.

But there is a prevailing problem. The people of Christ have never lacked for available power to accomplish the task set for them by their Master. But they have failed to make *disciples,* in the New Testament sense of the term. And naturally following upon this, they have failed even to *intend* to teach people to do all that Christ would have us do. Certainly this was, more often than not, because they thought it impossible. But in any case they have failed to seek his power to the ends he specified, and they have not developed the character needed to bear his power safely throughout the social order, or even within the church itself.

At this point in history, every leader among those who identify with Christ as Lord must ask himself or herself: "How can I justify *not* leading my people into the practice of disciplines for the spiritual life that would enable them to reign in their lives by Christ Jesus? How can I fail to give them this opportunity? How can I justify not giving myself to those practices until I am a spiritual powerhouse, the angels of God evidently ascending and descending upon me in my place?"

Ministers pay far too much attention to people who do *not* come to services. Those people should, generally, be given exactly that disregard by the pastor that they give to Christ. The Christian leader has something much more important to do than pursue the godless. The leader's task is to *equip saints until they are like Christ* (Eph. 4:12), and history and the God of history waits for him to do *this* job. It is so easy for the leader today to get caught up in illusory goals, pursuing the marks of success which come from our training as Christian leaders or which are simply imposed by the world. It is big, Big, always *BIG,* and *BIGGER STILL!* That is the contemporary imperative. Thus we fail to take seriously the nurture and training of those, however few, who stand constantly by us.

Everyone who has a pastoral role to others, whether as an official minister or not, must strive for a specific understanding of what is happening to those who come regularly under his or her influence and must pay individual attention to their development.[6] This is the absolutely sure way to "win the world" (John 17:21–23).

There is a special evangelistic work to be done, of course, and there are special callings to it. But if those in the churches really are enjoying fullness of life, evangelism will be unstoppable and largely automatic. The local assembly, for its part, can then become an academy where people throng from the surrounding community to learn how to *live*. It will be a school of life (for a disciple is but a pupil, a student) where all aspects of that life seen in the New Testament records are practiced and mastered under those who have themselves mastered them through practice. Only by taking this as our immediate goal can we intend to carry out the Great Commission.

THE PROPHETIC VISION

It is the prophetic vision that this commission *will* be fulfilled. The prophet Zechariah foresaw the time when masses of people around the world will exhort one another to worship God and seek his blessings. "In those days ten men from ten different nations will clutch at the coatsleeve of one Jew and say, "Please be my friend, for I know that God is with you" (8:23, LB). The "Jew" in this case is certainly the child of Abraham by faith (John 8:39; Isa. 63:16; Rom. 2:28–29), not just someone who *happens* to have originated from a certain line of DNA or a certain gene pool.

The vision of the prophet Jeremiah was that the law of God will become the natural habit patterns of God's people, written in their hearts, so that one person among them will not need to be taught by another to know the Lord (Jer. 33:33–34). This is to be fulfilled under the New Covenant in the "new and living way" (Heb. 8:10–

11; 10:17, 20) inclusive of both Jew and Gentile, all who are children of Abraham by faith.

The prophet sees the general outline of future facts, not the details. But there always *are* details, of course. What we are suggesting is that the details of Christ's coming reign consist in the reorganization of society on the model of the "judges," around those who assume loving responsibility for their neighbors with that fully developed character and power of Jesus Christ to which the ministry of the Kingdom of God has brought them, under the real, personal presence of Christ on earth.

OUR NEED TO IDOLIZE OUR GOVERNORS

Such people alone can fulfill the requirements of social and political leadership. This really is recognized by all, and explains why social and governmental leaders *must* be exhalted in the minds of those who follow them. The fantastic, often downright silly unrealism of political conventions and campaigns is a childish expression of the kinds of personal qualifications we know would be required if government really were to succeed with what it proposes to do.

This idolization—this willing self-delusion—about our leaders is not just a requirement for the naive and ignorant masses but is necessary for the sophisticates and the informed as well. A recent book on the life of a twentieth-century president tells how he used the secret service to hide the women he brought to the White House while his wife was away and used his adoring associates to provide respectable cover for liaisons outside the White House. The sober biographer who chronicles these facts then proceeds to state that this president could not be regarded as hypocritical or dishonest! One wonders what language means in such a case.[7] Our political leaders are lionized and idolized as they are because we know that it would take *that* sort of person to solve the problems of human society, or at least to prevent them from becoming worse.

But of course they are *not* like that. The bitter but all too truthful comment of Bertolt Brecht is:

Those who take the meat from the table
Teach contentment.
Those for whom the taxes are destined
Demand sacrifice.
Those who eat their fill speak to the hungry
Of wonderful times to come.
Those who lead the country into the abyss
Call ruling too difficult
For ordinary men.

And it *is* too difficult for ordinary people. In fact, it is *impossible,* as the record of human government shows. Turmoil, insurrection, and revolution are inevitable in an open society where the officials are corrupt. Ultimately, the saints—and by this we do *not* mean a political party of "saints"—*must* be the ones to judge the earth. Only saints of the faith of Abraham and Paul are capable of governing as God (*and* humans) would have it, because they work in the power of God and have the character to bear it without corruption.

COMMUNITIES OF JUSTICE AND PEACE

As the church of the Lord Jesus Christ turns its full energies to perfecting those in its fellowship in a life where they reign by and with Christ as in Romans 5:17, the power structures of this present world, which permit, even encourage the crushing waves of evil to roll over humanity, will be dissolved. They will be replaced by other structures anchored in the redeemed personalities distributed throughout society, stabilizing whatever evil may remain in the human heart so that it cannot build to the mass phenomena now seen. In most Western countries, and especially in the Americas, those who now have formal membership in our Christian churches would be far more than enough in number to receive the reign of Christ. Their leaders have only to bring them to the fullness of life which Christ has provided.

The *quality* of our social life then—though no doubt to be very different in many details and particular arrangements—is accurately captured in these words of Athanasius, characterizing the Egyptian communities under the influence of St. Antony:

Their solitary cells in the hills were like tents filled with divine choirs— singing Psalms, studying, fasting, praying, rejoicing in the hope of the life to come, and laboring in order to give alms and preserving love and harmony among themselves. And truly it was like seeing a land apart, a land of piety and justice. For there was neither wrongdoer nor sufferer of wrong, nor was there reproof of the tax-collector [the most despised of people]; but a multitude of ascetics, all with one set purpose—virtue. Thus, if one saw these solitary cells again and the fine disposition of the monks, he could but lift up his voice and say: "How fair are thy dwellings, O Jacob—thy tents, O Israel! Like shady glens and like a garden by a river, and like tents that the Lord hath pitched and cedars beside the waters![8]

NOTES

Epigraph 1. Leo Tolstoy, *The Kingdom of God and Peace Essays,* trans. Aylmer Maude (London: Oxford University Press, 1974), 451f.

Epigraph 2. Alasdair MacIntyre, *After Virtue: A Study in Moral Theory,* 2d ed. (Notre Dame, IN: University of Notre Dame Press, 1984), 245.

1. *Los Angeles Times,* January 23, 1983, part 1, 4.

2. *Los Angeles Times,* May 23, 1983. Opinion Section.

3. O. Hardman, *The Ideals of Asceticism: An Essay in the Comparative Study of Religion* (New York: Macmillan, 1924), 190.

4. *Sources and Resources: A Newsletter for Christian Leaders,* #76, June 15, 1983 (published by Youth Specialties, 1224 Greenfield Dr., El Cajon, California).

5. Thomas à Kempis, *The Imitation of Christ,* in, Irwin Edman ed., *The Consolation of Philosophy* (New York: Random House, Modern Library 1943), 148.

6. The program of pastoral oversight explained by Richard Baxter in *The Reformed Pastor* (1656; reprint, Carlisle, PA: Banner of Truth Trust, 1979) could be adapted to today and improved as needed. Of course we are talking about a revolution in pastoral training and care. Nothing less would do.

7. *Los Angeles Times,* September 18, 1983, Book Review Section, 1.

8. Athanasius, *The Life of Saint Antony* (New York: Newman, 1978), 57.

Epilogue

With the beautiful words of Athanasius, quoting also "the man whose eyes are open" (Num. 24:3–7), we close our discussion of the spirit of the disciplines and of those special activities through which we "present our bodies a living sacrifice, well-pleasing to God, that being the rational way to serve and worship him." (Rom. 12:1) The new life begun in us at the touch of God's gracious word upon the depths of our soul is experienced by us as love of Jesus and his Kingdom. The spirit of the disciplines—that which moves us to them and moves through them to prevent them from becoming a new bondage and to deepen constantly our union with the heart and mind of God—is this love of Jesus, with its steadfast longing and resolute will to be like him.

At his last meal with his closest friends he taught them and comforted them about his going away by saying: "The one who obeys me is the one who loves me; and because he loves me, my Father will love him, and I will too, and I will reveal myself to him." (John 14:21, LB) Obedience would be the sign of love, as love was the sign of discipleship. (13:35) Not because obedience produces love or even proves it. We know that it does not. And Jesus is not—in that all too human manner—trying to "corner" us into doing what he says by saying, "*If* you loved me you would do as I please!" Instead, he is teaching that obedience and love go together because *love alone stays to find a way to obey.*

It is the love that is fundamental, both within the process of our endeavors and in the divine assistance that will meet our love. We cannot too often repeat: "*Because* I love Jesus, his Father will love me—and he will make himself known to me! And their presence will give me light and joy and strength to do all that is right and good." We cannot too often center our minds upon his loveliness and kindness, that we might love him more and more.

The disciplines for the spiritual life are available, concrete activities designed to render bodily beings such as we ever more sensitive and receptive to the Kingdom of Heaven brought to us in Christ, even while living in a world set against God. Lovingly practiced they join with grace to enable us matter-of-factly to "come boldly to the very throne of God and stay there to receive his mercy and to find grace to help us in our times of need." (Heb. 4:16, LB) Their wise use allows us to live our lives by this throne of God. This is what makes the yoke of Jesus easy, his "burden" light. His commandments are not "bad news," not grievous, once we have found the ways to be with him.

But now is the time for decision and especially for planning. God changes lives in response to faith. But just as there is no faith that does not act, so there is no act without some plan. Faith grows from the experience of acting on plans and discovering God to be acting with us.

Now you have studied a number of ways in which we can be with Jesus and with his Father. It is time to take what you have learned and make your own specific plan for your life with them. This will come down to what you do on Sunday, Monday, Tuesday, Wednesday, Thursday, Friday, and Saturday. More importantly, at the outset, it will come down to what you do *not* do, to how you will manage to step out of the everlasting busyness that curses our lives. Didn't God give you quite enough time to do what he expects you to do? (Careful how you answer that one!)

You will be challenged to consider how thoroughly you are committed to following Jesus, and you may find that your commitment is remarkably flabby and thin because it has never been translated into how you spend your time. You will, perhaps for the first time, encounter tremendous obstacles to your faith: But those obstacles were there all along. You didn't notice them, or perhaps could not correctly identify them, precisely because you were not clearly moving in opposition to them. (Perhaps you have complained, however, about how little faith you seem to have in times of distress.)

Don't be distracted by what others are doing. They are not your servants, nor are you theirs, except as you follow the Lord. God does not call us to the same things. Do not be surprised if you are led in a way which others do not go. Be surprised if you are not! Among the last discussions of Jesus with his right-hand man Peter, Jesus tells him about how he is to die, adding, "Follow me" (John 21:19). What does one do when just told he will die by crucifixion? It would be hard to say what was on Peter's mind, but he looked around and saw John, who always seemed to have the inside track with Jesus, and asked: "What's going to happen to this fellow? How is he going to die?" (v. 21) Jesus replied: "If he never dies, it doesn't matter to you. You follow me."

Now Jesus comes by where you are and says, "You follow me." It is for you to work out with him how you are going to do that. *How* are you going to follow him? You cannot follow him without a plan to serve as the vessel in which the treasure of his life is received. Your plan will also be the cross on which you die to your old self and meet him in his life beyond death. He said, "Whoever does not carry his own cross and come after Me cannot be My disciple" (Luke 14:27 NAS). Do you now see where to begin to carry your own cross?

Do you think you know him now? You don't know him yet, nor do I, but we will increasingly know him when we give our lives to him through the disciplines for the spiritual life.

He comes to us as One unknown, without a name, as of old, by the lake-side, He came to those men who knew Him not. He speaks to us the same word: "Follow thou me!" and sets us to the tasks which He has to fulfil for our time. He commands. And to those who obey Him, whether they be wise or simple, He will reveal Himself in the toils, the conflicts, the sufferings which they shall pass through in His fellowship, and, as an ineffable mystery, they shall learn in their own experience Who He is.[1]

Let everyone who can hear, listen to what the Spirit is saying to the churches: Every one who is victorious shall eat of the hidden manna, the secret nourishment from heaven; and I will give to each a white stone, and on the stone will be engraved a new name that no one else knows except the one receiving it. (Rev. 2:17, LB)

NOTE

1. Albert Schweitzer, *The Quest of the Historical Jesus,* translated by W. Montgomery, (London: A & C. Black, 1936), p. 401.

Appendix I:

Jeremy Taylor's Counsel on the Application of Rules for Holy Living

From the dedicatory preface to Jeremy Taylor's *Holy Living and Holy Dying: Together with Prayers, Containing the Whole Duty of a Christian, etc.* (1650; reprint, London: Henry G. Bohn, 1858).

I have told what men ought to do, and by what means they may be assisted; and in most cases I have also told them why; and yet with as much quickness as I could think necessary to establish a rule, and not to engage in homily or discourse. In the use of which rules, although they are plain, useful, and fitted for the best and worst understandings, and for the needs of all men, yet I shall desire the reader to proceed with the following advices.

1. They that will with profit make use of the proper instruments of virtue, must so live as if they were always under the physician's hand. For the counsels of religion are not to be applied to the distempers of the soul as men used to take hellebore; but they must dwell together with the spirit of a man, and be twisted about his understanding for ever; they must be used like nourishment, that is, by a daily care and meditation; not like a single medicine, and upon the actual pressure of a present necessity: for counsels and wise discourses, applied to an actual distemper, at the best are but like strong smells to an epileptic person; sometimes they may raise him, but they never cure him. The following rules, if they be made

familiar to our natures and the thoughts of every day, may make virtue and religion become easy and habitual; but when the temptation is present, and hath already seized upon some portions of our consent, we are not so apt to be counselled, and we find no gust or relish in the precept: the lessons are the same, but the instrument is unstrung, or out of tune.

2. In using the instruments of virtue, we must be curious to distinguish instruments from duties, and prudent advices from necessary injunctions; and if by any other means the duty can be secured, let there be no scruples stirred concerning any other helps: only if they can, in that case, strengthen and secure the duty, or help towards perseverance, let them serve in that station in which they can be placed. For there are some persons in whom the Spirit of God hath breathed so bright a flame of love, that they do all their acts of virtue by perfect choice and without objection, and their zeal is warmer than that it will be allayed by temptation; and to such persons mortification by philosophical instruments, as fasting, sack cloth, and other rudenesses to the body, is wholly useless; it is always a more uncertain means to acquire any virtue, or secure any duty; and if love hath filled all the corners of our soul, it alone is able to do all the work of God.

3. Be not nice in stating the obligations of religion; but where the duty is necessary, and the means very reasonable in itself, dispute not too busily whether, in all circumstances, it can fit thy particular; but "super totam materiam," upon the whole make use of it. For it is a good sign of a great religion, and no imprudence, when we have sufficiently considered the substance of affairs, then to be easy, humble, obedient, apt, and credulous in the circumstances, which are appointed to us in particular by our spiritual guides, or, in general, by all wise men in cases not unlike. He that gives alms does best not always to consider the minutes and strict measures of his ability, but to give freely, incuriously, and abundantly. A man must not weigh grains in the accounts of his repentance; but for a great sin have a great sorrow, and a great severity; and in this take the ordinary advices, though, it may be, a less rigour might not be insufficient; ακριβοδικαιον, or arith-

metical measures, especially of our own proportioning, are but arguments of want of love and of forwardness in religion; or else are instruments of scruple, and then become dangerous. Use the rule heartily and enough, and there will be no harm in thy error if any should happen.

4. If thou intendest heartily to serve God, and avoid sin in any one instance, refuse not the hardest and most severe advice that is prescribed in order to it, though possibly it be a stranger to thee; for whatsoever it be, custom will make it easy.

5. When many instruments for the obtaining any virtue, or restraining any vice, are propounded, observe which of them fits thy person or the circumstances of thy need, and use it rather than the other; that by this means thou mayest be engaged to watch and use spiritual arts and observation about thy soul. Concerning the managing of which, as the interest is greater, so the necessities are more, and the cases more intricate, and the accidents and dangers greater and more importunate; and there is greater skill required than in the securing an estate, or restoring health to an infirm body. I wish all men in the world did heartily believe so much of this as is true; it would very much help to do the work of God.

Appendix II:
Discipleship: For Super-Christians Only?*

The word "disciple" occurs 269 times in the New Testament. "Christian" is found three times and was first introduced to refer precisely to the disciples—in a situation where it was no longer possible to regard them as a sect of the Jews (Acts 11:26). The New Testament is a book about disciples, by disciples, and for disciples of Jesus Christ.

But the point is not merely verbal. What is more important is that the kind of life we see in the earliest church is that of a special type of person. All of the assurances and benefits offered to humankind in the gospel evidently presuppose such a life and do not make realistic sense apart from it. The disciple of Jesus is not the deluxe or heavy-duty model of the Christian—especially padded, textured, streamlined, and empowered for the fast lane on the straight and narrow way. He stands on the pages of the New Testament as the first level of basic transportation in the Kingdom of God.

UNDISCIPLED DISCIPLES

For at least several decades the churches of the Western world have not made discipleship a condition of being a Christian. One is not required to be, or to intend to be, a disciple in order to become a Christian, and one may remain a Christian without any signs of progress toward or in discipleship. Contemporary Amer-

*My article as it appeared in *Christianity Today,* October 10, 1980.

ican churches in particular do not require following Christ in his example, spirit, and teachings as a condition of membership—either of entering into or continuing in fellowship of a denomination or local church. Any exception to this claim only serves to highlight its general validity and make the general rule more glaring. So far as the visible Christian institutions of our day are concerned, discipleship clearly is optional.

That, of course, is no secret. The best of current literature on discipleship either states outright or assumes that the Christian may not be a disciple at all—even after a lifetime as a church member. A widely used book, The Lost Art of Disciple Making, presents the Christian life on three possible levels: the convert, the disciple, and the worker. There is a process for bringing persons to each level, it states. Evangelizing produces converts, establishing or follow-up produces disciples, and equipping produces workers. Disciples and workers are said to be able to renew the cycle by evangelizing, while only workers can make disciples through follow-up.

The picture of church life presented by this book conforms generally to American Christian practice. But does that model not make discipleship something entirely optional? Clearly it does, just as whether or not the disciple will be a worker is an option. Vast numbers of converts today thus exercise the options permitted by the message they hear: they choose not to become—or at least do not choose to become—disciples of Jesus Christ. Churches are filled with "undiscipled disciples," as Jess Moody has called them. Most problems in contemporary churches can be explained by the fact that members have not yet decided to follow Christ.

Little good results from insisting that Christ is also supposed to be Lord: to present his lordship as an option leaves it squarely in the category of the white-wall tires and stereo equipment for the new car. You can do without it. And it is—alas!—far from clear what you would do with it. Obedience and training in obedience form no intelligible doctrinal or practical unity with the salvation presented in recent versions of the gospel.

GREAT OMISSIONS FROM THE GREAT COMMISSION

A different model was instituted in the Great Commission Jesus left the church. The first goal he set for the early church was to use his all-encompassing power and authority to make disciples without regard to ethnic distinctions—from all "nations" (Matt. 28:19). That set aside his earlier directive to go only to "the lost sheep of the house of Israel" (Matt. 10:5–6). Having made disciples, these alone were to be baptized into the name of the Father, and of the Son, and of the Holy Spirit. With this twofold preparation they were to be taught to treasure and keep "all things whatsoever I have commanded you." The Christian church of the first century resulted from following this plan for church growth—a result hard to improve upon.

But in place of Christ's plan, historical drift has substituted: "Make converts (to a particular faith and practice) and baptize them into church membership." This causes two great omissions from the Great Commission to stand out. Most important, we start by omitting the making of disciples or enrolling people as Christ's students, when we should let all else wait for that. We also omit the step of taking our converts through training that will bring them ever increasingly to do what Jesus directed.

These two great omissions are connected. Not having made our converts disciples, it is impossible for us to teach them how to live as Christ lived and taught. That was not a part of the package, not what they converted to. When confronted with the example and teachings of Christ, the response today is less one of rebellion or rejection than one of puzzlement: How do we relate to these? What have they to do with us?

DISCIPLESHIP THEN

When Jesus walked among humankind there was a certain simplicity to being his disciple. Primarily it meant to go with him, in an attitude of study, obedience, and imitation. There were no correspondence courses. One knew what to do and what it would cost. Simon Peter exclaimed: "Look, we've left everything and followed you!" (Mark 10:28). Family and occupations were deserted for long periods to go with Jesus as he walked from place to place announcing, showing, and explaining the governance of God. Disciples had to be with him to learn how to do what he did.

Imagine doing that today. How would family members, employers, and coworkers react to such abandonment? Probably they would conclude that we did not much care for them, or even for ourselves. Did not Zebedee think this as he watched his two sons desert the family business to keep company with Jesus (Mark 1:20)? Ask any father in a similar situation. So when Jesus observed that one must forsake the dearest things—family, "all that he hath," and "his own life also" (Luke 14)—insofar as that was necessary to accompany him, he stated a simple fact: it was the only possible doorway to discipleship.

DISCIPLESHIP NOW

Though costly, discipleship once had a very clear, straightforward meaning. The mechanics are not the same today. We cannot literally be with him in the same way as his first disciples could. But the priorities and intentions—the heart or inner attitudes—of disciples are forever the same. In the heart of a disciple there is a desire, and there is decision or settled intent. Having come to some understanding of what it means, and thus having "counted up the costs," the disciple of Christ desires above all else to be like him. Thus, "It is enough for the disciple that he become like his teacher" (Matt. 10:25). And moreover, "After he has been fully trained, he will be like his teacher" (Luke 6:40).

Given this desire, usually produced by the lives and words of those already in The Way, there is yet a decision to be made: the decision to devote oneself to becoming like Christ. The disciple is one who, intent upon becoming Christlike and so dwelling in his "faith and practice," systematically and progressively rearranges his affairs to that end. By these actions, even today, one enrolls in

Christ's training, becomes his pupil or disciple. There is no other way.

In contrast, the nondisciple, whether inside or outside the church, has something more important to do or undertake than to become like Jesus Christ. He or she has bought a piece of ground, perhaps, or even five yoke of oxen, or has taken a spouse (Luke 14:19). Such lame excuses only reveal that something on that dreary list of reputation, wealth, power, sensual indulgence, or mere distraction and numbness still retains his or her ultimate allegiance. Or if someone has seen through these, he or she may not know the alternative—not know, especially, that it is possible to live under the care and governance of God, working and living with him as Jesus did, seeking first the kingdom of God and his righteousness.

A mind cluttered by excuses may make a mystery of discipleship, or it may see it as something to be dreaded. But there is no mystery about desiring and intending to be like someone—that is a very common thing. And if we intend to be like Christ, that will be obvious to every thoughtful person around us, as well as to ourselves. Of course, attitudes that define the disciple cannot be realized today by leaving family and business to accompany Jesus on his travels about the countryside. But discipleship can be made concrete by loving our enemies, blessing those who curse us, walking the second mile with an oppressor—in general, living out the gracious inward transformations of faith, hope, and love. Such acts—carried out by the disciplined person with manifest grace, peace, and joy—make discipleship no less tangible and shocking today than were those desertions of long ago. Anyone who will enter into The Way can verify this, and he or she will prove that discipleship is far from dreadful.

THE COST OF NONDISCIPLESHIP

In 1937 Dietrich Bonhoeffer gave the world his book The Cost of Discipleship. It was a masterful attack on "easy Christianity" or "cheap grace," but it did not set aside—perhaps it even enforced—

the view of discipleship as a costly spiritual excess, and only for those especially driven or called to it. It was right to point out that one cannot be a disciple of Christ without forfeiting things normally sought in human life, and that one who pays little in the world's coinage to bear his name has reason to wonder where he or she stands with God. But the cost of nondiscipleship is far greater—even when this life alone is considered—than the price paid to walk with Jesus.

Nondiscipleship costs abiding peace, a life penetrated throughout by love, faith that sees everything in the light of God's overriding governance for good, hopefulness that stands firm in the most discouraging of circumstances, power to do what is right and withstand the forces of evil. In short, it costs exactly that abundance of life Jesus said he came to bring (John 10:10). The cross-shaped yoke of Christ is after all an instrument of liberation and power to those who live in it with him and learn the meekness and lowliness of heart that brings rest to the soul.

"FOLLOW ME. I'M FOUND!"

Leo Tolstoy claimed that "Man's whole life is a continual contradiction of what he knows to be his duty. In every department of life he acts in defiant opposition to the dictates of his conscience and his common sense." In our age of bumper-sticker communications some clever entrepreneur has devised a frame for the rear license plate that advises: "Don't follow me. I'm lost." It has had amazingly wide use, possibly because it touches with humor upon the universal failure referred to by Tolstoy. This failure causes a pervasive and profound hopelessness and sense of worthlessness: a sense that I could never stand in my world as a salty, light-giving example, showing people The Way of Life. Jesus' description of savorless salt sadly serves well to characterize how we feel about ourselves: "Good for nothing, but to be cast out, and to be trodden under foot of men" (Matt. 5:13), and not even fit to mollify a manure pile (Luke 14:35).

A common saying expresses the same attitude: "Don't do as I do, do as I say." (More laughs?) Jesus said of certain religious leaders—the scribes and Pharisees—of his day: "All that they tell you, do and observe, but do not do according to their deeds: for they say, and do not do" (Matt. 23:3). But that was no joke, and still isn't. We must ask what he would say of us today. Have we not elevated this practice of the scribes and Pharisees into a first principle of the Christian life? Is that not the effect, whether intended or not, of making discipleship optional?

We are not speaking of perfection, nor of earning God's gift of life. Our concern is only with the manner of entering into that life. While none can merit salvation, all must act if it is to be theirs. By what actions of the heart, what desires and intentions, do we find access to life in Christ? Paul's example instructs us. He could say in one breath both "I am not perfect" (Phil. 3:12), and "Do what I do" (Phil. 4:9). His shortcomings—whatever they were—lay back of him, but he lived forward into the future through his intention to attain to Christ. He was both intent upon being like Christ (Phil. 3:10–14) and confident of upholding grace for his intention. He could thus say to all: "Follow me. I'm found!"

LIFE'S GREATEST OPPORTUNITY

Dr. Rufus Jones has reflected in a recent book upon how little impact the twentieth-century evangelical church has had on societal problems. He attributes the deficiency to a corresponding lack of concern for social justice on the part of conservatives. That, in turn, is traced to reactions against liberal theology, deriving from the fundamentalist/modernist controversy of past decades.

Causal connections in society and history are hard to trace, but I believe this is an inadequate diagnosis. After all, the lack of concern for social justice, where that is evident, itself requires an explanation. And the current position of the church in our world may be better explained by what liberals and conservatives have shared, than by how they differ. For different reasons, and with different emphases, that they have agreed that discipleship to Christ is optional to membership in the Christian church. Thus the very type of life that could change the course of human society—and upon occasion has done so—is excluded from the essential message of the church.

Concerned to enter that life we ask: "Am I a disciple, or only a Christian by current standards?" Examination of our ultimate desires and intentions, reflected in the specific responses and choices that make up our lives, can show whether there are things we hold more important than being like him. If there are, then we are not yet his disciples. Being unwilling to follow him, our claim of trusting him must ring hollow. We could never claim to trust a doctor, teacher, or auto mechanic whose directions we would not follow.

For those who minister, there are yet graver questions: what authority do I have to baptize people who have not been brought to a clear decision to be a disciple of Christ? Dare I tell people as believers without discipleship that they are at peace with God? Where can I find authority for such a message? Perhaps most important: do I as a minister have the faith to undertake the work of disciple making? Is my first aim to make disciples?

Nothing less than life in the steps of Christ is adequate to the human soul or the needs of our world. Any other offer fails to do justice to the drama of human redemption, deprives the hearer of life's greatest opportunity, and abandons this present life to the evil powers of the age. The correct perspective is to see following Christ not only as the necessity it is, but as the fulfillment of the highest human possibilities and as life on the highest plane. It is to see, in Helmut Thielicke's words, that "The Christian stands, not under the dictatorship of a legalistic 'You ought,' but in the magnetic field of Christian freedom, under the empowering of the 'You may.'"

BIBLIOGRAPHY

Albertus Magnus. *Of Cleaving unto God*. Translated by Elizabeth Stopp. London: Mowbray, 1954.

Athanasius. *The Life of St. Antony*. New York: Newman, 1978.

Baxter, Richard. *The Reformed Pastor*. 1656. Reprint. Carlisle, PA: Banner of Truth Trust, 1979.

———. *The Saint's Everlasting Rest*. 2 vols. London: Griffith, Farran, Okeden & Welsh, 1887.

Berdyaev, Nicolas. *Freedom and the Spirit*. London: Bles, 1935.

Bernard of Clairvaux. *The Love of God*. Edited by James M. Houston. Portland, OR: Multnomah, 1983.

Bonar, Horatius. *God's Way of Holiness*. Chicago: Moody, n.d.

Bonhoeffer, Dietrich. *Letters and Papers from Prison*. London: Fontana, 1953.

Bouyer, Louis. *A History of Christian Spirituality*. 3 vols. New York: Seabury, 1982.

Brightman, Edgar S. *The Spiritual Life*. New York: Abingdon-Cokesbury, 1942.

Bruce, Alexander Balmain. *The Training of the Twelve*. Garden City, NY: Doubleday, Doran, 1928.

Burton, Ernest DeWitt. *A Critical and Exegetical Commentary on the Epistle to the Galatians*. Edinburgh: Clark, 1952.

Chadwick, Owen. *Western Asceticism: Selected Translations with Introductions and Notes*. Philadelphia: Westminster, 1958.

Chafer, Lewis Sperry. *He That Is Spiritual*. Findlay, OH: Dunham, 1918.

Chambers, Oswald. *The Psychology of Redemption*. London: Simpkin Marshall, 1947.

Christenson, Evelyn. *Lord, Change Me!* Wheaton, IL: Victor, 1979.

Clark, Kenneth. *Civilization: A Personal View*. New York: Harper & Row, 1969.

The Cloud of Unknowing. Edited by Dom Justin McCann. London: Burns Oates and Washbourne, 1943.

Delitzsch, Franz. *A System of Biblical Psychology*. Translated by Robert E. Wallis. Edinburgh: Clark, 1869.

The Desert Fathers. Translations with Introduction by Helen Waddell. Ann Arbor, MI: University of Michigan Press, 1957.

Durant, Will. *The History of Civilization.* Vols. 3–5. New York: Simon and Schuster, 1944–1953.

Eckhart. *Meister Eckhart.* Translationed by Raymond Blakney. New York: Harper, 1941.

Fairlie, Henry. *The Seven Deadly Sins Today.* Washington, DC: New Republic Books, 1978).

Finney, Charles Grandison. *Revivals of Religion: Lectures.* London: Morgan and Scott, 1910. Numerous other editions.

Fosdick, Harry Emerson, ed. *Great Voices of the Reformation: An Anthology.* New York: Modern Library, 1954.

Foster, Richard. *Celebration of Discipline.* New York: Harper & Row, 1978.

Fox, George. *Journal of George Fox.* Edited by Norman Penney. London: Dent, 1948. Also in various other editions.

Francis de Sales. *Introduction to the Devout Life.* Translated by John K. Ryan. Garden City, NY: Doubleday, Image Books, 1957.

Fuller, Daniel P. *Gospel and Law: Contrast or Continuum?* Grand Rapids, MI: Eerdmans, 1980.

Goforth, Jonathan. *"By My Spirit"* Grand Rapids, MI: Zondervan, 1942.

Goforth, Rosalind. *How I Know God Answers Prayer.* Grand Rapids, MI: Zondervan, 1921.

Goldbrunner, Josef. *Holiness Is Wholeness and Other Essays.* Notre Dame, IN: University of Notre Dame Press, 1964.

Gutierrez, Gustavo. *A Theology of Liberation.* Translated by Caridad Inda and John Eagleson. New York: Orbis, 1973.

Hamilton, Neil Q. *Recovery of the Protestant Adventure.* New York: Seabury, 1981.

Hardman, O. *The Ideals of Asceticism: An Essay in the Comparative Study of Religion.* New York: Macmillan, 1924.

Hilton, Walter. *The Stairway of Perfection.* Translated with Introduction by M. L. Del Mastro. Garden City NY: Doubleday, 1979.

Hughes, Philip. *A History of the Church.* 2 vols. New York: Sheed and Ward, 1935.

Ignatius. *The Spiritual Exercises of St. Ignatius.* Garden City, NY: Doubleday, Image Books, 1964.

Inge, W. R.. *Goodness and Truth.* London: Mowbray, 1958.

———. *Personal Religion and the Life of Devotion.* London: Longmans, Green, 1924.

James, William. *The Principles of Psychology.* 2 vols. New York: Holt, 1890, especially chap. 25.

Jewett, Robert. *Paul's Anthropological Terms: A Study of Their Use in Conflict Settings*. Leiden: Brill, 1971.

John, Bishop of Bristol. *The Ecclesiastical History of the Second and Third Centuries*. London: Griffith Farran Browne, n. d.

Jung, Carl G. *Man and His Symbols*. New York: Dell, 1975.

Kadloubovsky, E., and G. E. H. Palmer, ed. *Early Fathers from the Philokalia*. London: Faber and Faber, 1963.

Kierkegaard, Søren. *For Self-Examination: Recommended for the Times*. Translated by Edna and Howard Hong. Minneapolis, MN: Augsburg, 1940.

King, Henry Churchill. *The Seeming Unreality of the Spiritual Life*. New York: Macmillan, 1908.

Kuhn, Thomas S. *The Structure of Scientific Revolutions*. 2d ed. Chicago: University of Chicago Press, 1973.

Law, William. *A Serious Call to a Devout and Holy Life*. Many editions.

Lawson, James Gilchrist. *Deeper Experiences of Famous Christians*. Anderson, IN: Warner, 1970.

Lewis, C. S. *The Screwtape Letters and Screwtape Proposes a Toast*. New York: Macmillan, 1962.

Lives of the Saints. Translated with an Introduction by J. F. Webb. Baltimore, MD: Penguin, 1973.

Lowen, Alexander. *The Betrayal of the Body*. New York: Collier, 1971.

Marshall, Walter. *The Gospel Mystery of Sanctification*. 1692. Reprint. Grand Rapids, MI: Zondervan, 1954.

Meisel, Anthony C. *The Rule of St. Benedict*. and M. L. del Mastro, eds. Garden City, NY: Doubleday, 1975.

Merton, Thomas. *The Seven Storey Mountain*. New York: Harcourt Brace Jovanovich, 1978.

Miles, Margaret R. *Fullness of Life: Historical Foundations for a New Asceticism*. Philadelphia: Westminster, 1981.

―――. "Toward a New Asceticism." *The Christian Century* (October 28, 1981): 1097–1101.

Miller, Donald. *The Case for Liberal Christianity*. New York: Harper & Row, 1981.

Needleman, Jacob. *Lost Christianity*. New York: Bantam, 1982.

Owen, John. *The Forgiveness of Sins, Illustrated in Psalm CXXX*. Various editions.

Parker, William R., and Elaine St. Johns. *Prayer Can Change Your Life*. Carmel, NY: Guideposts Associates, 1957.

Peck, M. Scott. *The Road Less Traveled*. New York: Simon & Schuster, 1978.

Penn, William. *No Cross, No Crown*. London: Philips and Fardon, 1806.

Phillips, J. B. *When God Was Man*. New York: Abingdon, 1955.

The Philokalia: The Complete Text. 3 vols. Translated from the Greek and edited by G. E. H. Palmer, Philip Sherrard, and Kallistos Ware. London: Faber and Faber, 1979, 1981, 1984.

Pollock, John. *The Man Who Shook the World*. Wheaton, IL: Victor, 1972.

Ramsay, William M. *The Cities of St. Paul: Their Influence on His Life and Thought*. New York: Hodder & Stoughton, 1907.

Robinson, John A. T. *The Body: A Study in Pauline Theology*. London: SCM, 1952.

Ruskin, John. *Ethics of the Dust*. In vol. 11 of *The Complete Works of John Ruskin*. New York: Crowel, n.d.

———. *Modern Painters*. Vol. 7 of *The Complete Works of John Ruskin*. London: Allen, 1905.

———. *The Seven Lamps of Architecture*. London: Dent, 1969.

Sanford, Agnes. *The Healing Gifts of the Spirit*. New York: Lippincott, 1966.

Schaeffer, Francis A. *True Spirituality*. Wheaton, IL: Tyndale, 1971.

Schrodinger, Erwin. *What is Life? and Other Scientific Essays*. Garden City, NY: Doubleday, Anchor Books, 1965.

Sertillanges, A. G. *The Intellectual Life*. Westminister, MD: Christian Classics, 1980.

Severus, Sulpicius, et al. *The Western Fathers*. Edited and translated by F. R. Hoare. New York: Harper & Row, 1965.

Smith, David. *The Life and Letters of St. Paul*. New York: Harper, n.d.

Steer, Roger. *Admiring God: The Best of George Mueller*. London: Hodder and Stoughton, 1987.

Stendahl, Krister, ed. *Immortality and Resurrection*. New York: Macmillan, 1965.

Stewart, James S. *A Man in Christ*. New York: Harper, n. d.

Streeter, B. H., ed. *Foundations*. London: Macmillan, 1920.

———. *The Spirit*. London: Macmillan, 1919.

Suso, Henry. *The Life of the Servant*. Translated by James M. Clarke. Cambridge: Clarke, 1982.

Taylor, Jeremy. *Holy Living and Dying*. London: Bohn, 1858.

Teresa of Avila. *Interior Castle*. Translated and edited by E. Allison Peers. Garden City, NY: Doubleday, 1961.

Thomas à Kempis. *The Imitation of Christ*. Many editions.

Trueblood, Elton. *Alternative to Futility*. Waco, TX: Word, 1972.

Underhill, Evelyn. *Mysticism*. New York: New American Library, 1974.

Watson, David. *Fear No Evil: A Personal Struggle with Cancer*. London: Hodder and Stoughton, 1984.

The Way of the Pilgrim and The Pilgrim Continues His Way. Translated by R. M. French. New York: Seabury, 1965.

Weatherhead, Leslie D. *The Transforming Friendship.* London: Epworth, Wyvern Books, 1962.

Wesley, John. *Sermons on Several Occasions,* 2 vols. New York: Waugh & Mason, 1836. Many later editions.

Whitchurch, Ira Goldwin. *The Philosophical Bases of Asceticism in the Platonic Writings and Pre-Platonic Tradition.* New York: Longmans, Green, 1923.

Willard, Dallas. *In Search of Guidance: Developing a Conversational Relationship with God.* Ventura, CA.: Regal, 1984.

Winkworth, Susanna. *The History and Life of the Reverend Doctor John Tauler of Strasbourg; With Twenty-Five of His Sermons.* New York: Wiley & Halsted, 1858.

Wuellner, Flora. *Prayer and the Living Christ.* Nashville, TN: Abingdon, 1969.

Yutang, Lin, ed. *The Wisdom of China and India.* New York: Modern Library, 1942.

Zaner, Richard. *The Problem of Embodiment.* The Hague: Nijhoff, 1971.

Zockler, Otto. *Askese und Monchtum.* Frankfurt am Main: Heyder & Zimmer, 1897.

Name Index

Subject Index

Scripture Index